COLUMBIA UNIVERSITY STUDIES IN ENGLISH
AND COMPARATIVE LITERATURE

JOHN HORNE TOOKE

JOHN HORNE TOOKE

BY

MINNIE CLARE YARBOROUGH, Ph.D.

ASSISTANT PROFESSOR OF ENGLISH
IN WHEATON COLLEGE

New York
COLUMBIA UNIVERSITY PRESS
1926

To
MY AUNT
MINNIE MACFEAT

CONTENTS

INTRODUCTION

THE eighteenth century produced few more versatile characters than John Horne Tooke. While his reputation in our day rests almost entirely upon the ingenious theory of language which he set forth in his once popular *Diversions of Purley,* a study of his varied career must center about public activities to which he subordinated every other interest of his life. Dominated by a passion for politics, he flung himself enthusiastically into every public contest of the eventful era in which he lived. " No man," says Lord Brougham, " out of office all his life, and out of parliament all but a few months of its later period, ever acted so conspicuous a part in the political warfare of his times as Horne Tooke." [1] The powerful ally of John Wilkes in the famous Middlesex election of 1768, the dictator through the Lord Mayor of London to the King on his throne, the sole victim among his countrymen to a championship of the American Colonists, and the most prominent figure in the State Trials of 1794, he was, in the words of John Bowles Daly, " a living chronicle of the great political events of his age." [2]

The neglect by posterity of this energetic reformer, who attracted such notice in his own generation, must be attributed very largely to the inadequacy of the few biographical records that we have. The sketch of his life by Hamilton Reid, which appeared in 1812, was justly described by the *Quarterly Review* as " a miserable perform-

[1] *Statesmen of the Time of George III,* Philadelphia, 1839, Second Series, Vol. I, p. 134.
[2] *The Dawn of Radicalism,* London, 1892, p. 235.

ance, below contempt as to style, information, and talent." [3]
Less satisfactory still is the account which was published
in 1828 by an American, Dr. John Graham, who made a
futile effort to prove that Tooke was Junius. Obsessed by
this idea and admiring Junius extravagantly, Dr. Graham
indulged in the following absurd eulogy of his subject:
" Of John Horne Tooke it may truly and emphatically be
said, that on his demise there set the brightest sun that
ever illumined the hemisphere of English literature." [4] Dr.
Graham, it should be stated, was not alone in his belief
that Tooke was Junius, for John Fellows, another American, was similarly deluded, and several of Tooke's countrymen, among them Philip Thicknesse and John Blakeway,
promulgated the same theory. While the honors of Junius
have been very generally awarded to another, it is a tribute to the ability and reputation of Horne Tooke that he
should have been identified by not a few of his critics with
the foremost political satirist of his day.

Alexander Stephens published in 1813 the most satisfactory account of Tooke that has been written. The biographer failed, however, mainly because of his formal and
tedious style, to arouse a general interest in his subject,
though his second volume is considerably enlivened by personal recollections of Tooke's wit and eccentricities. We
learn of Tooke from these *Memoirs*, says Trevelyan, who
enumerates the celebrities with whom Stephens compares
his subject, " that though like Pericles, he rarely laughed,
like Alcibiades he could suit himself to the humours of
other men; that he could enjoy his wine with Homer and
Ennius, could draw a character with Tacitus, and was as
ready to accept money from his friends as Pliny and
Cicero; that during his career he was as artful in counsel

---

[3] Vol. 7, June, 1812, pp. 313–314.
[4] *Memoirs of John Horne Tooke*, New York, 1828, p. 98.

as Ulysses, as cool in action as the Duke of Marlborough, and as self-confident as Michael Angelo; and that, when the end came, he was as ready to die, and as desirous to have a simple funeral, as Titus Pomponius Atticus." [5] The one worthy, the historian adds, whom we are informed he did not resemble, was John Wesley, who believed, as Tooke did not, that fasting and early rising are essential to growth in grace.

To set forth the character and accomplishments of this unique figure is no easy task. We are confronted at the beginning by a perplexing body of criticism. "Tooke's stubborn integrity," as Crabb Robinson states in his *Diary*, "was blended with so impassioned a hatred, that it is difficult to apportion the praise and the reproach which his admirers and enemies, with perhaps equal justice, heap upon him." [6] To the majority of his contemporaries, perhaps, his name came to typify all that was abhorrent in the radicalism of the day. Even after he had been cleared of the charge of treason, he continued to be regarded by some of his adversaries as an arch conspirator. In the fifth edition of *The Pursuits of Literature,* for example, which was published in 1798, Mathias, one of the most hostile of his critics, alludes to

All that Horne Tooke can plot or Godwin write,

and in a note which supplements the reference to Tooke, he prophesies that his crime against the Government will eventually be disclosed:

His plans were unfolded, and though he was acquitted, and "Execution was not done on Cawdor," yet it is not impossible

[5] George Otto Trevelyan: *Early History of Charles James Fox,* New York, 1880, pp. 439–440.

[6] *Diary, Reminiscences, and Correspondence of Henry Crabb Robinson,* Boston, 1870, Vol. I, p. 74.

that hereafter (after his decease) some honest chronicler may be found,

> "who will report (in private)
> That very frankly he confess'd *his treasons,*
> Implor'd *his country's* pardon, and set forth
> A deep repentance." [7]

Though vain and cantankerous, Tooke was not, it may be asserted at the outset, a mere officious and meddlesome disturber of the peace. While it cannot be denied that he derived immense satisfaction from tormenting his superiors, he was, as a careful examination of his conduct will reveal, an honest patriot, impelled in all of his self-imposed tasks by a keen sense of justice. " In his appeals to the throne and the public there is," says Percy Fitzgerald, " an earnest ring, with a sarcastic, vigorous power, which excites admiration." [8]

His restlessness in the Church, the turbulent age in which he lived, and a natural taste for public life, — all combined to make him the " electioneering, pamphleteering, and mob-leading cleric " [9] that he became. The enthusiasm which he would undoubtedly have given to the law, had an ironical destiny not forced him into the Church, he eventually gave to politics. Chafing under disabilities which his unfortunate choice of a career imposed upon him, he sought in the dramatic public conflicts of the time an outlet for his energies and talents.

While circumstances conspired to make him a political agitator, he was, however, we may agree with Massey, " as little suited for the vocation of a demagogue as for that of a parish priest. He might, perhaps, have accommodated himself with outward decency to a profession which he

[7] Mathias: *Pursuits of Literature,* Dublin, 1798, p. 273.
[8] *Life and Times of John Wilkes,* London, 1888, Vol. II, p. 164.
[9] *Blackwood's,* Vol. 34, 1833, p. 207.

hated as Swift had done before him; or he might have found that the conscientious discharge of the duties of his sacred calling was not incompatible with the most brilliant reputation, as Sidney Smith subsequently proved. But Horne Tooke was deficient in some of the essential qualities of a popular leader. He neither felt, nor could with any plausibility simulate, a hatred for the upper classes, because his habits and tastes were those of a scholar and a gentleman. For the same reason, he could not stoop to flatter the mob. While he abused the House of Commons as a sink of corruption, he talked about the hereditary nobility being disgraced by the intrusion of that ' skipjack, Jenkinson,' in the style of a Talbot, or a Howard. He denounced the Opposition, on whom many of the democrats affected to fawn, as ' a pack of scoundrels,' like the Ministerial party; and declared that both parties were equally combined to cajole ' that poor man the King,' and to deceive the people of England. But he never expressed any desire that these scoundrels should be superseded by his friends of the constitutional and corresponding societies." [10]

His views, as the preceding observations suggest, were seldom in harmony even with those of his associates. As a politician, moreover, he was decidedly lacking in powers of coöperation. His fiercest quarrels were with his former allies. His self-importance and his disregard for the convictions of others limited his powers of leadership. According to Hazlitt, " he had not one particle of deference for the opinions of others, nor of sympathy with their feelings; nor had he any obstinate convictions of his own to defend —

"Lord of himself, uncumbered with a *creed!*" [11]

[10] *History of England,* London, 1863, Vol. 4, pp. 109–110.
[11] *Works,* Vol. IV, p. 232.

As a linguist, he acknowledged little indebtedness to his predecessors, and he scorned the opinions of his scholarly contemporaries. As the master of a circle of acquaintances who gathered about his hospitable board, he assumed the air of an oracle, by his strong personality and superior accomplishments easily lording it over his guests. Though he accepted valuable gifts from his friends, he never schemed to receive a legacy and he fawned on none of his benefactors. In every relationship of life, political, literary, and social, he maintained an attitude of complete independence. "If you wish to be powerful," he observed on one occasion, "pretend to be powerful." [12]

His position as a writer and as a politician was curiously isolated, for his strong prejudices made him a harsh critic of the most prominent men of his time and provoked retaliation from them or their followers. In an author or a statesman holding political views at variance with his own he found little to admire or to tolerate. Many of his countrymen, in turn, hating him for his violent prejudices or for his political alliances, underrated his abilities as a reformer and as a scholar. "The Ishmael of literature and politics, his hand was against every man's hand, and every man's hand was against him." [13]

But Tooke, as we shall see, was far from miserable in playing the rôle of an outcast. He was immensely pleased to disagree with his contemporaries, and was happier, we must conclude, in advertising their errors than in establishing his own theories. "Negative success," says Hazlitt, satisfied this extraordinary individual, who would rather have been "*against* himself than *for* anybody else." [14]

---

[12] *Specimens of the Table Talk of the Late Samuel Taylor Coleridge*, London, 1856, p. 394.

[13] *Quarterly Review*, June, 1812, Vol. 7, p. 316.

[14] *Works*, Vol. IV, p. 236.

Though doomed to defeat, for example, each time that he entered a political race, he undoubtedly found enough pleasure in crossing swords with his antagonists to repay him for his exertions in a losing game.

Although he was at constant strife with the Law and the Administration, he had, it will be discovered, no great objects to achieve — no profound truths to defend. " His politics," says Leslie Stephen, " were rather cynical than sentimental." [15] He was inspired by no large ideas and was the promulgator of no new political gospel. His aims as a reformer were practical rather than idealistic. There were no clarion calls in his sermons and there was no burning enthusiasm in his public addresses. He was not revolutionist enough to dream of a new order of society. He was carried away by no Utopian schemes for the public betterment. In the opinion of this literal-minded and unemotional reformer, the Golden Age of politics was in the past, and a reform in the House of Commons was all that was necessary to abolish political evils.

In the course of his long life of more than three-score-years-and-ten he applied himself at one time or another to theology, law, politics, and language, but he achieved no lasting recognition in any of these ventures. Even in the realms of scholarship and politics, where he accomplished most, his reputation has suffered, in the one case, from the inadequacy of his knowledge, and in the other, from the narrowness of his objectives. He has been eclipsed by scholars better equipped to formulate a philosophy of language, and his notoriety as a reformer has faded with the passing of events which lured him into the field of politics. " Promptitude, acuteness, and activity, not grandeur and comprehension, were the characteristics of his mind," says Lord Dudley. " All its operations were

[15] See article on Tooke in *Dictionary of National Biography*.

confined to a narrow sphere. What he saw he saw clearly, but his vision did not extend far. Wholly occupied in the squabbles of the day and anxious about the petty point which it was his immediate desire to carry, he seems to have preserved no just sense of the relative magnitude of objects, and behaved as if the fate of mankind had depended upon the event of the Middlesex or Westminster election." [16]

We find reflected in him the lack of idealism and spirituality that distinguished an age dominated by Hume and Voltaire. The philosophical and reflective spirit of Burke was no more his than was the unselfish ardor of Fox. He was too cautious and moderate a reformer to be a commanding or an inspiring leader. "There was," to quote Hazlitt again, " a hard dry materialism in the very texture of his understanding, varnished over by the external refinements of the old school. Mr. Tooke had great scope of attainment, and great versatility of pursuit, but the same shrewdness, quickness, cool self-possession, the same *literalness* of perception, and absence of passion and enthusiasm, characterized nearly all he did, said, or wrote." [17] He left upon Coleridge the impression of being a " keen iron man." [18]

In him we shall discover, however, the most consistent and uncompromising public agitator of his generation. He was resourceful, intrepid, and resolute, and was the master of every situation in which he found himself. " Methinks," said Henry Grattan, " if Mr. John Horne Tooke proposed to drink his glass of wine, and that the bolts of heaven had rent asunder the earth beneath his feet, Mr. J. H. Tooke

[16] *Quarterly Review*, Vol. 7, p. 318.

[17] *Works*, Vol. IV, p. 231.

[18] *Specimens of the Table Talk of the Late Samuel Taylor Coleridge*, New York, 1856, p. 310.

would still drink his glass of wine." [19] It may be noted in this connection, that on one occasion when at a public dinner he had jumped on top of the table in the midst of confusion and some opposition, to express his thanks for his health having been proposed, he pointed to his glass after a degree of order had been restored, to call attention to the fact that the wine was unspilled.

Once committed to a policy, he defended his position with a stubbornness and a tenacity that maddened his opponents. "He was, perhaps," says Leigh Hunt, "the hardest-headed man that ever figured in the union of literature and politics." [20] "I make it my boast," Tooke declared on one occasion, "that upon all great public questions, neither Friends nor Foes, nor Life, nor Death, nor Thunder nor Lightning, shall ever make me give way the breadth of one hair." [21] It is doubtful whether any other individual of Tooke's humble birth, moderate means, and unimportant political connections ever assumed such a dictatorial attitude as did he to his superiors. For more than a generation he was "the terror of judges, ministers of state, and all constituted authorities." [22] There was no more zealous custodian in all England of the traditional rights of his countrymen. No one was more eager to attack and punish the abettors of public wrongs.

"The history of the eighteenth century," says Thorold Rogers, "has been treated too much as though it were a gallery of family portraits, to which events are the mere frames. Public life, to be sure, was at that time a Homeric

[19] O'Regan: *Memoirs of the Legal, Literary, and Political Life of John P. Curran,* London, 1817, p. 109.

[20] *The Town, Its Memorable Characters and Events,* New York, London, and Toronto, 1907, p. 413.

[21] *Westminster Speeches,* London, 1796, p. 12.

[22] Massey: *History of England,* Vol. 4, p. 108.

battle, in which a few prominent figures occupied the scene, and, I must add, divided the spoils. Among them there was one man who got no spoils, was always in earnest, always serious. ' The Parson,' said Wilkes, ' never laughs.' He was also patriotic and wise. He swam against the current which he could not stem. It is perhaps still impossible to forget him as the minister of New Brentford, but though his enemies called him a hoary traitor, and even his friends thought it necessary to apologize for him, as a retired clergyman, they who are willing to be just to one of the foremost men of his age, will find much that is wholesome in the career of the politician and philosopher of Wimbledon." [23]

An attempt has been made in the following chapters to trace Tooke's career in greater detail and to emphasize his unique contributions to the political, the literary, and the social life of the period.

It is a pleasure to record my gratitude to those who have aided me in making this study. To the attendants and officials of the Yale University Library, of the Harvard University Library, and particularly of the Columbia University Library, I owe thanks for many courtesies and for efficient services. To Mr. A. S. Salley, Jr., Secretary to the Historical Commission of South Carolina, I am indebted for assistance in discovering records bearing on my subject. I am grateful to Professor R. L. Rusk for offering many helpful suggestions; to Professor William P. Trent for referring me to sources containing important information; to Professor Ernest H. Wright for reading the manuscript and the proof, and making valuable criticisms; and to Professor George P. Krapp for giving me wise counsel, and supervising the preparation of the chapter on Tooke

[23] *Historical Gleanings,* London, 1870, Second Series, pp. 246–247.

as a philologist. My chief obligations are to Professor Ashley H. Thorndike, who suggested the subject, and who has been my constant adviser. Throughout the progress of the study he has given me patient and scholarly guidance and stimulating criticism.

Wheaton College
May, 1926.

JOHN HORNE TOOKE

CHAPTER I

EDUCATION AND TRAVELS

JOHN HORNE, known in later life as Horne Tooke, was born in Newport Street, Westminster, on June 25, 1736. He was christened at St. Ann's, Soho, the day after his birth, " a circumstance which," according to his biographer, Stephens, " seems to indicate either that his life had been in immediate jeopardy, or that he was of so puny and delicate a frame as to render a speedy dissolution probable."[1]

His father, the elder John Horne, was a well-to-do poulterer, who was highly respected in his community, and his mother, Elizabeth Horne, was a kind-hearted woman, whose liberality endeared her to her neighbors. It was largely through the influence of his wife that the Westminster tradesman became a generous supporter of Middlesex Hospital, an institution of which he later became first treasurer.

By his combativeness the younger Horne came naturally, for his father never yielded a point in a matter of principle. On one occasion he stubbornly held his ground against the demands of royalty itself. When certain officers of Frederick, Prince of Wales, who were seeking an opening to the street through his premises, ordered the cutting of a door without first asking his permission, he protested against their highhandedness, and when no attention was

[1] *Memoirs of John Horne Tooke*, London, 1813, Vol. I, p. 6.

1

paid to his objections, he went to law. After a court of justice had decided in his favor, and he had thus attained his object, he very graciously granted the Prince his doorway, whereupon his Royal Highness, pleased with his concession, at once appointed him official purveyor of poultry to his household. He served the Prince in this capacity for many years, but he paid dearly for the honor, since the heir to the throne died suddenly, owing him a debt of several thousand pounds, which George II never felt obligated to settle.

The philologist was the third son in a family of seven children. Benjamin, the eldest, who became an enterprising and prosperous market gardener at Brentford, died in the prime of manhood, leaving the large amount of property that he had acquired to his sisters and brothers. With his brother Benjamin in mind, Horne once observed:

No man can bring himself to believe that he shall die. My brother, who left me £100 a year, and pronounced himself at the point of death, desired that such and such things might be returned to him if he recovered.[2]

The second son, Thomas, had a very different career from that of his elder brother. Though trained as a fishmonger, he later followed the trade of poulterer, inheriting his father's shop. Since he had no business sense, however, he soon squandered both his share of his father's estate and the annuity of seventy pounds left him by his brother Benjamin. He was reduced to poverty by his extravagance and had to spend the last years of his life in the Fishmongers' Almshouses.

There were four daughters in the Horne household, all of whom, apparently, made successful marriages. Mary, the eldest, the belle of the family, married Tom Wildman,

2 Samuel Rogers: *Recollections,* Boston, 1859, p. 168.

a friend of John Wilkes; Sarah, the next daughter, became the second wife of Stephen Charles Triboudet Demainbray, at one time a tutor of George III, and afterwards astronomer at Kew; Elizabeth, the third sister, who enjoyed something of her brother John's reputation as a wit, married a haberdasher; and Anne, the youngest of the sisters, who also wedded a tradesman, came eventually into considerable wealth.

John, the youngest son, was evidently the favorite of his parents. Realizing, no doubt, that his mental powers were unusually keen, they spared no expense, as we shall see, in his education. Horne was, for his part, a devoted son, deferential whenever possible to the wishes of his elders.

As a child, he was characterized, we are told, by a maturity beyond his years. When an old lady, who had long known him, was asked whether she recalled him as a boy, she replied: "He never was a boy: with him there was no interval between childhood and age; he became a man all at once upon us."[3] He was an odd little lad, we may be sure, who occupied himself with games of his own invention. For the sports that were popular with his companions he cared little. The most exciting event of his childhood was a military expedition on which he accompanied his father, when the latter, as a commissioned officer of the Trained Bands, set out to oppose the claims of the grandson of James II to the throne. The pleasure that the nine-year-old John derived from the stir and excitement of those days can easily be imagined. Another memorable incident of his boyhood was a holiday visit to a French Protestant family living in Canterbury, where he had the delightful experience of running and playing on the walls of the old town.

[3] Stephens: *Memoirs of John Horne Tooke,* Vol. I, p. 22.

The tradesman's son enjoyed probably in his teens the rare privilege of being companion to a prince, for the position of his brother-in-law, Demainbray, in Leicester House led to his introduction to the future King, George III, who was just two years his junior. At a later period, when Horne had become a prominent radical and had incurred the hatred of both Church and Court party, the King had no doubt, says Thorold Rogers, " forgotten him, and the garden, and the surreptitious way which led to the old poulterer's larder, as his grandfather and he had forgotten Frederick's bad debts — into an infinity of forgetfulness." [4]

At the age of seven Horne was sent to a school in Soho Square. A year later, in 1744, he was sent to Westminster, and two years later, to Eton. Among his predecessors at the latter famous institution was William Pitt the elder, the idol of his young manhood; among his contemporaries was Lord North, whose policies in the American crisis he was to attack so vigorously; and among his immediate successors was Charles James Fox, a bitter foe of his later years. Because of his humble parentage Horne suffered no little embarrassment at Eton whenever noble birth became a topic of conversation. On one of these occasions he was called upon by his more aristocratic companions, who had been boasting of the rank of their respective parents, one asserting that he was the son of a baronet, another, that he was the son of an earl, and still another, that he was the son of a duchess, to report on his origin. He admitted reluctantly that there were no titles in his family. Under more rigid cross-examination, however, he satisfied his tormentors by declaring that his father was " an eminent Turkey merchant." [5]

[4] *Historical Gleanings,* Second Series, London, 1870, p. 218.
[5] Stephens: *Memoirs of John Horne Tooke,* Vol. I, p. 21.

Near the beginning of his Eton period, Horne had the terrible misfortune to lose the sight of his right eye, in a playful tussle with one of his comrades, who had a knife on his person. While his eye was healing, or possibly during a vacation period, he was sent for a time to a school in Kent. Disliking the institution heartily, however, he made up his mind to escape, a decision to which he came on two other occasions in his school career. To avoid suspicion, he wore no cap when he began his journey of twenty-five miles to London. On perceiving shortly after he had stolen away, that his efforts to conceal his flight had been in vain, he outwitted his pursuers by hiding himself in the chimney of a deserted summer-house. When the road was free again, he persistently trudged on, in spite of the rain, which was pouring in torrents. Late in the afternoon a peasant discovered his plight and took him home to shelter. The peasant's wife received him kindly and provided him with dry garments and a bed for the night. The next morning he resumed his journey in the company of a gardener, who allowed him to ride to town on the top of his wagon. During a period of rest for the horses on the roadside, the truant overheard customers at an ale-house talking of " a little wicked boy, with a cast of his eye, who had run away during the preceding day from the boarding school of the worthy Mr. ———." [6] Upon hearing this exact description of himself, Horne at once buried himself in the straw, from which he did not emerge again until he had reached his own neighborhood in London.

The excuse which he gave to his father for his unceremonious departure from school is prophetic of the future grammarian. He informed his parent that his master was not qualified to instruct him, for though he no doubt knew what a noun or a verb was, he understood nothing

[6] Stephens: *Memoirs of John Horne Tooke,* Vol. I, p. 19.

at all about prepositions and conjunctions. Later in life
Horne repaid generously, with an annuity of ten pounds,
the hospitality of the peasant woman who, with her husband, had aided him in making his escape from so ignorant
a preceptor.

Another story of his criticism of his instructors is related by Crabb Robinson, who heard it at a dinner party
several years after Horne's death: " At school, he was
asked why he put a word in some case or mood, and
answered, ' I do not know,' for which he was instantly
flogged. Another boy was then asked, who repeated the
grammatical rule, and took his place in the class. On this
Tooke [7] cried. His master asked him what he meant, and
Tooke said: ' I knew the rule as well as he did, but you
did not ask for the rule, but the reason. You asked *why*
it is so, and I do not know that now.' The master is said
to have taken him aside and given him a Virgil in memory
of the injustice done him, of which Virgil Tooke was very
proud." [8]

At Eton Horne won a reputation for shirking his work.
His later veneration for the classics did not, it is clear,
manifest itself at this time, for he failed to distinguish
himself in either Latin or Greek verse. In after years he
confessed very frankly to his lack of studiousness in his
youth, applying Shakespeare's famous schoolboy description to himself. While he was neglecting his prescribed
duties so shamelessly, however, he was profiting by a com-
panionship with books of his own selection. With his early
literary discoveries in mind, he later recommended a des-
ultory reading for the young. " It is best," he said, " to
let children read what they like best, till they have formed
a taste for reading: and not to direct what books they

[7] Horne took the name of Tooke in 1782.
[8] *Reminiscences of Crabb Robinson*, Boston, 1870, Vol. I, p. 366.

shall read. When young, and long afterwards, I read without method." [9]

Shakespeare, it seems, was his first literary inspiration. At the age of seven, he was a worshipper of the great dramatist, his inability to grasp much of the poet's meaning interfering not at all with his enjoyment of the plays. The word *avaunt,* among many other Shakespearean terms then incomprehensible to him, "struck him with a kind of awe, and seemed to imply something very terrible." [10] "When children read to you what they do not understand," he once wisely observed, "their minds are exercised in affixing ideas to the words. At least it was so with me." [11]

Milton, like Shakespeare, early captured his imagination, the prose of that great writer, rather than his verse, making an appeal to him first. Such an admirer was he of Milton's prose masterpieces that he transcribed all of them in his youth. After he became a public agitator, he often quoted from the famous *Pro Populo Anglicano Defensio,* and he was always ready to defend the character as well as the genius of the author. Though he was never a republican as Milton was, we shall see, when we come to study his political career, that he was at one with the poet in his attitude toward Charles I.

For some time after Horne left Eton, it appears from his statements in a "Chronologico-Biographical Table," which Stephens had in his possession and which he copied in the Appendix to his *Memoirs,* that he was prepared for Cambridge by private tutors at Sevenoaks, Kent, and at Ravenstone, Northamptonshire. Finally at the age of nineteen, he became a student at St. John's College, where

---

[9] Samuel Rogers: *Recollections,* Boston, 1859, p. 165.
[10] Stephens: *Memories of John Horne Tooke,* Vol. II, p. 412.
[11] Samuel Rogers: *Recollections,* Boston, 1859, p. 170.

he applied himself so zealously to his studies that in a period of three years he received with honors the degree of A.B.

While in residence at the University, he formed a lasting friendship with Richard Beadon, a fellow student, who was included with him in the Triposes of the year 1758. Both Beadon and Horne were intended for the Church, and the latter lived to see his friend become Master of Jesus College, Bishop of Gloucester, and afterwards Bishop of Bath and Wells. Had Horne been content to remain in the profession originally chosen for him, similar clerical honors might have been his.

The divergence of their paths after their graduation from the University did not alter the intimate relations of these former Cambridge students. It is related by Samuel Rogers that shortly before Beadon succeeded to the bishopric of Gloucester, he met Horne in St. Paul's churchyard, and informed him of his promotion in the Church. " I suppose," said Horne, after hearing the news, " I must never call you Dick again." " Why," replied Beadon, hesitating between his words, " I don't exactly — see the necessity — of that." [12] To his love for his Alma Mater and to his esteem for Beadon, Horne gave public expression in the Dedication of Part I of *The Diversions of Purley*. Beadon, for his part, testified at Horne's trial for treason to the forty years of unbroken friendship between himself and the prisoner. " Indeed you have borne your testimony for me in very trying situations where few besides yourself would have ventured so much honesty," [13] Horne represents himself as saying to Beadon in the dialogue of his treatise on language.

Horne, who felt entirely indisposed to accede to the

[12] Rogers: *Recollections,* Boston, 1859, p. 162.
[13] *Diversions of Purley,* Philadelphia, 1806, Part I, p. 100.

wishes of his parents by entering the Church, had as early as November 9, 1756, enrolled himself as a member of the Inner Temple, with the intention, it seems, of ultimately realizing his own ambitions for a legal career. After his graduation, therefore, when his family, no doubt, were insistent upon his taking holy orders, he did not at once commit himself to the Church, but postponed a final decision in regard to a profession by undertaking for a time the work of a tutor. We find him, accordingly, in the rôle of schoolmaster at Blackheath, where he was first associated with an educator by the name of Jennings, and afterwards with the latter's son-in-law, Williams.

Stephens expatiates in the following passage upon the miseries of Horne's life during this period: " Instead of the charms attendant on elegant, or the improvements resulting from learned society, in place of the amusements and variety of a public, or the happiness and repose usually incident to a domestic life; here was now only heard the unvaried note of the cuckoo, and the eternal gabble, added to the tormenting tricks, of threescore mischievous boys. He might with Dr. Johnson, when exposed to similar misfortune, have fairly exclaimed, that ' one single day was the faithful copy of a whole existence '; and it must be allowed that the ill requited fatigue and unrewarded industry of this laborious, but useful class of men, could not fail to be odious to a liberal and ingenious mind." [14] Notwithstanding this gloomy picture of his occupation, Horne probably enjoyed a fair amount of success in his work and found it by no means unendurable. Throughout his life, as we know, he took a lively interest in educational discussions and was a staunch advocate of public instruction, though he was violently opposed to the complete government control of education advocated by

[14] Stephens: *Memoirs of John Horne Tooke*, Vol. I, pp. 23–24.

Lord Monboddo. One of his former pupils testified in manhood to the impressiveness of Horne's voice and manner,
and to the awe which he inspired in the young.

During his short stay at Blackheath, Horne had a love
affair with a young woman who was an occupant of the
house in which he lived. He was an ardent suitor, it
seems, but the courtship, for some unknown reason, soon
came to an abrupt conclusion. After the years had healed
wounds which may have been painful enough in his youth,
he used to remark: " I luckily escaped from two evils —
matrimony and misery at the same time." [15]

Horne usually became facetious, as the preceding observation suggests, when the subject of marriage was introduced in his company. To the counsel, for example, once
offered him by his uncle: " Now, young man, as you are
settled in town, I would advise you to take a wife," he is
reported by Samuel Rogers to have replied: " With all my
heart, Sir, whose wife shall I take? " [16] On another occasion, he asserted that he would never take a beautiful
woman for his wife. " She would," he said, " be studious to
be admired by others and to please anybody more than
her husband." [17] He is credited, it may be added, with expressing the wish that " women would purr when they were
pleased." [18] Repenting almost immediately of his folly, at
one period of his later life, in having committed himself to
a written proposal of marriage, he hastened to the post office
and reclaimed his love letter.

Even after the unhappy ending of his romance at Blackheath, Horne was in no haste to quit the neighborhood or to
leave off tutoring. On the other hand, his family, it may be
supposed, were urging him throughout this period of inde-
cision, to seek a more dignified calling. In conformity,

---

[15] *Ibid.*, p. 28.

[16] *Recollections*, Boston, 1859, p. 170.

[17] *Ibid.*, pp. 154–155.

[18] *Ibid.*, p. 155.

finally, with their earnest wishes and entreaties, he consented to give up schoolmastering to take orders in the Church.

After his ordination as deacon on September 23, 1759, he was given a charge in Kent, where, to quote Bowles Daly, he was speedily " demoralized with tea and muffins." [19] He had discharged the duties of his new office only a few months in this hospitable community, however, when a sudden attack of ague forced him to resign his curacy.

Even before his illness he must have had serious misgivings as to his fitness for his work, and during his convalescence he had leisure to consider employment of a more congenial character. Upon his recovery, therefore, he determined to take no further orders in the Church. At the same time, he resolved to prepare himself for another profession, which, as we have seen, it had long been his desire to enter. Braving the opposition of his parents, therefore, who had their hearts set upon his continuing in the Church, he took up his residence in the Inner Temple, there, as he himself expressed it, " to eat his way to the bar." [20]

While he was keeping his terms, he made the acquaintance of John Dunning and Lloyd Kenyon, the former of whom was destined to become his defender, and the latter, his judge. Kenyon, who had entered the Middle Temple in 1750, and Dunning, who had entered in 1752, had both been called to the bar in 1756, shortly before Horne had enrolled. Since neither, however, succeeded for several years in securing advancement in his profession, they were still students of the law when Horne entered upon his residence in the Temple. The three legal aspirants, who were so congenial as to spend many hours together, had to live economically. They frequently dined in Chancery Lane for the sum of

[19] *Dawn of Radicalism,* London, 1892, p. 6.
[20] Stephens: *Memoirs of John Horne Tooke,* Vol. I, p. 30.

seven pence each. On these gala occasions, Dunning and Horne were decidedly liberal, for, says the latter, " We gave the girl who waited upon us a penny a piece: but Kenyon, who always knew the value of money, sometimes rewarded her with a halfpenny, and sometimes with a promise." [21]

Dunning and Horne remained fast friends until the death of the former in 1783. Long after their pleasant student days had come to an end, and Dunning had become a famous lawyer, Horne was fond of telling the following story at the expense of his loyal friend, who was very homely in appearance. On one occasion, he declared, Lord Thurlow requested a waiter to take a note to Dunning, who was playing a game of whist at Mando's, with Horne and two others. Upon discovering that the servant did not know Dunning by sight, the lord directed him to take the note upstairs and deliver it to the ugliest player at the table — to him, suggested Thurlow, most resembling the knave of spades. The note, said Horne, was immediately presented to Dunning.

If Horne had been permitted to follow the law as a calling, he might have outstripped his associates, Kenyon and Dunning, whose training and talents were not superior to his. Before he had been admitted to the bar, however, he was persuaded by his father, who never had approved of his choice of a vocation, to abandon his legal studies to take further orders in the Church. In yielding to the wishes of his parent, who, it seems, even made him certain financial promises should he cast his lot in the Church, Horne was taking a course far more important in its consequences than either he or his father could possibly have foreseen. The determination of the elder Horne to make his son a clergyman may be attributed, it has been suggested, not only to his religious zeal but to his conviction that in the Church the younger Horne might rely for pro-

[21] *Ibid.*, Vol. I, p. 33.

motion upon royal patronage. Since his son-in-law, Demainbray, had had influence in Leicester House and since
he himself had suffered financial losses in the services of
Prince Frederick, the poulterer was justified in believing
that the King might be disposed to advance the interests
of his son. At that time, it must be remembered, preferment in the Church was usually " an affair of backstairs." [22]

On November 23, 1760, Horne was ordained a priest of
the Church of England. In an age of higher ideals, he
might have hesitated to pursue a calling for which he was
obviously unsuited. In an era notorious for its lack of
spirituality, however, he entered upon his career as a
clergyman. The century, it is true, had witnessed the re-
vivals of Whitefield and Wesley, but the teachings of these
earnest reformers were at first too often misunderstood and
misapplied by ignorant and unenlightened followers to produce an immediate regeneration among either clergy or
laity. " There is nothing," says Thorold Rogers, " which
shows how vital are the powers which lie within Christianity, and how incessantly they aid an awakened conscience
and enforce social duties, more clearly than the fact that
after the utter darkness of that age, Christianity effected
a revival and renewed itself." [23] On one occasion many
years after he had renounced his calling, Horne observed
that he had known well the great body of clergymen of his
time, and that some of those who had managed to be ordained would have been much better employed in the making of hobnails. In spite of his unfitness for his vocation,
it must be admitted that he discharged his obligations at
New Brentford, a living worth two or three hundred pounds
a year, purchased for him by his father, far more efficiently

[22] Thorold Rogers: *Historical Gleanings,* Second Series, Boston,
1870, p. 204.
[23] *Ibid.,* p. 189.

and conscientiously than the average churchman of his day.

So anxious was he to serve his parishioners, that he even made an elementary study of medicine in order that he might minister to their physical needs. The assistance that he rendered his flock in this manner was far more effica- cious, he freely admitted, than were his spiritual ministra- tions. We hear, however, of a young woman beset by doubt, seeking an interview with him, and we learn that he dispelled her fears, and boasted afterwards that he had found her an infidel and had left her an orthodox member of the Church of England. He won a reputation for his doctrinal sermons and was often commended for his talks preparatory to confirmation.

His one published sermon, which appeared in 1769, dif- fers very little from the conventional religious discourses of the day. Choosing for a text the following verses from Psalm 55:

" It was not an open enemy that hath done me this dishonour; for then I could have borne it.

" But it was even thou, my companion, my guide, and my own familiar friend,"

he reflects upon the disappointments of friendship. " Listen to me," he says, " whilst I propose to you a method how you may escape this anguish, and never know ' how sharper than a serpent's tooth it is to have a faithless friend.' " [24] The burden of the sermon is that trust may be placed only in a Higher Power. " God is the friend who seeks you for *your* sake," says the preacher. " He seeks you — not yours." [25]

Horne upheld the national institutions whether civil or religious and was unsympathetic with any criticism of the

[24] *A Sermon*, by the Rev. John Horne, London, 1769, p. 10.
[25] *Ibid.*, p. 22.

Established Church. He was an uncompromising opponent of Roman Catholicism, and he had no patience with Dissenters. Of Methodists he spoke in the terms of contempt fashionable at the time. Aside from defending the Established Church mainly because it was established, however, he took no part in religious debates. He himself frankly admitted after he had renounced his calling that theological controversies, in which he was well read, had never aroused him as had the political disputes of his time. He had, obviously, no strong religious convictions to defend. According to Wilkes, the parson's creed from the first article in it to the last, was "known to be *non credo.*" [26] Certainly his beliefs were vague and undefined. Many years after he had laid aside the cloth, Horne, who wished to impress his audience with his liberal-mindedness, asked one of the witnesses at his trial for treason: " Did you suppose me a great bigot for the Church of England, or any other church? " and the witness, to the amusement of the court, replied: " No, I thought you had no religion at all," whereupon Horne hastened to suggest, " Do you mean by having no religion at all, that I had no preference? " and the witness asserted that was what he meant, or that Horne was " for letting everybody enjoy his own." [27]

The minister of New Brentford was no recluse. He was gay and affable in society and participated enthusiastically in whatever entertainment the neighborhood could offer. Of ombre and quadrille, the fashionable games of the time, he was inordinately fond, and he was, perhaps, the champion whist player of the parish. He was an in-

[26] *Controversial Letters of John Wilkes, Esq., the Rev. John Horne and Their Principal Adherents,* London, 1771, p. 29.

[27] Gurney: *Trial of Horne Tooke for Treason,* London, 1795, Vol. 1, p. 358.

veterate card-player. Even on Sunday he spent the afternoon at the whist table, selecting as the scene of this Sabbath pastime a room with windows wide open to the street,
where he played in full and frank view of his astonished
parishioners. His unclerical amusements, as might be expected, provoked criticism from some of his flock, but the
worldly-minded parson could not, we are assured by his
biographer, be " accused of indulging in games of chance,
or playing for any sums that might impair his fortune or
engender the remotest suspicion of avarice." [28]   Notwithstanding this testimony in his favor, he was not always, it
appears, so cautious a gambler when he took his continental vacations. Samuel Rogers relates that Horne won
3,500 lire one night at a party at Aix in southern France,
and thinking it not expedient to depart at once for Italy,
whither he was bound, played on, losing all but 500 lire.

In defence of his character, it should be stated that in
a period when drunkenness was a vice to which even the
clergy frequently succumbed, Horne was, during these early
years, at least, an example of sobriety. It was only after
the age of forty-one that he was gradually led by the society which he kept into immoderate drinking. From this
time until shortly before his death, when he became quite
temperate again, he gravitated between a policy of total
abstinence and one of surrender to his cups. The habit of
swearing, moreover, to which he was particularly addicted
in his old age, seems not to have been a pronounced fault
in the Brentford days.

In 1763 Horne accepted the position of traveling companion to the son of the well-known miser Elwes, member
of Parliament for Berkshire. The tourists reached their
destination immediately after the Peace of Paris, and remained abroad for more than a year, Horne taking ad-

[28] *Memoirs of John Horne Tooke,* Vol. I, p. 40.

vantage of this opportunity to study French, in acquiring which he was, according to his own account, rather slow. He bemoaned the fact that he had been in France nine months before he had command of the language, though he tried hard to master it. Eventually he became an excellent student of French and Italian literature, both ancient and modern. " After too long an interval of idleness and pleasure," he stated in *The Diversions of Purley*, " it was my chance to apply to some of the modern languages." [29] He was in the habit, it may be mentioned, of reading once a year the French translation of *The Arabian Nights*. Of French masters, however, he never became a great admirer. Italian writers, on the other hand, Machiavelli in particular, fascinated him. Italian literature was a rich storehouse, he said, from which the French had borrowed all that was best in theirs.

While Horne spent his vacation very profitably in visiting spots of interest to himself and his companion, he saw very little of the social or literary life of Paris, since he had few letters of introduction and was at this period anything but a literary figure himself. His visit to D'Alembert seems to have been the only outstanding literary experience of the trip. Arrayed in the height of fashion, he presented himself at D'Alembert's and was very graciously received by his host, who chatted with him about suppers, plays, and operas. Having anticipated discourse of a very different nature, Horne was disappointed not a little at the turn the conversation had taken. When at last, after his unsatisfactory call, he arose to go, a gentleman neatly and plainly dressed, who had been present at the interview, and who had seen his disappointment, followed him to the door and informed him that owing to his gay costume, D'Alembert had mistaken him for a dandy. The

[29] *Diversions of Purley*, Philadelphia, 1806, Part I, p. 11.

gentleman, it is interesting to learn, was no other than
David Hume, who had recently arrived in Paris in the
company of Lord Hertford, and was receiving an enthusiastic welcome from French men of letters. It is needless
to say that Horne, profiting by Hume's kindly explanation
of his reception by D'Alembert, wore more subdued ap-
parel on his second visit to the Frenchman, when the conversation was more to his taste.[30]

Horne, who found more to admire in Hume than he did
in most of his famous contemporaries, must have derived
great satisfaction from meeting him at D'Alembert's. He
had delighted in Hume's *Essays* as they appeared, reading and rereading them, he once said, " because they are so
sweetly written." [31]   The author of these masterpieces
was, in his opinion, " one of the finest writers of any country." [32]   Of Hume as a historian, he was more critical.
The History of England, he said, was " bad in its tendency," for Hume " first wrote the History of the Stuarts
falsely, and then wrote the others to accord with it." [33]   He
wrote his history, said Horne, " as witches say their pray-
ers — backwards." [34]

Upon his return to England Horne resumed his clerical
duties, but it soon became apparent that he was not ambitious for promotion in his profession.   Through the influence of his brother-in-law Demainbray and his friends
the elder Elwes and Levintz, receiver-general of customs,
he had been promised a chaplaincy to the King.   Indifferent
to his future in the Church, however, he began to take an
active interest in public affairs.

[30] This incident is related by Samuel Rogers (See Dyce's *Table
Talk of Samuel Rogers,* New York, 1856, p. 123).

[31] Rogers: *Recollections,* Boston, 1859, p. 160.

[32] *Ibid.*

[33] *Ibid.*

[34] Dyce: *Table Talk of Samuel Rogers,* New York, 1856, p. 123.

To understand the enthusiasm with which he eventually threw himself into politics, we must recall the public situation of the period. Upon his accession to the throne in 1760 George III had been idolized by his subjects until the sudden resignation of Pitt from office and the equally sudden elevation of John, Earl of Bute, to the highest office in the kingdom. The royal favorite had immediately become the victim of violent attack, since he was generally regarded as the usurper of Pitt's position, and the King lost some of his popularity. Nothing that Bute could do met with the approval of the opposite faction. He was hated and abused even after his voluntary withdrawal from office on April 7, 1763. The enemies of the court party had found a popular leader, in the meantime, in the person of John Wilkes after the latter had been prosecuted for writing " No. 45 " of the *North Briton,* a paper which he and Churchill had brought forth for the express purpose of opposing the official organ known as the *Briton.* The successive efforts made by the Administration to punish Wilkes for his daring criticism of the King's commendation of the Peace of Paris had only endeared him to the public and made a hero of a demagogue.

In this political crisis the alert parson of New Brentford could not remain silent or neutral. He detested Lord Bute, he joined in the popular hero-worship of Pitt, glorified after his retirement, and he brooded on the wrongs endured by Wilkes, whose release from the Tower he had commemorated in a poem. His indignation at what he conceived to be a violation by the Government of the traditional rights of his countrymen finally found expression, in 1765, in a pamphlet entitled *The Petition of an Englishman,* an arraignment of Lord Bute and Lord Mansfield, which a courageous publisher was at length prevailed upon to print. This satire, which is more vindictive than any of his later

compositions, deserves special consideration since it was his
first bold attempt to arouse the public against gross violations of popular rights. " Nothing can be more trifling and
contemptible in point of authorship than this performance,"
wrote one of Horne's most hostile critics, in 1833, " but its
insolence may be supposed to have made up for its meagre
mediocrity." [35]

The pamphlet, which is addressed " To the Right Honourable, Truly Noble, and Truly Scottish Lords, Morti-
mer and Jefferies," differs somewhat, the writer admits,
from the ordinary type of petitions, but he offers no apology on that score; nor, he adds, " can your Lordships be
offended at it; since the conduct of you both, in your political and juridical capacities, has proved you not only the
enemies of all common Forms and received Customs, but
the Violators even of the established Laws, Constitution
and Liberties of my Country." [36] He begs at the hands of
these autocrats a favor commonly awarded by their Lordships to his countrymen. " Disgrace is turned to Honour,"
he says; " punishments change their nature; and what was
intended by our Forefathers as the Brand of Infamy, becomes in your Hands the Reward of Virtue." [37] His burning patriotism will, therefore, be satisfied only with a trium-
phant march to the " Field of Glory " — the Pillory — the
new " Order of Merit " which these noble gentlemen have
instituted in the kingdom. " The Boon I beg of you," he
says, " is, to be admitted a Knight-Companion of this honourable Order; and that you would in consequence of this
my Request, speedily issue forth a Particular Warrant for
me to be invested with this noble Croix de St. Pillory," a
decoration much needed, since his countrymen have hith-

[35] *Blackwood's,* June, 1833, Vol. 33, p. 965.
[36] *Petition of an Englishman,* by John Horne, London, 1765, p. 5.
[37] *Ibid.,* p. 6.

erto been distinguished by no title save that of Englishman and " their noble Bosoms decorated with no Jewel, but Precious Liberty." [38] He begs the public to remember " with what *universal contempt*, what *hisses*, and Execrations was viewed the Star that glitters on the Breast of Bute; and what Shouts of Joy, what hearty triumph, and what loud applause attended the plain rug coat of a poor and obscure Printer in the Pillory." [39] The only refuge remaining to the writer and his outraged countrymen from one who is not their countryman, and in whom " the distinct and inconsistent Offices of Prosecutor, Judge, and Jury " [40] are combined, is the Pillory, which, without apologies to Milton, is glorified in the following verses: —

Here at least we may be free. The Fav'rite hath not built
Here for his Envy: will not drive us Hence.
Here we may rest secure; and, in my Mind,
Honour is worth Ambition — in a Pillory.[41]

In this asylum alone can the patriot dwell in peace — " free from the Violence of Secretaries, Warrants and State Messengers," for in Wilkes, as the writer points out, all are outlawed. " Sentence is passed on all." [42]

Horne not only aspires to the honor of being placed in the pillory, but he even dares to hope for the burning of his Petition at the hands of the common hangman. His imprisonment, which he accepts as a matter of course, he leaves to the discretion of his judges, as he does the question of mutilation, though he quite agrees with their lordships " that from the natural Body, as well *as from the Body politic, should be lopped without Mercy the Members that offend.*" [43] In the following passage, therefore,

---

[38] *Ibid.*, p. 7.   [41] *Ibid.*
[39] *Ibid.*, p. 10.   [42] *Ibid.*
[40] *Ibid.*, p. 11.   [43] *Ibid.*, p. 13.

in which his irony reaches a climax, he instructs his superiors in the tortures that should be inflicted upon their critics: —

Squeeze out therefore the Eyes that presume to pry into your Mysteries and Intrigues of State or Lust.

Slit the nose that dares to smell a Rat.

Wring off the Ears, and root up the Tongues that listen to or whisper the words — Liberty and Laws.

And for the sake of *congruity*, for your own Satisfaction, and certainty of a punctual Performance, — be yourselves the Executioners of the Sentences you pass — and let Fulvia, with her Bodkin, pierce through again the Tongue of Cicero.[44]

Having concluded this bitter arraignment of the Administration, he anticipates the martyrdom which he has courted: —

Even I, my countrymen, who now address myself to you, — I, who am at present blessed with Peace, with Happiness and Independence, a fair character, and an easy fortune, am at this moment forfeiting them all.

Soon must I be beggared, vilified, imprisoned. The Hounds of Power will be unkenneled and laid upon the scent. They will track out diligently my footsteps from my cradle.[45]

Calling upon the spirits of Hampden, Russel, and Sidney to inspire his fellows, he concludes his Petition with the following eloquent passage: —

My Heart in its first Pantings, beat to Liberty. She is twisted with my Heart-strings, and cannot be torn from them.

They have formed together a Gordian Knot; which cannot be *untwisted* by the subtle Finger of Corruption, nor loosened by the Touch of Fear. Nothing can separate us. No! not the cruel and bloody Sword of Tyranny.

Her Union with me is lovely and honourable through Life; and even in Death I will not be divided from her.[46]

The daring satirist came near suffering the prosecution

44 *Ibid.*, p. 13.　　45 *Ibid.*, pp. 23–24.　　46 *Ibid.*, pp. 24–25.

which he invoked, his escape being generally attributed to his having very adroitly introduced into his pamphlet " a true and accurate plan of some part of Kew-Green," [47] along with a detailed explanation of the location of the residences of Lord Bute and the Princess-Dowager of Wales, a clever allusion to the popular gossip of the time, which the Ministry hesitated to bring into the courts.

After thoroughly enjoying the perils to which he had exposed himself by his bold criticism of the authorities, Horne settled down once more to the uneventful life of his parish until he was offered another opportunity for taking a vacation on the Continent. Leaving his duties to be discharged by a curate, he went abroad in the autumn of 1765, as travelling companion to young Taylor, the son of a gentleman living near Brentford.

At the beginning of their tour the travellers met in Calais the talented parents of Richard Brinsley Sheridan, who had arrived in France the year before to take up their residence at Blois. Thomas Sheridan was interested at the time in a linguistic scheme which so amused the future philologist that he ridiculed it in the famous letter which he addressed to Wilkes from Montpellier. " Sheridan is at Blois," he wrote, " *by order of his Majesty*, and with a pension; inventing the method to give a proper pronunciation of the English language to strangers, by means of sounds borrowed from their own. And he begins with the French.

" I remember, a few years ago, when an attempt was made to prove Lord Harborough an idiot, the council on both sides produced the same instance; one of his wit, the other of his folly. His servants were puzzled once to unpack a large box, and his lordship advised them to do with it, as they did with an oyster, put it in the fire, and it would gape!

[47] *Ibid.*, p. 17.

"This commission of Sheridan appears to me equally equivocal. And should a similar statute be at any time attempted against his Majesty, they who do not know him may be apt to suspect that he employed Sheridan in this manner, not so much for the sake of foreigners as his own subjects, and had permitted him to amuse himself abroad to prevent his spoiling our pronunciation at home." [48]

In Paris the travellers met a number of Englishmen, among them John Wilkes, to whom Horne was introduced by a letter from Humphrey Cotes, a patriotic wine merchant of Westminster. The author of *The Petition of an Englishman* was elated at meeting the victim, as he regarded Wilkes, of political injustice, and Wilkes, as we may judge from the letters which he directed to Cotes shortly after his introduction to the clergyman, was ready enough to cultivate the friendship of one whom he already knew as a warm defender of his cause. "I have had the pleasure several times of seeing Mr. Horne, and I thank you heartily for so valuable an acquaintance," [49] Wilkes wrote to Cotes on October 7, 1765, and in another letter to the wine merchant, dated October 13, he described his growing intimacy with Horne: —

I have this afternoon your very kind letter of the 8th, and I must leave you to imagine the impatience of my soul for the long one you mention by Mr. Horne. I have often seen that gentleman and I give you my repeated thanks for so valuable an acquaintance. He is still at Paris and we are much together. [50]

Before Horne left Paris, it is important to note, he had promised to correspond with Wilkes.

After their departure from the French capital Horne and

---

[48] Stephens: *Memoirs of John Horne Tooke*, Vol. I, pp. 77–78.

[49] John Almon: *Letters of Wilkes to His Friends*, London, 1805, Vol. II, p. 207.

[50] *Ibid.*, p. 209.

his companion set out for Ferney, famous since 1758 for being the home of Voltaire, who was visited in his retreat by throngs of admirers, representing almost every rank, occupation, and nationality. Although Horne made the customary pilgrimage to Ferney and had the privilege of meeting Voltaire, he was not at all impressed, it seems, by his visit. In his Montpellier letter to Wilkes, which contains some account of his continental experiences, there is no reference to Ferney. Horne was never an appreciative reader of Voltaire. Once in his later years he went so far as to declare that the influential French writer was " inferior in everything — inferior as a poet, a biographer, and an historian." [51] Dryden was, in Horne's opinion, a far more universal author than Voltaire.

From Ferney the English travellers journeyed to Lyons, where they met the author of *Tristram Shandy*. Horne and Sterne were soon on intimate terms, it appears, though, according to Cross, we may conclude from the following paragraph in Horne's letter to Wilkes that the novelist was " clearly bored " [52] by the clergyman's eulogies of the exiled patriot:

I passed a week with Sterne, at Lyons, and am to meet him again, at Sienna, in the summer — Forgive my question, and do not answer it, if it is impertinent. Is there any cause of coldness between you and Sterne? He speaks very handsomely of you, when it is absolutely necessary to speak at all; but not with that *warmth* and *enthusiasm*, that I expect from everyone that knows you. Do not let me cause a coldness between you, if there is none. I am sensible my question is at least impudent and my jealousy blamable. [53]

Horne and his companion went directly from Lyons to

[51] Stephens: *Memoirs of John Horne Tooke*, Vol. II, p. 435.

[52] Wilbur L. Cross: *Life and Times of Laurence Sterne*, New York, 1909, p. 375.

[53] Stephens: *Memoirs of John Horne Tooke*, Vol. I, p. 77.

their destination, Italy. At Genoa, the first Italian city
which they visited, they stayed under the same roof with
Rosenhagen, who was so distinguished a person as to be
identified by some with Junius. In Genoa, too, they made
the acquaintance of a native family through whom they
met the élite of the city, and Horne, who remarked on one
occasion that love at first sight ought to be acted upon,
now became the ardent admirer and constant attendant of
Signora Durazzo. After he had devoted himself to the
Genoese beauty for several weeks, however, he was surprised to learn at an evening party that she was highly
displeased with him, and that the other guests were also
ignoring him. " Now," said Horne, when he was relating the incident many years later, " what do you imagine
was the cause of this? Why, they had discovered *that I
was a Protestant clergyman.* But I was resolved not to be
brow-beaten; and I made myself so agreeable, that, before
the party broke up, we were all again on the very best
terms; some of them even waited on me home, with music,
in a sort of triumph." [54]   The young woman's failure to
recognize her suitor as a clergyman from the first was due
to the fact that at Dover he had laid aside his clerical costume, and was " flaunting through the continent in very
unclerical suits of flowered silk and gold lace." [55]

For this love affair with a daughter of Italy, Horne came
near paying dearly, for certain hot-blooded relatives of the
lady, angered by his attentions to her, determined to have
redress. When he finally left Genoa, he was advised by the
brother of Signora Durazzo to stop on the first day of his
journey at a villetta to avoid meeting these members of his
family who had sworn to take his life. The warning was
timely, for on the road Horne heard shots, and soon after-

[54] Dyce: *Table Talk of Samuel Rogers,* New York, 1856, p. 125.
[55] Bleackley: *Life of John Wilkes,* London, 1917, p. 176.

wards found an Englishman wounded in his chaise. " Mr. Horne," explained his countryman, " this was intended for you." [56]

The tourists visited all of the principal Italian cities, spending the Carnival season in Venice. Both Naples and Pisa delighted Horne, while Venice, Rome, and Vesuvius surpassed his dreams of them. In every other spot or city, however, he was disappointed. It is to be regretted that he did not keep some systematic record of his continental adventures and impressions. Such a diary would have been a fascinating document, for we may rest assured that nothing escaped the keen eye of this " robust little dandy." [57]

By the end of the year, Horne and Taylor were at Montpellier, a popular winter resort, where they made the acquaintance of many French and English families of high social standing. Here, too, they met Adam Smith, who was acting during this period as travelling tutor to the young Duke of Buccleuch. We have no reason to suppose that Horne and Smith became intimately acquainted, though both of them spent some time at Montpellier. In after years Horne ridiculed Smith's theories. He remarked on one occasion that Smith was inferior to his master, Hume, that his *Theory of Moral Sentiments* was " nonsense," and that his *Wealth of Nations*, though full of important facts, was " written with a wicked view." [58]

It was from Montpellier that Horne, remembering his promise to Wilkes, finally addressed to him on January 3, 1766, an extraordinary letter, which came, as we shall see, to have far-reaching consequences for the author. " You are

---

[56] Clayden: *Samuel Rogers and His Contemporaries,* London, 1889, Vol. I, p. 78.

[57] Bleackley: *Life of John Wilkes,* p. 176.

[58] Rogers: *Recollections,* Boston, 1859, p. 160.

now," declared Horne, with the obvious intention of amusing and flattering Wilkes, " entering into a correspondence with a parson, and I am greatly apprehensive lest that title should disgust; but give me leave to assure you I am not ordained a hypocrite. It is true I have suffered the infectious hand of a bishop to be waved over me; whose imposition, like the sop given to Judas, is only a signal for the devil to enter." [59]

" A clergyman in these times, who wrote in such a fashion," says Thorold Rogers by way of commenting upon this passage, which was quoted so often against Horne a few years after it was written, " would be interpreted to have abjured his relations with the church, and to have abjured them indecently. In those days, the language of this letter might have shocked some, and would have amused many. Even when the letter was published, Walpole, speaking of him, said that ' no reproach was cast on the morals of Horne, but that to please Wilkes he had ridiculed his lords, the bishops, and to please himself, had indulged in more foppery than became his profession.' " [60]

Horne, as might be expected, could not close his letter without reminding Wilkes of his responsibilities to the popular cause. After stating that he has just seen a communication from England to the effect that Fitzherbert has authorized Wilkes to draw on him to the amount of one thousand pounds a year, he adds:

I am afraid this is Eutrapelian generosity, and that, by furnishing you with the means of pleasure, they intend to consign you over to dissipation, and the grand points of national liberty and·your glory to oblivion. I am sure they will be mistaken; nothing little or common is for the future to be pardoned you.

[59] Stephens: *Memoirs of John Horne Tooke*, Vol. I, p. 76.
[60] Rogers: *Historical Gleanings*, Second Series, London, 1870, p. 209.

The public have done you the justice to form extravagant notions of you; and though they would be very sorry to see you neglect any opportunity of serving your private interest; yet they hope never to have cause to reproach you as Brutus did Cicero, — " That it was not so much a *Master* that he feared as Antony for that Master."

You perceive how freely I deliver my sentiments; but all this is uttered in the openness of my heart, and ought not to offend you, as it proceeds from a man who has always both felt for your sufferings and spoken highly of your conduct in the public cause.[61]

To this communication Wilkes did not reply. It might have occurred to Horne that Wilkes would not be so pleased by his flattery as to relish his meddlesome interest in his private affairs. He had intended no offence by his frankness, however, and was apparently at a loss to understand Wilkes's silence. Upon his return to Paris the following spring, therefore, he sought Wilkes and asked for an explanation. With the object, it may have been, of punishing the indiscreet parson for his presumption, Wilkes at first evaded his inquiries or treated them as a joke. At last when hard pressed by Horne for an answer, he denied having received the letter. Horne must have known that he was lying, but he accepted his statement and even ignored his duplicity after learning positively that he had displayed his letter on several occasions and had threatened to publish it.

Despite this revelation of Wilkes's character, Horne continued to seek his society. Resolved, apparently, to overlook his personal failings because he represented the public cause and was, besides, a fascinating companion, he remained on such intimate terms with him during the rest of his stay in Paris, that when he was ready to leave the Continent, he entrusted to his care the fashionable clothes

[61] Stephens: *Memoirs of John Horne Tooke*, Vol. I, pp. 79–80.

which he was in the habit of donning on his travels.   In
a note that accompanied the consignment of his elaborate
wardrobe of varied style and color, to the keeping of the
exile, the parson observed wittily:

If you have any fellow feeling, you cannot but be kind to them,
since they too, as well as yourself, are outlawed in England.[62]

[62] *Ibid.*, p. 83.

CHAPTER II

THE MIDDLESEX ELECTION

AFTER spending almost two years abroad in the fashionable resorts of Italy and France, where he played the gallant, indulged in frivolities that were hardly in keeping with his holy calling, and consorted with a rake and an avowed atheist, Horne returned to his parish in the summer of 1767, and for a time, it seems, applied himself in earnest to his clerical duties. He even became a popular preacher, and was often requested to speak in the London churches, particularly at St. Paul's, Covent Garden, in the vicinity of his early home. Notwithstanding his erratic conduct he had won the affection and confidence of his parishioners and he might even yet have found advancement in his profession had he not been tempted again by public issues, which were becoming more and more clearly defined, to neglect the Church for politics. His stay abroad among men who loved her not, had, no doubt, intensified his love for England, and his acquaintance with other lands may have convinced him, too, of the privileges which he enjoyed as a Briton. Little incentive was needed to arouse him to further political activity, and the occasion that was to call forth his powers of leadership was not long in presenting itself.

In spite of the growing discontent manifested by the nation, " public affairs," says Lord Campbell, " remained in a state of considerable tranquillity till the sudden reappearance in England of the notorious John Wilkes, which threw the whole nation into a ferment." [1] Wilkes, as we

---

[1] *Lives of the Chancellors,* London, 1857, p. 390.

have seen, had been a popular hero ever since he had demonstrated the illegality of general warrants, had been prosecuted for libel, and had been driven into exile. And now, when still unpardoned for a series of offences against the Government, he audaciously offered himself as a candidate to represent the City of London, and when failing to win the metropolis, he boldly presented himself as a candidate for Middlesex, he won still greater notoriety and inaugurated one of the most exciting campaigns in the whole history of elections. It was this dramatic situation that furnished Horne with an opportunity for appearing before the public as a champion of popular rights. "The Middlesex election," says Bowles Daly, "brought the scene before his eyes and the actors to his door." [2]

Wilkes was fortunate, upon his reëntrance into politics, to win the support of Horne. Though he numbered among his followers such influential personages as Lord Temple and the Duke of Portland, he found in the country clergyman his ablest assistant. The alliance between Horne and Wilkes seems the more astonishing when it is learned that there had been no intercourse between them since their separation in Paris the previous year. "From the time I left you in Paris in 1767," said Horne in a letter to Wilkes, in 1771, when the two former associates were engaged in a violent public controversy, "I held no communication with you of any kind whatsoever; nor did I upon your arrival in England in 1768 even pay you a visit, till it was very evident you had lost your election in the city." In defence of his former championship of his correspondent he adds: "Then indeed I went to you, because I knew I could be useful to you in Middlesex; and I did then and still do think that there was no method by which I could do greater service to the public, than by espousing your cause,

[2] *Dawn of Radicalism,* London, 1892, p. 26.

which the weakness and wickedness of our court had made, to a certain degree, the cause of every Englishman." [3]

Horne's principal motive in throwing himself wholeheartedly into the cause of a demagogue, in whose character he surely was not deceived, was, undoubtedly, to defeat through Wilkes a stupid Administration. It was only human, however, if he welcomed an opportunity to prove to his leader that the parson had power and influence enough to turn the tide in his favor.

Horne's family and friends, as may be supposed, heartily disapproved of the course that he was following, and implored him not to take part in the campaign. His brother-in-law Demainbray was active on the Ministerial side. Heedless to all remonstrances, however, he persisted in his fight for Wilkes. Since the candidate was too poor to open a single house at the places of election, Horne even provided for his use the two best inns at Brentford. To win the county for his leader, moreover, he canvassed the country on foot or on horseback, alone or with Wilkes, extolling the latter's virtues, depicting his sufferings, and excusing his follies and sins. His earnestness and ardor, indeed, completely overbalanced his judgment at times, and led him into extravagances of abuse. He made violent attacks upon the two Ministerial candidates, to one of whom, Sir William Beauchamp Proctor, he dispatched a series of communications. A single quotation from one of these letters will show the extremes to which the writer's partisanship led him. " Were I," said Horne, " to adopt the coarsest language which is used by honest indignation to the most prostitute and abandoned characters, I think I should be justified in this address to you." [4]   On one

---

[3] *Controversial Letters of John Wilkes, Esq., the Rev. John Horne, and Their Principal Adherents*, etc., London, 1771, pp. 34–35.

[4] Quoted in Stephens' *Memoirs of John Horne Tooke*, Vol. I, p. 97.

memorable occasion the parson, carried away by his enthusiasm, so completely forgot himself as to declare in the presence of his parishioners " that in a cause so just and holy he would dye his black coat red." [5] His participation in the election, it is needless to say, blasted his reputation with both Court and Church party.

There is abundant testimony to the excitement that accompanied this extraordinary campaign. Benjamin Franklin, who was a witness to the popular demonstrations, wrote to his son that there was hardly a door or a shutter for a distance of five miles from the metropolis on which the words " Wilkes and Liberty," the reminder of the popular candidate's martyrdom, were not inscribed, and that the same patriotic sign adorned the road for a distance of sixty-four miles. When the actual voting began, a mob of six thousand spectators occupied every entrance to the polls and made the upper classes pay tribute to their hero. Before a traveller could pass the crowds stationed at prominent posts on the roadside, he must display the magic number or must submit to its being chalked upon his clothes or upon his conveyance. Even the Austrian Ambassador did not escape, infuriated though he was at the indignity, without having the soles of his shoes decorated with the popular number. Women of high birth were compelled to descend from their coaches to exclaim " Wilkes and Liberty," words which were so familiar that a wit of the time, we are told, began one of his letters: " I take Wilkes and Liberty to assure you," etc. [6] The young prince, the future King George IV, is said to have rushed into his royal father's presence shouting the popular phrase. Many years after his break with Wilkes, Horne, commenting on the desire of his

[5] *Ibid.*

[6] Quoted in Jesse's *Celebrated Etonians,* Edition de Luxe, Vol. II, p. 319.

former ally to have his tomb bear the inscription: " J. W. a friend of Liberty," remarked: " I am glad he was not ashamed to show a little gratitude to her in his old age, for she was a great friend to him." [7]

While many circumstances combined to aid Wilkes in winning a victory at the polls, he owed his election, without question, chiefly to the indefatigable exertions of John Horne. The result of the balloting at Brentford on March 28, 1768, was an overwhelming majority for Wilkes, who polled 1292 votes, the rival candidates, Cooke and Sir William Beauchamp Proctor, obtaining 827 and 807 votes, respectively. Wilkes and Cooke were, therefore, declared winners in the election, and there was great rejoicing in London and elsewhere.

Shortly after his election, Wilkes, who had still to make his peace with the law, surrendered to the Court of King's Bench and after being formally arrested, was ordered to jail. Horne, it is interesting to learn, was allowed to accompany him to prison, and on the way, at Westminster Bridge, where a mob surrounded the carriage and liberated the prisoner, he was acclaimed with Wilkes as a popular hero. Wilkes had the discretion, fortunately, to deliver himself to the authorities as soon as he could free himself from his admirers, and Horne, who had no desire to incite the populace to violence, returned quietly to his parish. On June 8, Wilkes procured from Lord Mansfield a reversal of his outlawry on a technical point, but on June 18, the court sustained the former verdict against him for publishing " No. 45 " of the *North Briton,* and the *Essay on Woman.* He was thereupon fined one thousand pounds and was sentenced to twenty-two months' imprisonment in the Tower.

In the riots that followed the refusal of the Government

[7] Samuel Rogers: *Recollections,* Boston, 1859, p. 167.

to permit Wilkes to take his seat in the House, Horne was the self-appointed investigator of disorders and murders. Not lacking in personal courage, he exposed himself to grave dangers to gather witnesses for the purpose of apprehending the offenders. In a lengthy address which he delivered before the freeholders of Middlesex in 1770, he related in detail his efforts to bring to justice the murderers of a young man by the name of Allen, the victim of soldiers who had fired upon the mob waiting outside the prison to see whether their representative would be allowed to take his seat in Parliament.

"On the ever memorable 10th of May, 1768," said Horne, " I was told in Westminster Hall, about two o'clock, of a murder committed in St. George's Fields. I went thither with another gentleman. I found there a great multitude of people and soldiers, but everything very quiet. And it is worth remarking, that on the 10th of May, 1768, when that cowardly massacre was committed, there was not a pane of glass broken, nor a nail wrenched, nor a tile displaced of the King's Bench Prison. As soon as I came, I was applied to by a gentleman, then a stranger to me, to assist him in discovering the murderers. He said he had been requested so to do by the deceased's mother; but that the Justices of the Peace would pay no regard to his application. I would have excused myself as one extremely unfit for such a purpose, and unacquainted with such matters. However, I yielded to his pressing intreaty, and with my friend and others, sought after those who were present at the death of Allen. I discovered the evidence, the soldiers, and officer concerned. I applied for a warrant. The Justices of the Peace refused to grant any, or to receive the information. After much ill treatment and many rebuffs from the Justices, the gentleman who was with me (*and whom I now see in the room*) told me he

thought it in vain to stay there any longer; that he saw
the Justices would not discharge their duty; that they
seemed bent on mischief and on blood; that for his part he
had a wife and family, whom he was to consider, as well
as his own safety; that therefore finding himself unable
to do any good, he should retire; and that he would advise me for my own sake to do the same; I replied, that I
had neither wife nor children, nor any connexion or concern to which my life was of much consequence; that I was
determined to stay till I could procure a warrant, and apprehend the offenders; that if I fell I hoped he would do
me justice and bear witness to the honesty of my intentions; and that I did not risque my life from idle curiosity
or any other unworthy motive. He left me, and I continued my endeavors with the Justices — They behaved as
men who had no other business there but to use the soldiers *effectually*, and as men who expected to be *thanked*
and *rewarded substantially* too, for their *alacrity*. I bore
their coarse and scandalous treatment with an affected hu-
mility, and with the most abject submission, which in any
other situation would have disgraced a beggar; but I would
not depart without a warrant. Mr. Gillam behaved with
much less rudeness than any of the others; he sometimes
inclined to civility, and seemed at last to be very desirous
to do anything — but his duty. At last I collected my witnesses together, and did through shame prevail on Mr. Gillam to go with me into the Marshal's house, to receive
their depositions. The other Justices soon followed. Mr.
Ponton ordered me out of the room, for a *rude fellow,*
to *trouble gentlemen that were going to dinner about a
murder*.

" They dined. They sat down with unwashed hands,
after all that bloodshed, comfortably and joyously to eat
and drink. I waited with the witnesses in the passage. It

is impossible for me, in these few minutes, to tell you all the tricks and shuffling which the Justices practiced through the afternoon. The Marshal commanded me to get out of his house: I refused to obey, because there was a bench of Justices there. He did not, however, think proper to take me into custody." [8]

Horne, who was not to be dissuaded from his purpose, was now approached, he continued, by a certain attorney, familiar with at least some of the incidents just described. The officers, said the latter, evidently did not know who Horne was, and should be informed. A few minutes later one of the justices apologized to Horne, declaring that he had been mistaken for an attorney, after which one of them tried to persuade him to give up all attempts to secure a warrant, assuring him that the soldiers had orders for their act. Upon inquiring from whom the justices had their commands and upon being told that they had them from the Ministry, the astonished parson exclaimed: " Good God, Sir, from the Ministry! The Justices are bound to be guided by the laws; and I never yet found the word *Ministry* in any law book that ever I read." [9]

In due time Horne was allowed to enter the room where sat the representatives of the law. One official, who had been outrageously rude, was now particularly anxious to conciliate the intruder, " and," declared Horne, " for fear I should suspect from his behavior, that he was not a gentleman, told me he had been brought up at Oxford, and professed very great esteem for men of letters." [10]   Horne was

[8] *An Oration Delivered by the Rev. Mr. Horne at a Numerous Meeting of the Freeholders of Middlesex,* etc., London, 1770, pp. 13–15.

[9] *Ibid.,* p. 15.

[10] *Ibid.,* p. 16.

now treated with the greatest civility by the justices, who sought to divert him from his intentions by flattery. " At length," he said, " when they found compliments had no more effect on me than rudeness, the witnesses were called in, and a trial, rather than an examination ensued. The depositions with various delays and interruptions, were taken by Mr. Pardon. Mr. Gillam complained that he made the depositions all alike. Mr. Pardon threw up the pen. The Justices said they could not send for the soldiers accused. However, I had them brought. They were sworn to." [11]

After furnishing his audience with additional details connected with the examination of the witnesses, Horne added: " I can with truth aver that, from the Chief Justice down to the lowest Clerks, there was scarce one honest man who dared to do his duty in this business." [12] When he had concluded his account of the events that had taken place in St. George's Fields, and of the trial of young Allen's murderers, the audience was much moved by the unfortunate father of the victim, who, bursting into tears, exclaimed, " It is true, it is true." [13]

During the Middlesex campaign of December, 1768, Horne again endeavored to see justice done by furthering the prosecution of Edward M'Quirk, who had brutally killed an innocent man by the name of George Clarke. Although convicted by a jury, the murderer, a ruffian in the hire of the Ministerial party, was pardoned. In the course of the trials a surgeon, John Foot, testified that Clarke had died from the effects of a blow on the head, and soon afterwards a pamphlet giving the full details of the case was published under the signature of Foot. Horne, however, confided to Stephens and to Holt White, an acquaintance living near Endfield, Middlesex, that the entire

[11] *Ibid.*, p. 16.   [12] *Ibid.*, p. 18.   [13] *Ibid.*, p. 40.

production, aside from the surgical facts, was written by himself.[14]

By 1769 Horne was influential enough politically to be elected a burgess of the town of Bedford, opposing successfully by this means the Duke of Bedford, who had aroused his displeasure by his alliance with the Grafton administration. He was able at approximately the same time to secure, upon the death of Cooke, the election of a candidate of his own choosing, to fill the vacancy in Parliament. " I beg leave," he had said in addressing the voters, " to present Mr. Glynn to your choice. I know his principles to be as firm, and his heart as incorruptible, as his conduct is modest and moderate, and his abilities uncontradicted. Complete your work and place by the side of your persecuted patriot, Wilkes, his strenuous and disinterested defender, Glynn! " [15]

While Horne was gaining notoriety as a critic of the Administration, he was not forgetful of his former chief, who instead of occupying a seat in the House was serving a sentence in the Tower. He soon devised a plan to reward Wilkes for his services and at the same time to promote the popular cause. On February 20, 1769, Horne founded a society, later to be called the Society for Supporting the Bill

[14] On the cover of a copy of this pamphlet, which was owned by Holt White and which may now be consulted in the Library of Yale University, White states: " Mr. H. Tooke told me this was written by him."

The pamphlet is entitled:

" An Appeal to the Public Touching the Death of Mr. George Clarke, who received a blow at Brentford on Thursday the Eighth of December last, of which he languished and Died on Wednesday the Fourteenth of the same month."

By John Foot, Surgeon

Of Holes-Street, Cavendish Square.

[15] Quoted in Stephens's *Memoirs of John Horne Tooke*, Vol. I, p. 103.

of Rights, which had for its primary object the payment of Wilkes's campaign debts. The discharging of Wilkes's obligations was in Horne's opinion the most effective means of serving the cause in which the debts had been incurred. Because of his exertion in Wilkes's behalf, Horne, according to Percy Fitzgerald, appears " to have been the first that introduced the ' paid patriot ' on the scene, who had hitherto to content himself with applause as his remuneration." [16]

Associated with Horne as active members of the new society were the prisoner for whose benefit it had been established, such patriots as Glynn, Sawbridge, Oliver, and Townshend, all members of the House of Commons, and William Tooke, Horne's future patron, who was first treasurer of the organization. The following advertisement was drawn up by Horne, approved by the Society, and published on February 27, 1769:

" Many gentlemen, members of parliament and others, *divested of every personal consideration* and *unconnected with any party,* have formed themselves into a Society at the London Tavern under the title of *Supporters* of *the Bill* of *Rights.* Their *sole aim* is to maintain and defend the *legal, constitutional liberty* of the subjects. They mean to support Mr. Wilkes and his cause, *as far as it is a public cause.* For this purpose they solicit the countenance and encouragement of the public *whose advantage and emolument alone are intended.*" [17]

At the third meeting, on March 7, the Society voted that three hundred pounds be sent to Wilkes for meeting his immediate needs. A committee was appointed at the same time to investigate the extent of his obligations. The So-

---

[16] *Life of Wilkes,* London, 1888, Vol. I, p. 74.

[17] *Controversial Letters of John Wilkes, Esq., the Rev. John Horne, and Their Principal Adherents,* London, 1771, pp. 150–151.

ciety was soon actively engaged, however, not only in paying Wilkes's debts, but in furthering the cause of Parliamentary reform. The members of the Society were " required
to aim at a full and equal representation of the people in
Parliament, annual Parliaments, the exclusion from the
House of Commons of every member who accepted any
place, pension, contract, lottery ticket or other form of
emolument from the Crown; the exaction of an oath against
bribery; the impeachment of the ministers who had violated
the rights of the Middlesex freeholders, and instigated the
'massacre' of St. George's Fields; the redress of the grievances of Ireland, and the restoration of the sole right of
self-taxation to America." [18] The new organization, which
received subscriptions from far and near, flourished until it
was disrupted by the unscrupulous conduct of its beneficiary.

Having once demonstrated his ability as a political
leader, Horne found himself busy from morning till night,
organizing meetings, making speeches, and taking part in
every political contest of the time. He came to be publicly
regarded, says one of his critics, " as a kind of traveling
counsel to every man who thought himself capable of being
made an object of public commiseration; an advocate-
general for all the empty querulousness, extravagant irrita-
tion, and unmeasured antipathies of the multitude." [19]

Added to his political duties and closely connected with
them, certainly, was his self-imposed task of disclosing the
violations of justice in the courts. On several occasions
he embarrassed the authorities not a little by displaying his
familiarity with the law. His knowledge of legal precedents enabled him to interfere so effectually, for example,

[18] Lecky: *England in the Eighteenth Century,* New York, 1892,
Vol. III, p. 374.
[19] *Blackwood's,* Vol. 33, p. 969.

in the Bigby case as to disconcert the court completely. Of the criminality of two brothers by the name of Kennedy, who had been convicted of the murder of Bigby, there was absolutely no question. When, therefore, they were pardoned by the King, through the intercession of a nobleman, infatuated by the beautiful sister of the murderers, Horne, who was not content with voicing the universal disgust at so outrageous a scandal, set to work to discover some means of punishing the offenders. By investigating an old English law ratified by Magna Charta, and other statutes, he found that all private wrongs could have recourse to " the right of appeal of blood," a privilege which could be claimed by the widow of the victim. In the case of a conviction under such an appeal, the King was powerless to grant a pardon. After persuading Bigby's wife to claim the privileges of this old statute against her husband's murderers, Horne anticipated with satisfaction a recall of the King's pardon or at least a public exposure of the proceedings. A defeat of justice and an escape from the grave disclosure was found, however, by the same nobleman who had interfered in the first instance. By presenting the widow of Bigby with 350 guineas, he persuaded her to waive her right of appeal.

Two condemned Spitalfields weavers next claimed Horne's attention. " I took no small pains, with other gentlemen," he said, " to save the lives of some innocent men; but though one was petitioned by the lord-mayor and all the aldermen who sat on the bench at his trial, with the strongest circumstances in his favour, and though another was unanimously and strongly recommended to mercy by the jury, they were hanged. Their crime was not murder." [20] Having discovered an alteration in their death sentence, Horne astonished the authorities by declaring not only that

[20] *Controversial Letters of John Wilkes, the Rev. John Horne,* etc., p. 20.

such a deviation from the original sentence was illegal but that adherence to the warrant would be murder. Realizing that such a statement came from an authority on the law, the sheriffs decided to seek advice. A lengthy and involved legal correspondence ensued, but Horne's efforts were futile and the execution finally took place at Bethnal Green. The questions raised by this critic of the law courts, were, however, the means of altering the mode of passing sentence. There was no disparity, in the future, between the sentence and the command for execution.

Under the title of *Genuine Copies of All the Letters Which Passed between the Lord Chancellor and the Sheriffs of London and Middlesex, etc. relative to the Execution of Doyle and Valine,* Horne himself published the entire correspondence connected with this legal dispute. The two city magistrates involved in the transaction were friends of his, and it is generally conceded that he wrote or dictated all of the letters ascribed to them.

Horne found time during what may be called the Wilkes Era not only to criticize the law courts but to advertise on every occasion the popular grievances against the Administration. He became, chiefly through the notoriety that he had won in the Middlesex elections, the favorite spokesman of those patriots who were restless under the injustice that they had suffered in the treatment of their chosen representative. In the course of his address to the freeholders of Middlesex, who had met in 1770 to consider the advisability of petitioning the King to dissolve Parliament, Horne dwelt upon the popular cause of discontent:

The violation of our rights in the person of Mr. Wilkes, is one plentiful source of our complaints. Notwithstanding the protection offered to that gentleman by the *privilege of* parliament, he was *closely* confined by an illegal *General Warrant;* and an illegal seizure was made *of his Papers.* He was continued in custody by an evasion of the *Habeas Corpus*. He was prevented from making his complaint to the House of Commons, by the collusion of the late Speaker with the Minister, and a message from his Majesty was admitted before the complaint for breach of privilege. He was expelled unheard, tho' detained from his attendance on the House by the wound of an assassin. In order to prevent his obtaining a legal satisfaction from Lord Halifax, his outlawry was expedited by the alteration of records, and he was convicted of publishing what he carefully concealed. To justify in some measure the former illegalities, and to screen the offenders, the Commons, contrary to law, which the Judge is bound by oath to observe, voted away the privilege of Parliament in case of a libel. On his appearance and surrender, an unjust attempt was made to prevent the reversal of his outlawry; and a scandalous delay was used of pronouncing judgment when that attempt was frustrated. When he was elected Member for the county of Middlesex, his seat was, by the Minister, made to depend on his with-holding his petition from the House of Commons. Mr. Fitzherbert waited on Mr. Wilkes from the Duke of Grafton, to inform him, that if he presented his petition, he should be expelled; but if he withheld it, he should keep his seat. Mr. Wilkes disdained to hold a seat in parliament by any other tenure than by your free choice. After that petition had been received, and severe punishment denounced if *every Tota* (that was the expression) was not proved. After witnesses for that purpose had been prepared, at a very great expense; after all this, six out of eight articles were struck out of the petition; and, in conformity to the Duke of Grafton's threats, he was again unjustly expelled, unheard, on an accumulated charge. After repeated reëlections, he was, contrary to law, incapacitated by a vote of the Commons; and a *vicious* writ, which alone is sufficient to make the acts of this parliament *null* and *void*, was, contrary to law, ordered to be issued by the same Commons, who had before pretended and usurped a power to disqualify.[21]

At approximately the same time that he was taking a conspicuous part in the deliberations of the Middlesex

[21] *An Oration Delivered by the Rev. Mr. Horne at a Numerous Meeting of the Freeholders of Middlesex*, London, 1770, pp. 9–10.

petitioners, Horne was interested in two remonstrances which the City of London presented to the King. The first of these was probably of his authorship, at least in part, and it is certain that he gave a copy of it to the *Public Advertiser*. Moreover, for writing the following paragraph, which concluded his description of the manner in which King George received this plea from his subjects, he narrowly escaped prosecution:

> When his majesty had done reading his speech, the lord mayor, aldermen, etc. had the honor of kissing his hand; after which, as they were withdrawing, his majesty instantly turned round to his courtiers and *burst out a laughing*.
> " Nero fiddled whilst Rome was burning." [22]

Horne subsequently apologized for his effrontery by publishing a solemn statement to the effect that Nero did *not* fiddle while Rome was burning.

Although Parliament promptly drew up a loyal address to the King to express its disdain for the petitioners, the City of London decided to present another remonstrance. This famous document, which was read to King George, seated on his throne, on May 23, 1770, was, without doubt, wholly the composition of Horne, whose political principles are embodied in the following paragraph:

> Your majesty cannot disapprove, that we here assert the clearest principles of the constitution, against the insidious attempt of evil counsellors to perplex, confound, and shake them. We are determined to abide by those rights and liberties, which our forefathers bravely vindicated at the ever memorable revolution, and which their sons will always resolutely defend; we therefore now renew, at the foot of the throne, our claim to the indispensable right of the subject, a full, free, and unmutilated parliament, legally chosen in all its members; a right, which this house of commons have manifestly violated, depriving at their will and pleasure, the county of Middlesex of one of its legal

[22] Stephens: *Memoirs of John Horne Tooke,* Vol. I, p. 150.

representatives, and arbitrarily nominating as a knight of the shire, a person not elected by a majority or the freeholders.[23]

Foreseeing that the answer to this request would be unfavorable, the resourceful clergyman, in addition to composing the remonstrance, had prepared for his friend Beckford, the Lord Mayor, a reply to the King. It is quite possible that Beckford, somewhat confused when the moment for his rejoinder arrived, may have made little use of the speech originally written for him by Horne, but the totally unexpected and unprecedented liberty taken by the petitioner in replying to the King astounded King George and his courtiers.

Horne, thinking it essential that the public be acquainted with the particulars of this unusual occurrence, published an account of the ceremony, the address of the recorder, and the reply which he himself had composed for the Lord Mayor. So popular did Beckford become for his audacity in responding to the King that when he died, not long afterwards, it was unanimously voted by the City of London to erect a monument to him, and Horne's speech, ascribed to the Lord Mayor, was engraved in gold letters on the base of the statue. Horne himself informed his biographer that the address was his. Having Beckford's statue in mind, he was accustomed to declare that no one could call him vain, inasmuch as he had secured statues for others but none for himself.

The last paragraph of the memorable reply to the King, attributed to Beckford but really the composition of Horne, must be quoted:

Permit me, sire, to observe, that whoever has already dared, or shall hereafter endeavor, by false insinuations and suggestions, to alienate your majesty's affections from your loyal subjects in general, and from the city of London in particular, is an enemy

[23] *Ibid.*, p. 154.

to your majesty's person and family, a violator of the public peace, and a betrayer of our happy constitution, as it was established at the glorious revolution.[24]

According to one writer, who saw nothing significant in the reforms which Horne was trying to effect, the latter, during the period that we have just been describing, " was flying all round the horizon for a grievance, canvassing every quarter of public caprice for a grievance. He must have found one, or made one, or sunk into the obscurity that was torture to his bustling and bitter soul." [25] Even this unfriendly critic is willing to admit, however, that Horne's officiousness and alertness played no small part in bringing about at least one important reform — the freedom of the press. His services in this instance were called forth, as were his earlier public activities, by issues growing out of the Wilkes situation. The publication of the proceedings in Parliament against Wilkes had led to such criticism of the authorities that the House, after deciding that the printing of the debates was a modern practice entirely without precedent, passed a resolution making the publication of proceedings in the House a direct offence against the privileges of that body. This autocratic measure, of course, immediately aroused the liberals to action, and as usual they found a ready exponent of their cause in Horne, who by artful planning soon brought matters to a climax between the opposing factions. By persuading two newspapers to ignore the resolution of the House forbidding the publication of Parliamentary debates, and by exacting the promise of such city officials as Brass Crosby, the Lord Mayor, and Aldermen Oliver and John Wilkes [26] to sustain

[24] *Ibid.*, p. 157.

[25] *Blackwood's Magazine,* Vol. 34, p. 307.

[26] Wilkes was discharged from the Tower on April 17, 1770. Before his release he had been elected alderman for the ward of Farringdon Without.

the cause of the printers, he staged a dramatic scene in the House of Commons. The conflict which the wily parson thus precipitated between the City of London and the House of Commons resulted eventually in the triumph of the press.

CHAPTER III

ONSLOW, WILKES, AND JUNIUS

THREE notable controversies in which Horne engaged during the first period of his political career were occasioned either directly or indirectly by his relations to Wilkes. His legal contest with George Onslow followed the withdrawal of that official from the camp of Wilkes; his notorious quarrel with Wilkes himself was provoked by the unprincipled conduct of his former ally; and his controversy with Junius was caused by his rupture with Wilkes, Junius making his attack just at the conclusion of that famous dispute.

In the year following the Middlesex elections, Horne, whose enthusiasm in the popular movement made him eager to detect traitors to the cause, attacked Onslow after the latter had aroused his distrust by accepting office under the Grafton administration. At a public meeting of the freeholders of Surrey at Epsom, Horne declared that Onslow was " a man who would promise fair, but was incapable of keeping his word," adding that " if Mr. Onslow would lay aside his privileges, he would lay aside his gown." [1] Following this arraignment of Onslow, there appeared in the *Public Advertiser* a letter signed " A Freeholder of Surrey," which contained insinuations of corrupt dealing on the part of Onslow. That official indignantly denied the charges against him, but his reply did not prevent the publication of still more violent and scurrilous accusations. He had

[1] Quoted in Stephens' *Memoirs of John Horne Tooke,* Vol. I, p. 121.

not, his libeller insisted, allayed the suspicions against him. Resolved, therefore, to resort to the law for a vindication of his character, Onslow applied to the printer for the name of his assailant. He was informed that the writer was the Rev. Mr. Horne, who had authorized the publisher to divulge the secret.

Shortly after this disclosure of his identity, Horne found himself involved in a suit for libel. The case, which was tried in 1770, before Sir William Blackstone, at Kingston, was opened by Sergeant Leigh, the counsel for the plaintiff. In making the charge, the latter reminded the court that the defendant and the plaintiff were strangers, that there had been no personal differences between them, and that nothing could explain or excuse the presumption of the defendant's accusations. For some time before publishing his libel, Horne had " conceived great malice," said Sergeant Leigh, " against Mr. Onslow; he had affected upon all occasions to treat him with contempt, and to cast reflections upon his character, which if they were true — which if Mr. Onslow really deserved — he was unfit for either of those offices which he is stated on the declaration to have held; he was unfit undoubtedly to be trusted with the public money of this country, or the disposal of offices and employments; he must be most unworthy to be of the privy council of his majesty, or to represent so respectable a county as this of Surrey." [2] The plaintiff, who had been unable to understand the defendant's insinuations against him at the meeting of the freeholders of the county, had, his counsel continued, been still further disconcerted to see in a newspaper Horne's criticism of his character.

Horne's letters, which were, of course, produced in court

[2] *Whole Proceedings in the Cause on the Action brought by the Rt. Hon. Geo. Onslow, Esq., against the Rev. Mr. Horne,* London, 1770, pp. 4–5.

as evidence, are fair examples of his satirical manner. The very first publication is a bold, unequivocal denunciation of Onslow. After referring to one of the Lords of the Treasury as having recently secured a thousand pounds for securing an individual by the name of Burns a place in America, the writer makes his charge: " The Lord of the Treasury kept his word, and the gentleman was appointed to the office he had paid for! and stranger still, Lord ———, who discovered this Bargain and Sale, is offended at it, and insists on the Dismission of this Lord of the Treasury. Now, Sir, I must intreat you to favour one of your Constituents with the name of this Lord of the Treasury, for you, no doubt, who sit at that Board yourself, must be acquainted with him." [3]

Onslow, who, it seems, was, at the time of Horne's attack, in correspondence with Burns in an honest effort to discover the recipient of the money, which undoubtedly had been paid to someone, termed the accusation " a gross and infamous Lie from Beginning to End." [4] All the information that he had concerning the hated fraud, was contained, he urged, in two letters which he now published. He indignantly concluded: " I defy the whole World to prove a single word in your libellous Letter to be true, or that the whole is not a barefaced, positive, and entire Lie. That it is I do assert, and I call upon anybody, if they can to disprove what I say." [5]

At the outset of his reply to this angry denial of his charges, Horne makes an insulting interpretation of one of his adversary's sentences. With a wit and a sarcasm nothing short of malicious, he asserts:

If with another innocent man, Lord Holland, you too were ambitious to add to the List of Mr. Walpole's Right Honourable

---

[3] *Ibid.*, pp. 7–8.   [4] *Ibid.*, p. 12.   [5] *Ibid.*, p. 13.

Authors, you might like him have exposed yourself with more Temper, and have called names in better English.

I should be sorry to libel you by mistaking your meaning, but the strange manner of wording your first sentence leaves me at a Loss to know whether you intend that my Letter, or . . . your own character is a gross and malicious Lie from Beginning to End.[6]

After protesting against Onslow's having cleared himself, Horne introduces an illustration to suggest his guilt: "Archbishop Laud thought to clear himself to Posterity from all aspersions relative to Popery by inserting in his Diary his Refusal of a Cardinal's Hat; not perceiving the Disgrace indelibly fixed on him by the offer."[7] In closing, he warns his correspondent not to prosecute him for an Insinuation: "Alter your Charge before it comes upon record to prevent its being done afterwards, for though Lord Mansfield did not know the difference between the words when he substituted the one for the other, we all know very well now that it is the *Tenor,* and not the *Purport,* that must convict for a Libel, which indeed almost every student in the Law knew before."[8]

The counsel for Onslow recognized the wit and ability of the libeller, but considered that he had prostituted these talents "to so bad a purpose, as to attack wantonly and without foundation,"[9] a neighbor's character. It seemed, indeed, from the evidence that was advanced and from the attitude of the court that Onslow would win his case, when Glynn, who was Horne's lawyer, raised certain legal technicalities that made a decision impossible. He contended, for example, that there was a discrepancy between the printed letter and that which the printer had stated to be the wording of the original. The first indictment, there-

---

6 *Ibid.,* p. 18.
7 *Ibid.,* p. 23.
8 *Ibid.,* p. 26.
9 *Ibid.,* p. 31.

fore, ended in a mistrial, and Horne escaped for the time. A new trial, over which Lord Mansfield presided, was soon ordered, however, and the defendant had now to answer, in addition to the former accusations, for maligning Onslow before the Middlesex freeholders. The decision finally arrived at by the court, in spite of Horne's masterly efforts in his own behalf, was a verdict of £400 in favor of the plaintiff.

Refusing to accept this decree as final, Horne appealed to a higher court on the ground that the words used in the indictment against him were not actionable. The court, after complicated and lengthy proceedings, finally decided on April 17, 1771, to favor the defendant, with the result that the second verdict was set aside. This triumph over Mansfield in the Onslow case was, says John Foster, " a proud commencement of that series of interviews which Horne was destined to have with his lordship, under the relation of judge and culprit, and might contribute not a little to his maintaining ever afterwards such an attitude of intrepidity and equality as no other man did, in the same relation, to the great despot of the law." [10]   Onslow, it should be stated, lost £1,500 in the lawsuit, while Horne lost only £200.

Even before a final decision had been rendered in the preceding case, Horne had quarreled with Wilkes, whose interests he had been defending, as we have seen, when he attacked Onslow. The disregard of Wilkes for all principles and his ingratitude to his supporters had estranged the former compatriots. Horne, who had never been deceived as to Wilkes's private failings, had tried in vain to curb his personal extravagances and to arouse in him some sense of obligation to those who had made sacrifices in his behalf. When, for example, Wilkes secured a verdict of £4,000 dam-

[10] *Critical Essays*, London, 1856, Vol. II, p. 167.

ages from Lord Halifax for the latter's action against him
in the matter of general warrants, Horne had urged him
to apply the sum to his debts. The patriot, it is needless
to say, had scorned the suggestion. After it became quite
obvious to Horne that Wilkes was taking advantage of the
organization founded primarily for the purpose of paying
his campaign debts, to indulge in outrageous expenditures
of a purely personal nature, he protested against his un-
scrupulousness and sought to divert at least a part of the
society funds to other purposes. He called the attention of
the members to the necessity for considering the case of
Bingley, who had been imprisoned shortly after he had
published in the *North Briton* one of the most daring of
Wilkes's letters in condemnation of the law courts. Finding
the evidence against the printer too slight for a conviction,
Lord Mansfield had endeavored to force a confession of
guilt from him by making a rule of court and setting a
date when he was to answer certain questions. Instructed
by Horne, who had discovered the illegality of Lord Mansfield's procedure, Bingley refused to reply to his examiners
and was confined on November 7, 1768, for contempt of
court. Although the sufferings of the prisoner for whom
Horne now interceded before the society entitled him to
the support of the organization almost as much as did those
of Wilkes, the first motion in his behalf failed to carry,
the society, controlled by the Wilkes faction, voting on
January 22, 1771, to pay Wilkes's debts before relieving
Bingley. On February 12, nevertheless, Horne succeeded
in carrying a motion that £500 be subscribed for the prisoner. Horne's victory in the society was only tempo-
rary, however, for on February 26, it was moved and carried that no new subscriptions should be undertaken until
all of Wilkes's debts should be paid. Following this resolution, Horne moved that the society be dissolved, and

when his proposal was rejected by a vote of 26 to 24, the minority withdrew from the organization and founded soon afterwards the Society for Constitutional Information. In his public correspondence with Wilkes, Horne dwelt upon the futile efforts for compromise in the original society when the Bingley motion was under discussion. " It was proposed," he said, " that every person might be permitted in that society to subscribe for whatever good purpose he should adopt: It was shown plainly, that by their vote they should exclude from the society everyone who wished to do public good, and who yet might not consent to subscribe to Mr. Wilkes, or who having given something might not consent to subscribe any more. Mr. Wilkes would listen to no terms; he was now sure to accomplish his wishes, and saw that from this day the society would either exist no longer, or would exist for him only." [11]

Two months before matters had come to a crisis in the society on account of the Bingley episode, Horne and Wilkes had already attacked each other in the *Public Advertiser*. With his usual alacrity to explain matters to the public, Horne had published on October 31, 1770, an anonymous account of a meeting of Westminster electors, who had deliberated upon the advisability of instructing their representatives to impeach Lord North. Wilkes had taken exception to Horne's description of the meeting, especially to the reflections cast upon him as chairman on the occasion, and had published on November 7 his own account of the proceedings. He confessed that he had favored a drastic step against the Ministry but he denied that he had attempted, as Horne's letter had implied, to dictate to the electors. In reply to Wilkes's letter Horne wrote on November 12:

[11] *Controversial Letters of John Wilkes, the Rev. John Horne and Their Principal Adherents,* London, 1771, p. 216.

I find myself in a situation which most of your friends have
at some time or other experienced. It is painful to me, but not
surprising. I have long foreseen it, and most earnestly endeavored to avoid it. You are in possession of my name, and
needed not to have called for it in the public papers. When I
gave the Printer the account of the proceedings at Westminster, I ordered him to acquaint you with it, and on the day
of its appearance in the paper I avowed it to yourself at a meeting of some freeholders at the Denmark Tavern, and I offered
to give you a justification of it, if you would afford me an opportunity by retiring with me after the meeting should be over.
I shall take it as a favour if you will not insist on a public
justification; for though I agree with you that " the public have
a right to truth," yet I must confess that there are some " imposi-
tions on mankind " which I would fain be excused from the office
of " detecting and exposing." [12]

The letter was, of course, a direct challenge, which Wilkes
lost no time in answering. Addressing his reply " to the
Author of the Letter to Mr. Wilkes," he stated that the
printer ordered to acquaint him with his name had not
complied with the request. " When I saw him the next
day," he continued, " I said that I guessed at the author
of that very erroneous *account*, but thought it an improper
question to *ask him*," [13] whereupon the printer had smiled.
" At the Denmark Tavern," Wilkes added, " I complained
to yourself of that *false account*, and declared that I would
answer it, nor did you mention a word of justification." [14]
After Horne's conduct had been criticized by several
anonymous writers, in particular by two signing themselves
" Scourge " and " Cat-o'-nine Tails " who accused him at
Wilkes's suggestion, no doubt, of misapplying funds, Horne,
on January 14, 1771, addressed to Wilkes, under his own
signature, a still more vindictive letter, at the very beginning of which he asserted: " An agent of yours declared
some time ago that it would be useful to you and your

[12] *Ibid.*, pp. 8–9.   [13] *Ibid.*, p. 9.   [14] *Ibid.*, pp. 9–10.

affairs to come to an open rupture with me. From this opinion has flowed all the abuse which has lately been bestowed upon me in the public papers. I believe you have mistaken a strong inclination for policy, and have yielded to a natural bias in opposition to honesty and your interest."[15] For almost three weeks, the writer explained, he had been ill, and, with the exception of the *Public Advertiser*, had seen only those papers which his friends had brought him. He had discovered in the papers little deserving a reply, with the exception of certain specific charges in the *Gazetteer* of the preceding Tuesday. Thinking that he owed it to his friends and to the public to take note of these particular accusations, he would answer each charge, he said, not copying Wilkes's example of recrimination. He would reserve for the future an explanation of his difference with his former ally.

The definite charges against him he enumerated as follows:

1. That "I subscribed to the Society of the Bill of Rights, but never paid one shilling." 2. That "I have received amazing sums for Mr. Sergeant Glynn's election, ten guineas each from most of his friends." 3. That "I have received subscriptions for the widow Bigby's appeal." 4. That "I have received subscriptions for Mr. Gillam's trial." 5. That "I have received subscriptions for the affair of the weavers in Spitalfields."[16]

Proceeding in a clear and convincing manner to state the facts in connection with each of these charges, Horne acquitted himself in each instance of duplicity or corruption. His refutation of the second accusation contained the following interesting reference to the thankless task that fell to his lot as a reformer:

I must premise that I have always carefully avoided three things; I mean the being placed upon any public occasion in any

[15] *Ibid.*, p. 13.　　　　　[16] *Ibid.*, p. 14.

situation of honour, trust, or profit from which my name, and my station, and inclination equally dissuaded me. I have been regularly and indefatigably the drudge of almost every popular election, prosecution, and public business, — never the object of any one. For three years past my time has been entirely, and my income almost wholly, applied to public measures.[17]

After repudiating the five charges against him and calling upon three of his colleagues, Richard Oliver, Sergeant Glynn, and William Tooke, to authenticate his statements, Horne added ironically: " But, Sir, there is one subscription more that I have received, and with which you have not charged me; I mean a subscription of £94 17s. 9d. raised for you in my neighborhood, which I have brought in to the Society very lately at the last meeting but one at the London Tavern." Before this subscription had been raised, Horne had advanced a payment to Wilkes of £38 8d., " which," he said, " I am still to receive, and of the subscription itself seven guineas still remain unpaid to me." [18]

The following replies to Horne's request for vindication from his friends, who hastened to testify to his honesty, would have disconcerted any one but Wilkes:

" I think it my duty ," said Richard Oliver, " to declare that the charge brought against Mr. Horne, relating to the Society at the London Tavern, of which I am Treasurer, is false, scandalous, and groundless; and all the other charges, as far as I know or believe, are the same." [19]

" The charge against the Rev. Mr. Horne," declared Sergeant Glynn, " as far as it respects my election, is false and groundless: with regard to the other charges, my experience of the integrity and disinterestedness of Mr. Horne entitles him to my testimony, if his general character had not made it totally unnecessary." [20]

---

[17] *Ibid.*, pp. 15–16.

[18] *Ibid.*, p. 22.

[19] *Supplement to the Letters of John Wilkes, Esq., the Rev. John Horne and Their Adherents*, p. 239.   [20] *Ibid.*

" The charge brought against Mr. Horne relative to the subscription for the Widow Bigby's appeal," William Tooke asserted,
" is entirely false and groundless: What Mr. Horne has said concerning it, in his letter of this day, is true. I have the list of the
subscribers, and the account of the money paid to the attorney,
and the balance due Mr. Horne is £39 4 s. I believe the other
charges have as little foundation." [21]

After Wilkes had replied briefly to " the feeble, languid,
and weary pages," [22] as he called them, of Horne's lengthy
defence of his character, there was a lull in the controversy
until May, 1771, when upon Wilkes's announcement of his
candidacy for the office of sheriff of London, Horne revived the old quarrel. From now on the correspondence of
the former allies became more violent and unrestrained.
For two months the public was amused and scandalized by
the furious letters which they exchanged. All barriers of
good taste were broken down and the readers of the *Public
Advertiser* were entertained with accounts by each writer
of the depravity of the other. Horne disclosed the true
character of Wilkes, furnishing minute and explicit details
of his personal extravagances, accusing him of dishonesty
in handling the sum of £1000 which he had held in trust
for the Foundling Hospital, of cheating a Jew by the name
of Silva, and of pawning the fashionable clothes which he
had left in his custody on the Continent. He challenged
Wilkes, moreover, to publish the fatal Montpellier letter,
inasmuch as there was in it nothing of which he needed to
be ashamed, except the compliment to his correspondent.
He pleaded his services in the public cause, giving in detail the history of the Society for Supporting the Bill
of Rights, and reminding Wilkes of his base ingratitude

[21] *Ibid.*
[22] *Letters of John Wilkes, Esq., the Rev. John Horne, and Their
Principal Adherents,* p. 25.

to the founder of the society. "You will not say that I courted you in your prosperity and forsook you in your adversity, you will not say that I have been ungrateful, or that I ever received any favours at your hands," said Horne. "I found you in the most hopeless state; an outlaw; plunged in the deepest distress; overwhelmed with debt and disgrace; forsaken by all your friends, and shunned by everything that called itself a gentleman, at a time when very honest men who could distinguish between you and your cause, and who feared no danger, yet feared the ridicule attending a probable defeat. Happily we succeeded, and I leave you by repeated elections the legal Representative of Middlesex, an Alderman of London, and about twenty thousand pounds richer than when I first knew you; myself by many degrees poorer than I was before; and I pretend to have been a little instrumental in all these changes in your situation." [23]

Wilkes, who contented himself with contributing to the controversy only about half as many letters as Horne published, ignored the real issue between himself and Horne and parried the latter's thrusts with characteristic wit and facility, while attacking his character, ridiculing his pretensions to the priesthood, and informing him that he must publish his last letter before Midsummer Day, since his correspondent would probably, by vote of the City of London, be preparing after that date " for the duties of a very important office and the faithful discharge of the Sheriff's oath." [24]

"The pair of patriots," says Trevelyan, " had abundance of mutual secrets connected with the money-lender, the vintner, the horse-dealer, and even the old-clothes man, which Horne did not scruple to unpack and display before the eyes of a laughing public, and Wilkes retaliated by

[23] *Ibid.*, p. 33.   [24] *Ibid.*, p. 29.

extracting from the parson of Brentford's letter of January, 1766, that sentence which unluckily for its author, is the only passage in his works that any living man, except a lecturer on etymology can repeat by heart." [25]   A few quotations from this voluminous correspondence will illustrate the extremes to which the notorious quarrel was carried.   Wilkes's reply to Horne's accusations of pawning his wardrobe must not be omitted: " As to your *old clothes*, I have already said that they continued in my home, the Rue des Saints Pères, From May 25 till November 1767, and were then sent to the great English banker's, Mr. Panchaud's.   Your assertion of the pawning is an impudent falsehood and a rascally return for the care I took of such trifles at your desire during the time I staid at Paris, and even on my leaving France." [26]   In a later communication Wilkes in denying Horne's accusations declares: " No courtier seems to me to enjoy the luxury of lying equal to the minister of New Brentford," [27] and in alluding to the Montpellier letter, by this time public property, he adds: " Scorpion-like you have stung yourself to death." [28]

Horne, who excelled in the power to write satire of the most vilifying quality, found no difficulty in matching the sarcasm of Wilkes.   " I have not changed my opinion of you," he informs his opponent, " since I knew you at all, except in *degree:* in that I think I am excusable: my small experience of mankind and my reading, even the exaggerated bad characters of plays and romances, had never furnished me with any example of a character so

[25] Otto Trevelyan: *Early History of Charles James Fox,* New York, 1880, p. 441.

[26] *Controversial Letters of John Wilkes, the Rev. John Horne,* etc., p. 74.

[27] *Ibid.,* p. 101.   [28] *Ibid.,* p. 106.

hideous as you: should I ever find a second *John Wilkes,* my whole system of philosophy would be altered." [29]

The correspondence of Horne and Wilkes includes without doubt a considerable amount of able composition, but as John Foster observes, it is " so completely of a personal nature as that it would require the combatants to be of much greater historical importance to give it any permanent interest. It explains why they became virulent and implacable enemies, and exhibits a graceless picture of strong talent on the one side, and alert talent on the other, earnestly exerted and delighted to tear, and stab, and poison, and ready, apparently, to join in a most devout prayer to the nether world for more efficient implements of offence. Horne's letters are composed with a grave, intense, argumentative acrimony. Wilkes's with still more deadly rancour, are more volatile, satiric, affectedly careless, and captiously smart: they display the boldest impudence of depravity, with wit enough to render it both amusing and mischievous. In point of success, relatively to the main matters in dispute, there is no manner of comparison between the two. Horne's part of the correspondence, though it may not completely vindicate himself in all points, perfectly explodes his opponent to atoms." [30]

After the futile controversy had dragged on for weeks, Wilkes again reminded his foe that he must complete his charges against him by the Wednesday preceding Midsummer Day, adding wittily that should the letters of Horne swell to " Number 45 " he would discontinue his correspondence on that date. On June 20, therefore, Wilkes, in accordance with this promise to close at that time a correspondence of which the public were weary, penned his last words in the controversy. In his final epistle, after

[29] *Ibid.,* p. 130.
[30] *Critical Essays,* London, 1856, Vol. II, p. 168.

enumerating carefully and concisely " a catalogue of lies in the letters of the Rev. Mr. Horne addressed to Mr. John Wilkes, not mentioned before," [31] and which he asserts to be twenty in number, he concludes: " Whether you proceed, Sir, to a thirteenth or, a thirtieth letter, is to me a matter of the most entire indifference. You will no longer have me for a correspondent. All the efforts of your malice and rancour cannot give me a moment's disquietude. They will only torment your own heart. I am wholly indifferent about your sentiments of me, happy in the favorable opinion of my valuable friends, in the most honourable connections, both public and private, and in the prospect of rendering myself eminently useful to my country. Formerly in exile, when I was *urbe patriaque extorris,* and torn from every sacred tie of friendship, I have moistened my bread with tears. The rest of my life I hope to enjoy my morsel at home in peace and cheerfulness, among those I love and honour; far from the malignant eye of the false friend, and the insidious hypocrite." [32]

After completing his account of the final scenes in the Society for Supporting the Bill of Rights, Horne depicts unflinchingly the consequences of his part in the contest with his former chief. " The poor parson," he confesses, " has been buffetted on the hustings where he did not appear, and hissed out of playhouses which he never entered; he has been sung down the streets, and exalted to a conspicuous corner with the pope and the devil in the print shops; and finally to complete the triumph over this mighty adversary, you have caused him to be burnt in effigy." [33]

As his last letter suggests, Horne undoubtedly sacrificed

---

[31] *Controversial Letters of John Wilkes, Esq., the Rev. John Horne,* etc., p. 200.

[32] *Ibid.,* pp. 202–203.

[33] *Ibid.,* p. 314.

his personal popularity to the contest with Wilkes, and his candidate, Richard Oliver, who, along with the founder and the more respectable members of the Society for Supporting the Bill of Rights, had withdrawn from that organization, was beaten in the city election of Sheriffs by Wilkes and by the Administration candidates. The controversy was most unfortunate for Horne, inasmuch as it injured his reputation with many of his admirers, who regarded him, after his break with his former leader, as a deserter of the popular cause. He was even accused, as we shall see presently, of siding with the Government. Moreover, the extended quarrel divided patriotic citizens in their allegiance to the advocates of liberal principles, and thus weakened not a little the solidarity of the radical movement.

Perhaps much of the odium which attached itself to Horne's name as a result of this controversy, was due to the general opinion that a minister of the Gospel should have refrained from a combat so obviously worldly and degrading. Public criticism of his conduct was voiced in the following description of a parson forgetful of his duties: "When a clergyman himself appoints the day for the christening of a gentleman's child and neither comes in person, nor takes care of another to do his duty, nor sends an excuse, he is guilty and insolent. When he leaves his parish, and in the morning goes to a tavern, and, among bottles and glasses, *jumps on a table* to harangue on a business in the decision of which he has no vote, he becomes at once impertinent and ridiculous."[34]

Before this prolonged quarrel with Wilkes had fairly come to an end, Horne was engaged in another controversy, in this instance with the foremost political writer of his

[34] *Supplement to Controversial Letters of John Wilkes, the Rev. John Horne*, etc., p. 302.

day. " While everybody with leisure for such a problem
was discussing," says Trevelyan, " whether it was worse
to apologize for having submitted to ' the infectious hand
of a bishop,' or to have shirked paying for three chintz
dressing-gowns and twenty-five bottles of old Jamaica rum,
Junius infused a spark of common-sense and high feeling
into the ignoble altercation by reminding Horne that the
Wilkes whom he formerly worshipped was the same man
as the Wilkes whom he had reviled, and that the sincere
friend of a great cause should find other means to evince
his love for it than by gloating over the frailties of its most
prominent advocate." [35]

The attack from Junius was like a bolt from the blue,
for Horne was not aware of having antagonized that mysterious personage, who now appeared in the rôle of a defender of Wilkes against his criticism. In a letter addressed to " His Grace the Duke of Grafton," written on
June 9, 1771, Junius not only refers to " Mr. Horne's new
zeal in support of the Administration," [36] but assails his
character. " The unfortunate success of the reverend Mr.
Horne's endeavors in support of the ministerial nomination
of sheriffs, will I fear obstruct his preferment," he states.
" Permit me to recommend him to your grace's protection.
You will find him copiously gifted with those qualities of
the heart which usually direct you in the choice of your
friendships. He too was Mr. Wilkes' friend, and as incapable as you are of the liberal resentment of a gentleman.
No, my lord, it was the solitary, vindictive malice of a
monk, brooding over the infirmities of his friend, until he
thought they quickened into the public life, and feasting,
with a rancorous rapture, upon the sordid catalogue of his

[35] *Early History of Charles James Fox,* New York, 1880, pp.
441–442.

[36] *Letters of Junius,* London, 1796, Vol. II, p. 131.

distresses. Now, let him go back to his cloister. The church is a proper retreat for him. In his principles he is already a bishop." [37]

Horne, who had already displayed his controversial powers in the contests with Onslow and Wilkes, accepted immediately the challenge of this new and formidable opponent. After enumerating the various antagonists apparently in league against him, he comes directly to the issue between him and his new correspondent when he says: " You charge me with ' a new zeal in support of administration ' and with ' endeavors in support of the ministerial nomination of sheriffs.' The reputation which your talents have deservedly gained to the signature of Junius, draws from me a reply, which I disdained to give to the anonymous lies of Mr. Wilkes. You make frequent use of the word gentleman; I only call myself a man, and desire no other distinction: if you are either, you are bound to make good your charges, or to confess that you have done me a hasty injustice upon no authority." [38]

Far from upholding the Administration, says Horne, he utterly abhors their policies and has always shown himself a violent opponent of their measures. He puts the matter strongly and honestly when he declares: " I say, that I have not, and never have had, any communication and connexion of any kind, directly or indirectly, with any courtier or ministerial man, or any of their adherents: that I never have received, or solicited or expected, or desired, or do now hope for, any reward of any sort, from any party or set of men in administration or opposition, etc." [39] Junius must, therefore, recant or lose his reputation for veracity as a writer.

The rewards of a servant of the public are, moreover, strikingly painted by Horne in the concluding paragraph of

[37] *Ibid.*, p. 134.　　[38] *Ibid.*, p. 137.　　[39] *Ibid.*, p. 138.

this answer to Junius: " Singular as my present situation is, it is neither painful, nor was it unforeseen. He is not fit for public business who does not even at his entrance prepare his mind for such an event. Health, fortune, tranquillity, and private connexions,. I have sacrificed upon the altar of the public; and the only return I receive, because I will not concur to dupe and mislead a senseless multitude, is barely, that they have not yet torn me in pieces. That this has been the only return, is my pride, and a source of more real satisfaction than honours or prosperity." [40]

To this spirited and eloquent defence of himself Horne received, on July 24, 1771, from the " Great Unknown," a long acknowledgment, imperious in tone, from the outset. " Sir," began the author, " I cannot descend to an altercation with you in the newspapers. But since I have attacked your character, and you complain of injustice, I think you have some right to an explanation." [41] The writer explains that he does not suspect Horne of the folly of soliciting votes or championing the cause in the papers. It is from his letters that Junius draws his conclusions. In gratifying personal feelings against Wilkes, Horne has, according to his correspondent, sacrificed the interests of his country. " The mode of your attack upon Wilkes (though I am far from thinking meanly of your abilities) convinces me," says Junius, " that you either want judgment extremely, or that you are blinded by your resentment. You ought to have seen that the charge you urged against Wilkes could never do him any mischief. After all, when we expected discoveries highly interesting to the community, what a pitiful detail did it end in! — Some old clothes, a Welch poney, a French footman, and a hamper of claret. Indeed Mr. Horne, the public should, and will forgive him

[40] *Ibid.*, p. 139.   [41] *Ibid.*, p. 141.

his claret and his footmen, and even the ambition of making his brother chamberlain of London, as long as he stands forth against a ministry and parliament who are doing everything they can to enslave the country, and as long as he is a thorn in the king's side." [42]

The implication that his professions are not in conformity with his conduct arouses Horne to the greatest warmth in his defence. In reply to Junius, he declares that his own demeanor has been frank and open and that, unlike his antagonist, he has not concealed himself in his " chamber to shoot my arrows out of the window; nor contented myself to view the battle from afar; but publicly mixed in the engagement, and shared the danger." [43] He condemns Junius, moreover, for his attitude to Wilkes, inasmuch as Wilkes *is* a " thorn in the king's side," and he exposes again the personal character of his former ally.

In his last letter Junius repudiates an opinion of Wilkes's conduct that coincides with Horne's and takes his correspondent to task again for his desertion of the popular hero: " How shameful it is in a man who has lived in friendship with him, to reproach him with failings, too naturally connected with despair! Is no allowance to be made for banishment and ruin? Does a two years' imprisonment make no atonement for his crimes? The resentment of a priest is implacable. No sufferings can soften, no penitence can appease him. Yet he himself, I think, upon his own system has a multitude of political offences to atone for." [44]

Horne congratulates Junius after the publication of his last letter upon the recovery of his usual style, though it has cost him a fortnight to regain it, and he indulges at the same time in a commendation of his own facility. " I compassionate your labour in the composition of your let-

[42] *Ibid.*, pp. 143–144.   [43] *Ibid.*, p. 155.   [44] *Ibid.*, p. 183.

ters," he has the audacity to tell the great satirist, " and will communicate to you the secret of my fluency. Truth needs no ornament, and in my opinion, what she borrows from the pencil is deformity." [45] He then reveals the indirectness and subterfuges of his correspondent: " You brought a positive charge against me of corruption. I denied the charge, and called for your proofs. You replied with abuses, and reasserted your charge. I called again for proofs. You reply again with abuse only, and drop your accusations. In Junius's last letter," Horne concludes triumphantly, " there is not one word upon the subject of my corruption." [46]

This letter closes the famous controversy between Horne and Junius, for although the latter referred to Horne in other letters, he addressed no further communications to him. Horne, it is generally conceded, had got the better of his accuser. He had won a decided victory over " the most perfect wielder of slanderous polemics that had ever arisen in English political controversy." [47]

In the *Quarterly Review* for June, 1812, Lord Dudley, who had been impressed by Horne's replies to Junius, praises his controversial style. " The most finished specimen of his composition," he declares, " is probably to be found in the two or three letters written in answer to the attacks of Junius; and he had the honor, which in those days was deemed no inconsiderable one, of being the only knight that returned with his lance unbroken from a combat with that unknown, but terrible champion. The great fault of Junius is a sort of stiffness and appearance of labor. His compositions smell too much of the lamp. He wanted nothing to be a perfect master of his art, but the

[45] *Ibid.*, p. 192.
[46] *Ibid.*, pp. 192–193.
[47] *Cambridge History of English Literature*, Vol. X, p. 406.

power of concealing it." Horne's letters, on the other hand, says the reviewer, have " the flow, unity, and simplicity which belong to writings struck off at a heat, and which depend for their effect, rather upon the general power of the writer, than upon great nicety and labor in the particular instance.

" In justice to Junius, as a writer, we must add, that he was laboring under the disadvantage of a weak case. It is evident that he was early and deeply sensible of his mistake; and he was therefore glad to put an end to the contest as soon as possible, even at the price of leaving his adversary in possession of the field; a humiliation to which he would not have submitted, but from the consciousness of his having originally selected an unfavorable ground." [48]

[48] Vol. 7, p. 319.

CHAPTER IV

RELATIONS TO AMERICA AND TRIAL FOR
SEDITIOUS LIBEL

AFTER Horne had thrown away his chances for promotion in the Church, he resolved to change his profession. The following passage from a letter which was addressed on May 25, 1769, by the Reverend Weeden Butler to his friend John Alleyne, reveals the disfavor into which Horne had fallen with the Church authorities even before his controversy with Wilkes and the publication of the fatal Montpellier epistle:

Our attendance at the Bishop's Visitation was very interesting; his Lordship gave a solemn, clear, and judicious charge. Mr. Horne's name had been previously called over with the rest of the cloth in the present department of the diocese: and, luckily for him, I believe he was either not present, or did not answer to the call. If I can see an inch into the mill-stone, a rod lays in brine for his political cleverness.

What a pity our young clerical cobbler will not attend more decently to his last! The charge would have afforded him a paragraph or two of pertinent and very wholesome cogitation; and it is not likely to end there.[1]

After formally resigning his living in 1773, Horne moved to a house in Windmill Lane, in the vicinity of New Brentford. " The great luxury of my life," he remarked in the progress of his trial for seditious libel, " is a very small but a very clean cottage." [2] Here at the age of thirty-seven, he returned with enthusiasm to the study of law,

[1] Nichols: *Illustrations of the Literary History of the Eighteenth Century*, London, 1828, Vol. V, p. 839.

[2] T. B. Howell, *State Trials*, London, 1816–1828, Vol. 20, p. 786.

which his parents, both of whom were now dead, had induced him thirteen years earlier to give up for a career in the Church. It seems that certain of his London friends, who had urged him to take the course upon which he was now entering, even guaranteed him an annuity of £400 until he should be admitted to the bar, though he never, it may be said to his credit, took advantage of their generosity.

Besides reading for the bar, Horne devoted some of his time during this period to the study of philology, a subject in which he had been interested since his undergraduate days. He now had leisure in which to organize material that he had previously collected and to add to his knowledge of the field. Two years before he renounced his calling he had still further prepared himself for scholarly investigation or for a distinguished professional career by becoming a candidate at Cambridge University for the degree of Master of Arts, an honor which he won only after a struggle with the University authorities. We read in the *Annals of Cambridge:*

Some excitement prevailed at the Commencement in consequence of an organized opposition to John Horne (afterwards Tooke) of St. John's College, proceeding to his degree of M.A. The avowed ground for this very unusual step was, that he had in his correspondence with Mr. Wilkes spoken disrespectfully of the episcopal character.[3]

Paley, Hubbard, and Bromley were among those who opposed his candidacy, while conspicuous among those who favored his application were Beadon and Jebb, both of whom testified that he had been distinguished at the University by the propriety of his conduct and his zeal for learning. The degree which was thus contested in his case was an honor, said Horne many years later in allud-

[3] Cooper: *Annals of Cambridge*, Cambridge, 1852, Vol. IV, p. 362.

ing to the injustice that had been done him, to which " any
creature that could answer two rational questions " [4] might
aspire. The degree " would to-morrow be conferred upon
a great dog," he declared on another occasion, " if he could
pay the fees and call out *Pro Domino Rege*." [5]

Shortly after Horne had become established in his new
home at Windmill Lane, he was called upon to abandon
his studies for a time to interest himself in the affairs of
his friend William Tooke, who, after purchasing an estate,
including Purley Lodge, near Croydon, Surrey, had become
involved in frequent disputes with Thomas de Grey, the
owner of the adjoining territory. In 1774, matters came
to a culmination between the two landowners when an en-
closure bill favoring De Grey was introduced into the
House by Sir Edward Astley. As soon as the proposition
was presented, Tooke petitioned for a delay of action
on the plea that the customary notice had not been given
to the inhabitants, whose interests, as well as his own,
would be seriously affected by the passage of the bill. In
spite of this protest, there was every indication that the
bill, which was to be read again at an early date, would
speedily be approved by the House.

It was at this crisis in his affairs that the master of
Purley Lodge sought the advice of Horne, who was delighted, as usual, to employ his talents against the perpe-
trators of a public wrong. Realizing the seriousness of
his friend's situation and believing that direct opposition
to the bill would now be futile, he decided to resort to a
desperate device for defeating the proposed measure. To
attract public attention to the bill and to provoke an investigation of the proceedings, he published a violent attack against the Speaker of the House, Sir Fletcher Norton,

---

[4] Gurney: *Trial of Horne Tooke,* London, 1795, Vol. II, p. 161.
[5] *Parliamentary History,* Vol. XXXV, p. 1380.

whom he accused of partiality in the handling of petitions.
The libel, which, of course, aroused immediate action on the
part of the House, against the printer and the author, resulted eventually, in accordance with the writer's expecta-
tions, in an inquiry into the proposed legislation.

When his name was announced by the printer, who had
been hastily summoned by the House to disclose the identity of the libeller, Horne, prepared to defend his action,
was in the gallery, no doubt enjoying the scene to the
full. Sir Fletcher Norton, it is said, was astonished to
discover that he had antagonized John Horne, and the
whole House was surprised at the revelation of the reviler's name. The former clergyman, now neatly dressed
in gray, hastened to present himself before the bar to explain the object of his attack. In an ingenious address in
which he disclaimed any lack of respect for Sir Fletcher
on either private or public grounds, he confessed that he
had been driven to extreme methods by his desire to serve
his friend and by his horror of a tyrannical measure.

Since only indirect testimony could be advanced against
the bold libeller, who maintained in the course of the
proceedings against him that he had been incorrectly described as a clergyman in the warrant that had been served
on him, he was finally, after being subjected to close ques-
tioning, acquitted and released from custody. His plan,
in the meantime, had succeeded, for the House, having
been given full time for deliberation and thought on the
proposed inclosure bill, eventually eliminated or withdrew
the objectionable clauses. Horne's initiative and resourcefulness had won another victory, the benefits of which were
enjoyed by his friend and by others who would have been
affected by the passage of the bill. William Tooke, grateful to his champion for his timely assistance, gave him
valuable presents and selected him as the heir to his prop-

erty. It was not until 1782, however, that Horne adopted
the name of his benefactor after the latter had apparently
long insisted upon it.

Having interfered in the settlement of his friend's affairs
and decided the fate of the inclosure bill, Horne returned
to his cottage and resumed his studies. He was not to
lead a leisurely life very long, however, for rumors of im-
pending conflict between Great Britain and her American
Colonies aroused him again to an active interest in public
affairs. The part which he played in the struggle of the
Colonists for independence deserves particular consideration since he was the only public man in England who
suffered trial and imprisonment for the avowal of sym-
pathies that were expressed by almost every Whig statesman of the period. His sentiments were in complete accord, for example, with those uttered by Rockingham,
Richmond, Grafton, Chatham, and Shelburne, in the House
of Lords, and with those voiced by Dunning, Fox, and
Burke, in the House of Commons. In the opinion of these
Opposition leaders, the triumph of the King over the
Colonies would mean a defeat of those ideals for which
they themselves stood at home. We have only to recall the
famous speech of Chatham in 1775, the bold declarations
of the Duke of Richmond even after the battle of Bunker
Hill, and the never-to-be-forgotten arraignment of the war
party by Burke, to be convinced that these influential personages were certainly not less emphatic in their condemnation of the Ministry than was Horne. So opposed, indeed, were many of the Whigs to the course which the
nation had adopted, that many of them, among them
Chatham's son, refused to take up arms against the rebels.

The numerous publications that appeared during the
first stages of the Revolution record the extremes to which
sentiment went, on the one hand, in its denunciation of the

Colonists for their rebellious spirit, and on the other, in its criticism of the Administration for its efforts to coerce America into submission. One type of patriotism that flourished before all hope of conciliation had been abandoned, found expression in a pamphlet written by the Reverend J. Fletcher, Vicar of Madeley in Shrewsbury. This optimistic clergyman, after making some observations on the "Dangerous Politics Taught by the Reverend Mr. Evans, M.A., and the Reverend Dr. Price," makes a scriptural plea for the revolting Colonists, who are obviously in the wrong, but whom royal clemency may yet reduce to the state of beautiful submission described in the following passage:

A *Lee* and a *Washington* are resolute enough to stand for a time the shock of thy forces: An *Adams* and an *Hancock* are obstinate enough to bury themselves in the ruins of their country: But, resolute and obstinate as they are, thy mercy confounds — thine indulgence disarms them. — The paroxysm is over — Candor and loyalty return together — The fiery heroes come back to sober heroism: and the rash patriots to true patriotism. Thy royal mercy has melted them into tears. With shame they fix their weeping eyes to the ground, with admiration they lift them up to heaven. — They claim the honour of bringing in person the restitution money thou insistest upon for thy injured subjects. — They haste to throw themselves at the feet of a Sovereign, who knows how to protect, to conquer, *and* pardon.[6]

Horne, who labored under no sentimental delusions as to the intentions of the Colonists and their desire for forgiveness, attempted for several years preceding the Revolution to mould public opinion in favor of a fairer attitude toward America. He could not, for example, conclude his

[6] *American Patriotism farther Confronted with Reason, Scripture, and the Constitution: Being Observations on the Dangerous Politicks Taught by the Reverend Mr. Evans, M.A., and the Reverend Dr. Price, etc.,* London, 1776, p. 122.

address before the freeholders of Middlesex, in 1770, without alluding in the following terms to the gravity of the American situation:

I have detained you too long to enter now into the grievances of our countrymen and fellow-subjects in America; I shall only say, that the security of their Freedom and their Rights, is essential to the enjoyment of our own. We should never for a moment forget this important truth, that when the people of America are enslaved, we cannot be free; and they can never be enslaved whilst we continue free. We are stones of one arch, and must stand or fall together.[7]

Versed in constitutional law and fully awake to the importance of the principles that were at stake, he denounced the Administration for its alienation of the Colonies through the Stamp Act and the Tea Duty. To such an uncompromising supporter of the popular cause neutrality and inactivity in a crisis that involved the traditional privileges of Englishmen were not to be thought of. Not satisfied with a mere criticism of the Ministry, he endeavored, through the medium of the patriotic organizations to which he belonged, to promote legislation favoring America. If he did not actually write the following resolution, adopted on July 23, 1771, by the Society for Supporting the Bill of Rights, he heartily subscribed to it:

You shall endeavor to restore to America the essential right of taxation by representation of their own free election, repealing the acts passed in violation of that right since the year 1763, and the universal excise so notoriously incompatible with every principle of British Liberty, which has been lately substituted in the colonies, for the laws of customs.[8]

The pioneer radical society, which was thus committed to a support of the American demands, came, as we shall

[7] *Oration Delivered by the Rev. Mr. Horne at a Numerous Meeting of the Freeholders of Middlesex*, London, 1770, p. 36.

[8] Stephens: *Memoirs of John Horne Tooke*, Vol. I, p. 166.

see, to sustain immediately after its establishment, a unique relation to the quarrel between King George and at least one of his colonial possessions. Inasmuch as Horne was the founder of the organization, and the dictator of its policies, it is perhaps no exaggeration to state, in this connection, that he was at least indirectly responsible, therefore, for the serious controversy which arose between the province of South Carolina and his Majesty George III, after the former had expressed approval of the Society for Supporting the Bill of Rights by appropriating funds for its use.

We read in the *Journals of the Commons House of Assembly of the Province of South Carolina*, that on December 8, 1769, it was resolved in the affirmative by the House " That the Public Treasurer do advance the sum of Ten thousand five hundred Pounds Currency, to be paid to certain Gentlemen, who are to remit the same to Great Britain, for the support of the just and Constitutional Rights and Liberties of the People of Great Britain and America." It was ordered at the same time " that the Public Treasurer do advance the sum of Ten thousand five hundred Pounds Currency, out of any money in the Treasury, to be paid into the Hands of Mr. Speaker, Mr. Gadsden, Mr. Rutledge, Mr. Parsons, Mr. Ferguson, Mr. Dart and Mr. Lynch, who are to remit the same to Great Britain for the Support of the just and Constitutional Rights and Liberties of the People of Great Britain and America," [9] the House pledging itself to reimburse the Public Treasurer the amount thus appropriated.

His Majesty's Council and his Majesty himself were astounded, of course, and highly incensed at the audacity of the House in providing funds to be used for purposes of in-

[9] *Journals of the Commons House of Assembly of the Province of South Carolina*, 1761–1771, No. 38, p. 215.

structing the Ministry and the British public in principles of constitutional government. Against such unprecedented legislation the Council protested violently in the following communication to the House:

Fully sensible that we live under a kind and generous prince, and are blessed with a Constitution, which has perhaps arrived at as great a state of perfection as human wisdom can extend to, we cannot persuade ourselves that a grant of such a sum, is in any sense honourable, fit or decent, not fit or honourable, as we conceive your Jurisdiction to Grant, is local and merely for provincial purposes, and not Decent, as the Grant by the Tax Bill to answer the Estimate thereto annexed, is expressly declared to be to His Majesty, and yet contains a provision, which tacitly affronts His Majesty's Government, which has been in our opinion, Gracious, Mild, and Good to all his faithful people.[10]

In spite of this threatening remonstrance, the Commons House stubbornly maintained "that to grant money for the Support of the Just and Constitutional Rights and Liberties of the people of Great Britain and America, can not be construed to be disrespectful or affrontive to His Majesty, the great patron of the Liberty and Rights of all his subjects."[11]   Even after being apprised of the King's commands to the Governor of the province to restrain the action of the House in the future in the matter of appropriating money " for services or purposes not immediately within or incident to our said Province of South Carolina, unless upon special Requisition from us, our Heirs and Successors, etc.,"[12] a Committee of the refractory House reported "that the order and Resolution of this House on the preceding 8th day of December last, cannot be deemed dangerous or unwarrantable, that the same would not have been so represented or the power of the House on that point, drawn into question, if the money borrowed had not been applied towards frustrating the unjust and

[10] *Ibid.*, p. 387.   [11] *Ibid.*, p. 391.   [12] *Ibid.*, p. 404.

unconstitutional measures of an arbitrary and oppressive ministry." [13]

In replying to the resolutions of the Commons House asserting their right to dispense funds for furthering the cause of liberty in England, his Majesty's Council, it may be added, referred contemptuously to the radicals composing the society which had been the beneficiary of the House, as a "set of people, who have been daily disturbing the repose and embarrassing the Councils of the best of Princes, alarmed at the unprecedented gift, and apprehending that the people of this Province ought not to be taxed," etc.[14]

The preceding quotations reflect the seriousness of the altercation between the King and the obstinate Commons House of the South Carolina province, and point clearly to the development of issues that were decided only by the Revolution. Nothing, of course, would have pleased Horne more than an acquaintance with the details of this dramatic contest, which he himself had indirectly provoked. He was apparently ignorant, however, that the action of South Carolina in appropriating funds for the support of the newly established radical society had precipitated a crisis in the history of that province.

He was involved, however, in another controversy of a very different kind, which was occasioned by the ingratitude of Wilkes to his benefactors across the water. At a time when Wilkes's debts were the subject of anxious and embarrassing deliberation by the Society for Supporting the Bill of Rights, that organization, Horne tells us, received, on February 6, 1770, a generous gift from South Carolina. "It was resolved," he goes on to say in his record of this donation to the society, "that a letter of thanks should be returned to the Speaker, etc., of the

<hr>

[13] *Ibid.*, p. 432. [14] *Ibid.*, p. 434.

Commons House of *South Carolina*. One of the members of the society, a gentleman of the clearest public principles and of much merit, drew up *very hastily* a letter of thanks on the occasion, which he showed to Mr. Wilkes for his opinion. Mr. Wilkes commended it extravagantly, and earnestly pressed the committee to adopt the letter; and he took some extraordinary measures that it might be adopted by the Society. When the committee had read it, they judged it for many reasons highly improper. It was not difficult to see the motives of Mr. Wilkes for making so strong a point of this measure. He was displeased at the Commons house of South Carolina, for not sending the *money to himself;* and he enjoyed the opportunity of making both them and the Society ridiculous. Some of us waited on Mr. Wilkes to dissuade him from pushing this letter: he persisted strenuously in recommending it; I desired him to tell us seriously upon his honour whether he did recommend it to us to send that letter. He put his hand formally upon his bosom, and declared *upon his honour* that he did most seriously approve and recommend it. We were amazed at his effrontery: however, upon my pressing him with particular passages, and desiring his justification of them, he was forced to declare that ' to be sure it would not be fit to send such a letter to the gentlemen of *Yorkshire,* or any other county in England; but was admirably calculated for the meridian of *South Carolina.'* Such was his sincerity to the friend who consulted him! Such was his gratitude to South Carolina! Such was his zeal for the public cause, that he wished to expose and undo in this treacherous manner a society which was evidently more capable of serving the public than any that had ever before been established in this country! Mr. Wilkes had always hated the Americans, was always the declared foe of their liber-

ties, and condemned their glorious struggles for the rights
of humanity, not only when he ignorantly expected to be
sent out Governor of Canada, but even after his confinement in the King's Bench; and many gentlemen as well as
myself, can remember the disputes which he has often
maintained with us before large companies in the King's
Bench, against the liberties of America. The *personal*
compliment of a letter to him from Boston softened his
language; but not so much as to make it proper for him
to take the advice I gave him before several gentlemen,
that he should burn the flattering answer he had read to
us, and write to the Bostonians his real sentiments, which
he was then *talking* to us against them. The compliment
paid to him by the letter from *Boston,* was effaced by the
affront, as he thought it, offered him by South Carolina.
He considered this subscription to the London Tavern as
£1500 out of his pocket, and no doubt felt the contempt
he expressed for them, who could prefer the payment of his
debts to furnishing him with *ready* money." [15]

The society would have been wrecked, said Horne, in
concluding his account of the disgraceful behavior of
Wilkes had the latter's stubbornness been unchecked.
Through Horne's exertions a suitable communication was
at length dispatched to the Commons House of South
Carolina.

When the society was finally dissolved on account of the
unscrupulous conduct of Wilkes, who, according to Horne,
had determined to convert it into " a sponge which should
suck up the generosity of the public to be squeezed into
his pocket," [16] the interests of America were looked after

[15] *Controversial Letters of John Wilkes, Esq., the Rev. John
Horne, and Their Principal Adherents,* etc., London, 1771, pp. 153–
159.

[16] *Ibid.,* p. 153.

by the new organization founded by the seceders from the pioneer society. Indeed, one of the chief objectives of the Society for Constitutional Information was to express emphatically the contempt of Horne and of his colleagues, and of the friends of liberty throughout the country, for the policies persisted in by the Government as a means of conquering the rebellious colonies. Of the members enrolled in the new organization no one was more unreservedly disposed to favor the American cause than was Major Cartwright, of whom Horne said: " If England possessed half a dozen men of his character and firmness in the different counties, they would have put a stop to the American War." [17]

As late as 1775, and perhaps even later, Horne believed as did Dr. Price and other opponents of the War party, that conflict with America might be averted, or at least shortened, if public sentiment could be aroused against the Administration. His criticism of the Government finally reached a climax, when after the clash between the Colonists and the royal troops at Lexington and Concord, he proposed at a meeting of the Society for Constitutional Information that funds be appropriated by the society, for the widows, the orphans, and the aged parents of the American soldiers killed in the recent conflict. His motion was adopted and the sum of one hundred pounds was subscribed out of the society funds, after which the resolution, made official by Horne's signature, was dispatched to the newspapers for publication.

Although this bold action provoked no little comment at the time of its advertisement, the Government took no immediate notice of it. After the Americans were officially declared to be rebels, however, the attitude of the Administration toward sympathizers with the Colonists be-

[17] Daly: *Dawn of Radicalism,* London, 1892, p. 128.

came more severe, and the authorities were anxious to make an example of such offenders. Horne's part in the resolution was accordingly remembered, and in 1777, when he was engrossed in his legal studies, anticipating at such a late date no inquiry into his share in the transaction, he was called upon to answer to a charge of seditious libel. Upon learning that three of the printers of the resolution had been fined and that he was to be prosecuted, he at once appeared before the Attorney-General to demand that the proceedings, which he did not intend to pay for, should be read to him. His request having been granted, he withdrew, after informing the authorities that he would conduct his own case.

His trial, which was opened on July 4, in the Court of King's Bench, Guildhall, was presided over by Lord Mansfield, before whom, as we have seen, he had formerly been arraigned on a charge of libel. With that audacity, indeed, which characterized his behavior in a court of law, Horne reminded the Judge that he had previously been the victim of his errors. Upon being informed by Lord Mansfield that he would have a remedy if it were proved that a certain ruling of the court to which he objected was irregular, he had replied: " O, my Lord: I have already suffered under your lordship's directing me to remedies. The most cruel of all poisoners are those who poison our remedies." [18] The remedy he had been offered in the Onslow case was almost as bad, he said, as the verdict would have been, for it had cost him £200. " I have always found," he added, " that such kind of remedies from your lordship are like giving a man a wound, and then telling him where he may find a plaster." [19] Horne's " great object," says Lord Campbell, " seems to have been to provoke

[18] Howell: *State Trials*, London, 1816–1828, Vol. 20, p. 664.
[19] *Ibid.*, p. 667.

Lord Mansfield to a sally of impatience of which he might have taken advantage." [20]

The Chief Justice, it must be remembered, had been the object of satiric attack by Horne from the time that the latter had appeared in the rôle of a political pamphleteer. On one occasion, he had even expressed the wish that an old law dating from the reign of James I, forbidding a Scotchman's becoming a judge, still existed. " This wish," he explained to the freeholders of Middlesex whom he was addressing, " does not proceed from any national prejudice, or from any disesteem or want of affection for those our fellow-subjects; but it would have been happy for us, and for the great bulwark of our Rights and Liberties, if the Common Law, which he despises, had known as little of Lord Mansfield as Lord Mansfield does of the Common Law. For since he has presided in that court, almost the whole practice of the King's Bench has been altered. Those extraordinary discretionary powers which the equity of former judges had rarely ventured to exercise on the most extraordinary occasions, he has brought into common use. He bails murder whenever it is pleasing to the Court. He grants new trials. He alters Records when the Crown prosecutes. He makes the plaintiff swear to his debt, thereby acting as in Chancery. He sets Jurymen aside. He does a hundred things of the same nature as mere matters of course; and has converted all the *extraordinary* into the *ordinary* powers of the Court; at the same time assuming new powers whilst he abuses the old." [21]

The prisoner was charged by his prosecutor, Attorney-General Thurlow, with being a " wicked, malicious, sedi-

[20] *Lives of the Chief Justices of England,* New York, 1873, Vol. III, p. 407.

[21] *Oration Delivered by the Rev. Mr. Horne at a Numerous Meeting of the Freeholders of Middlesex,* London, 1770, p. 21.

tious, and ill-disposed person," who, disloyal to the King, had purposed and contrived " to stir up and excite discontents and seditions among his Majesty's subjects and to alienate and withdraw the affection, fidelity, and allegiance of his said Majesty's subjects " [22] from their sovereign. The defendant had declared " that divers of his majesty's innocent and deserving subjects had been inhumanly murdered by his said majesty's troops in the province, colony, and plantation of the Massachusetts-Bay in New England, in America, belonging to the crown of Great Britain," and in conformity with these convictions he had written and published " a certain false, wicked, malicious, scandalous, and seditious libel of and concerning his said Majesty's government and the employment of his troops according to the tenor and effect following: ' King's Arm's Tavern, Cornhill, June 7, 1775 — At a special meeting this day of several members of the Constitutional Society, during an adjournment, a gentleman proposed that a subscription should be immediately entered into by such of the members present who might approve the purpose, for raising the sum of £100 to be applied to the relief of the widows, orphans, and aged parents of our beloved American fellow subjects, who, faithful to the character of Englishmen, preferring death to slavery, were for that reason only inhumanly murdered by the King's (meaning his said Majesty's) troops at or near Lexington and Concord, in the province of Massachusetts (meaning the said province, colony, or plantation in America) on the 19th of last April; which sum being immediately collected it was thereupon resolved that Mr. Horne (meaning himself the said John Horne) do pay tomorrow into the hands of Messrs. Brownes and Collinson, on account of Dr. Franklin, the sum of £100 and that Dr. Franklin be re-

[22] Howell: *State Trials,* London, 1816–1828, Vol. 20, p. 652.

quested to apply the same to the above mentioned purposes," etc.[23] The prisoner was condemned, furthermore,
for his boldness in publishing these proceedings shortly
afterwards in *The Morning Chronicle, The London Advertiser,* the *London Packet,* or *New Lloyd's Evening Post,*
and the *Public Advertiser.*

Tooke's audacity in signing his name to the resolution
was, in the opinion of the Attorney-General, who prosecuted him for being the original publisher of the libel, an
aggravation of his offence against the Government. "It
seemed to imply," he said, "a bolder insult upon manners and decency, and the laws of the country, than a
simple publication of a libel without that name would
have been. It *seemed* to imply this because while that
name lay hid behind the printer of the paper, the stout-
est champion of sedition could not have defied the laws
with greater security; for, though it stood in capitals upon
the front of many thousand pages, yet it was as inscrutable
and impossible for me to follow, as if the name had not
appeared upon the paper at all. For the rest of it, I put
it upon the publication, chiefly because that seems to be
the whole object and drift of the composer of the libel; for
as a composition it is absolutely nothing. I do not mean to
speak of it by derogation from the parts and talents of
the ingenious gentleman (whose parts and talents I never
heard so much of as I have done today) I do not mean to
speak in derogation of them; no doubt he could have writ
a better thing: but his understanding was industriously let
down and suppressed: and the very purpose of this writing
was to make it ribaldry and trash. For the intention of it
was (as it appears to me) nothing more than to defy the
laws and justice of the country, proclaiming, as it were,

[23] *Ibid.,* pp. 652–653.

thus: either punish the libel, or confess that there are no laws in the country by which a libel can be punished." [24]

Horne, who, it is obvious, had made no attempt from the first to conceal his authorship of the advertisement, boasted in the course of his defence that he was entirely responsible for the daring action taken by the Society for Constitutional Information. In referring to the apprehension of the printers, he informed the court:

Gentlemen, for every minute of imprisonment that those printers suffered I do freely and frankly confess that I deserve at least a year, comparatively. If they deserved a minute, for every minute I certainly deserve a year, and for every farthing of that hundred pounds which they were fined, proportion only our guilt (if there is any guilt in the case) a million of money will not be sufficient for my crime. If they can justify their sentence on the printers, I will justify the court for the most ample punishment they can inflict on me. If I am guilty, no man upon earth so guilty. It was the most deliberate act of my life; it was thought of long before I did it. I made the motion; I called the meeting; I subscribed a great part of the money; I procured the rest from my particular intimate friends.[25]

Not content, moreover, with this audacious confession, he added: " I am out of the reach of the intended consequences of this prosecution; I say, intended consequences: for rely upon it, I am better known to those who have caused this prosecution, than for them to have only in view the consequences of imprisonment and fine. No, they know better: they know that no men act as I have always done who mean to be stopped by imprisonment and fine." [26]

Maintaining that he was not the original author of the charge against the King's troops, Horne read a communication which he asserted was the original charge, signed by the agent of the province in which the murders had been

[24] *Ibid.*, pp. 668–669.   [25] *Ibid.*, p. 710.   [26] *Ibid.*, p. 711.

committed. "The original affidavits confirming it," he declared, "are here said to be lodged with the lord-mayor for inspection. It is very lucky for Mr. Lee that his receiving them, and causing them to be advertised, has caused no prosecution against him. We shall know presently whether this affidavit be a forgery or not: the gentleman for whose it is given attends by my subpoena to prove or to disprove it." [27]

The following illuminating account of the engagement at Lexington was then produced in court:

"I Edward Thoroton Gould, of his majesty's own regiment of foot, being of lawful age, do testify and declare that on the evening of the 18th instant, under the orders of General Gage, I embarked with the light infantry and grenadiers of the line, commanded by Colonel Smith, and landed on the marshes of Cambridge, from whence we proceeded to Lexington. On our arrival at the place we saw a body of provincial troops armed to the number of about sixty or seventy men. On our approach they dispersed, and soon after firing began; but which party fired first I cannot exactly say, as our troops rushed on shouting and huzzaing previous to firing, which was continued by our troops as long as any of the provincials were to be seen. From thence we marched to Concord. On a hill near the entrance of the town we saw another body of the provincials assembled. The light infantry companies were ordered up the hill to disperse them. On our approach they retreated towards Concord. The grenadiers continued the road under the hill towards the town. Six companies of light infantry were ordered down to take possession of the bridge, which the provincials retreated over: the company I commanded was one. Three companies of the above detachment went forward about two miles. In the meantime the provincial troops returned, to the number of about three or four hundred. We drew up on the Concord side of the bridge. The provincials came down upon us; upon which we engaged and gave the first fire. This was the first engagement after the one at Lexington. A continued firing from both parties

[27] *Ibid.*, p. 712.

lasted through the whole day. I myself was wounded at the attack of the bridge, and am now treated with the greatest humanity and taken all possible care of by the provincials at Medford." [28]

To justify his charge against the King's troops Horne himself undertook to describe the peacefully disposed Colonists on the eve of the battle:

Now, gentlemen, picture to yourselves the Americans of Lexington and Concord sleeping quietly in their beds, their wives and infants by their sides, roused at the dead of night, with an alarm that a numerous body of the king's troops (their number, perhaps augmented by fear and report) were marching towards them by surprise in an hostile manner — these troops who were not to be brought to justice by them for any murders which they might commit! What shall they do? Shall they stay, and submit themselves and their families to the licentiousness of these ruffians? I suppose there might be amongst them (as amongst us) some of both these sorts: but, however, for the honour of human nature, there were also some of another temper. They hastily armed themselves as well as they could; they collected together as they might, and they staid waiting the event, determined not to attack, but to defend themselves from lawless insult, or to sell their lives as dearly as they could. There is nothing surely in this that will justify the slaughter of them which ensued. [29]

Horne emphasized in the course of his defence the motives which had impelled him to take sides with the Colonists. He had been aroused to their support, he said, purely by convictions and principles and not by self-interest or personal ties. " I have never had occasion," he declared in this connection, " to promote an election, or to vote, or to do anything for any particular connections; they have always been absolute strangers to me, and men taken up upon the footing of oppression. Friends! — Yes, if friendship received from me could make them my friends.

[28] *Ibid.*, pp. 712–713.   [29] *Ibid.*, p. 737.

But friends! No, if friendship received from them was necessary to make it so. My motive has been constantly the same: I know no American." [30]

Although Horne was a stout champion of the cause of the Colonists, he never, it should be said, expressed any enthusiasm for them as individuals. Americans were, in his opinion, " of a very inferior cast; a prodigious number of pigmies, and but few giants among them. Extraordinary talents had neither occurred, nor were to be expected, perhaps, in that quarter of the globe: a man who knew but little, thought himself an extraordinary character there, and was actually so when compared with the common herd." [31] In contrast to the poor opinion that Horne entertained of the average American, was his admiration for Thomas Jefferson, whom he met in the eighties and considered a great figure. Another American whom he held in high esteem was Joel Barlow. The proscription by the British Government of the *Advice to the Privileged Orders,* and Barlow's interest, during his residence abroad, in the London Society for Constitutional Information, recommended him, no doubt, to Horne, who was instrumental in introducing him to France.

In pleading his case, Horne adopted a critical attitude toward the information against him, maintaining that it really charged him with no crime. He could not, he declared, be accused of seditious libel merely for reserving to himself the right to condemn the action of the King's troops, which, he said, " I did then call, and do still, and will tomorrow call, because contrary to law, a murder." [32] He reminded the court that after the riot in St. George's Fields he had accused the King's troops of murder, that he

[30] *Ibid.,* p. 715.
[31] Stephens: *Memoirs of John Horne Tooke,* Vol. II, p. 337.
[32] Howell: *State Trials,* Vol. 20, p. 663.

had not been accused of libel at the time, and that to charge the soldiers with murder was not to arraign the Government and the King. To impress the jury with the injustice of his being prosecuted on such a charge, he referred to the famous condemnation of the royal troops by Wilkes, who was present at the trial. " There sits near the Judge," he declared, " one of the most distinguished members of the House of Commons: he is as liable to an information of libel as I am at this minute. In his book the charge of murder is as completely made as in my advertisement: it is lately published in his letter to the Freemen of Bristol: he stands as liable to be expelled, to be punished, to be shut up from society as a mad dog as I do, and with the same pretense." [33]

Lord Mansfield's observation that Wilkes was "the pleasantest companion, the politest gentleman, and the best scholar that he ever knew," [34] was made, suggests Thorold Rogers, after the patriot had sat beside him at Horne's trial.

Horne amused his audience not a little in the course of his defence, by his witticisms at the expense of the Attorney-General. After listening to the long speech of the latter, who had exhausted his eloquence in an effort to convince the court of the defendant's crime and to impress upon them his own solemn duties as a prosecutor, Horne observed that if a stranger had come into the room at the moment when the Attorney-General was " talking of his integrity, his conscience, and his duty," [35] he might have mistaken the prosecutor for the defendant then pleading his cause. He aroused merriment, too, by his exposition of

[33] *Ibid.,* p. 700.

[34] Rogers: *Historical Gleanings,* Second Series, London, 1870, p. 178.

[35] *State Trials,* Vol. 20, p. 679.

the manner in which special juries were chosen and by his subsequent comments on the privileges of the Attorney-General.

" The Sheriff's officer," said the prisoner, " stands by, the Solicitor of the Treasury, his clerk, and so forth; and whilst the names are taken, if a name (for they know their distinction) which they do not like occurs and turns up, the sheriff's officer says, ' O, Sir, he is dead! ' The defendant who does not know all the world, and cannot know all the names in that book, does not desire a dead man for his juryman. ' Sir, that man has retired.' ' That man does not live any longer where he did.' ' Sir, this man has failed and become a bankrupt.' ' Sir, this man will not attend.' ' O ' (it is said very reasonably) ' let us have men that will attend, otherwise the purpose of a special jury is defeated.' " [36]

Horne had written down the names and saved two to whom the officer had objected. " I begged him," he said, "not to kill men thus without remorse, as they have done in America, merely because he understood them to be friends to liberty; that it was very true, we shall see them alive again next week and happy; but let them be alive to this cause. The first name I took notice of was Mr. Sainsbury, a tobacconist on Ludgate Hill. The sheriff's officer said he had been dead seven months. That struck me. I am a snuff-taker, and buy my snuff at his shop; therefore I knew Mr. Sainsbury was not so long dead. I asked him strictly if he was sure Mr. Sainsbury was dead, and how long he had been dead? ' Six or seven months.' ' Why, I read his name today; he must then be dead within a day or two: for I saw in this newspaper that Mr. Sainsbury was appointed by the city of London one of the committee (it happened to be the very same day) to re-

[36] *Ibid.,* p. 690.

ceive the toll of the Thames navigation,' and as the city
of London does not often appoint dead men for these purposes, I concluded that the sheriff's officer was mistaken;
Mr. Sainsbury was permitted to be put down amongst you,
gentlemen, appointed for this special jury." The other
gentleman " saved " by the defendant, had gone to the country, it was said. After some delay his name was included.
" Now what followed? " asked Horne. " This dead man
and this retired man were both struck out by the Solicitor of the Treasury; the very men whom the sheriff's
officer had killed and sent into the country were struck
out, and not admitted to the jury. Now, gentlemen,
what does that look like? There were many other names
of men that were dead, and had retired, which were left
out." [37]

After making further illuminating remarks on the manner
of selecting the jury, Horne continued: " Well, gentlemen,
having then got such a special jury as he usually does get
(for it seldom happens that twelve gentlemen have sense
enough of their duty to attend, as happens to be now my
case) the Attorney-General brings on the trial." [38] If the
Attorney-General secured a verdict, he punished whom he
pleased and when he pleased. " I think," said Horne,
" there were eight convictions for this advertisement, yet
but three have been called up to judgment. One, I think,
was let off because there was a little false swearing in the
case by an officer under the Crown (I allow it to have been
a mistake, because he is a gentleman of character) and
therefore it is accounted for how this one got off; but how
the other printers escaped, whether from the benevolence
of the Attorney-General, I do not know.

" That is not all. He aggravates the punishment of the
person against whom he gets a verdict, if he pleases. I was

[37] *Ibid.*, pp. 690–691.　　　　[38] *Ibid.*, p. 692.

present in court when I heard the judge who now tries me
(and who will perhaps give the same intelligence in my
case) tell the Attorney-General of that time (who is now
Chief Justice of the Common Pleas) when he moved that
the convict (who was the gentleman who now sits next to
the judge) when the Attorney-General moved that Mr.
Wilkes might be committed to the King's Bench prison,
Lord Mansfield instantly said to Mr. De Grey, ' The King's
Attorney-General may chuse his prison: all the prisons are
the King's.' " [39]

In addressing himself finally to the consideration of the
jury, Horne, abandoning the ironical and humorous tone
that had characterized a great part of his defence, declared
that he wished for no verdict that would " abate a hair " [40]
from that which the court deemed essential for the justice
of his country. His masterly efforts to vindicate his attitude toward the rebellious Colonies were in vain, however,
for after approximately an hour and a half's deliberation
the jury delivered a verdict of guilty, and though the trial
was later reopened, upon the defendant's motion in arrest
of judgment, Horne's attempt to prove that the information
against him really charged him with no crime, proved futile,
and he was forced to abide by the following decision of his
judges:

The court have considered of the punishment fit to be inflicted upon you for this offence: and the sentence of the court
is, — That you do pay a fine to the king of £200, that you
be imprisoned for the space of twelve months, and until that
fine be paid; and that upon the determination of your imprisonment, you do find sureties for your good behaviour for three
years, yourself in £400 and two sureties in £200 each.[41]

Horne received the sentence with composure, inquiring
particularly for an explanation from Lord Mansfield as

[39] *Ibid.*, pp. 693–694.   [40] *Ibid.*, p. 787.   [41] *Ibid.*, p. 788.

to the finding of sureties for three years. Upon Justice Ashton's and the Judge's interpreting it as not repeating similar offences or being guilty of any misdemeanor, the prisoner declared: " If your lordships would imprison me for three years, I should be safer; because I can't foresee, but that the most meritorious action of my life may be construed to be of the same nature." [42]

For his bold efforts in behalf of the American strugglers for independence Horne was consigned to the King's Bench Prison, a jail most unhealthy as to location, situated as it was in the midst of a swamp, and unspeakably bad from the standpoint of the accommodations provided for the prisoners. After a disagreeable experience when he first entered the jail, however, he was permitted to make a financial arrangement whereby he was allowed to occupy comfortable quarters outside the prison walls. Here, during his confinement, he was visited by his friends and associates in the popular cause. With Aldermen Oliver, Townshend, and Sawbridge, Sir John Bernard, William Tooke, and several other intimate companions, he enjoyed a dinner every Wednesday at " The Dog and Duck " in St. George's Fields, a weekly gathering which may have suggested the famous Sunday dinners at Wimbledon many years later.

In spite of the consideration with which Horne was treated during his imprisonment, his health was impaired by jail-distemper, to relieve which he drank much more wine than had been his habit. In consequence of this dissipation he contracted gout, a disease from which he suffered periodically from this time until his death.

Horne had boasted that fine and imprisonment would not silence his protests against tyranny. He had been released from prison only a few months, therefore, when he resumed

[42] *Ibid.*, p. 789.

his efforts to arouse sentiment against the War party. Undaunted by his previous sufferings in the cause, he resolved to make the struggle with the Colonists unpopular, in the hope of shortening its duration. With this object in view, he published in 1780, in collaboration with Dr. Richard Price, who composed the second and eighth chapters, which pertain to finance, a pamphlet entitled *Facts addressed to Landholders, Stockholders, Merchants, Farmers, Manufacturers, Tradesmen, Proprietors of every Description, and generally to all the Subjects of Great Britain and Ireland.*

Throughout the progress of the war there had been a notorious waste and misapplication of the public funds for war commodities. Horne and Price were, therefore, determined that an account of public expenditures should be presented to the nation. In the preparation of this record, the two patriots received at first the support of the Earl of Shelburne, who was opposed to the Ministry, but when the account was completed, the earl, for some reason, objected to certain passages in the pamphlet and tried to dissuade Horne from publishing it. Horne, however, who held a different opinion as to the advisability of presenting the *Facts* to the public, arranged for its immediate printing in spite of Lord Shelburne's protest.

The need of an immediate reduction of public expense is urged by the pamphleteers. Specific attention is called through statistics to the cost of the war even had peace been declared at Christmas, 1779, and the public are reminded that there is " a limit beyond which taxation cannot be carried with effect." When taxes become a burden, it is added, they will be evaded. "They will lessen consumption; destroy trade; encroach upon one another; engender rage; and terminate in revolt. It will be strange if two or three years more of the present war do not bring us to this crisis." [43] Such evils as the diminishing of trade, depopulation, private hoarding to avert financial ruin, embarrassment of the banks, complaints of the populace, and a general despondency on the part of the people, are enumerated, the economical and well-managed conduct of French expenses being contrasted with the looseness of the English administration.

The chapter entitled " The King's Civil List " is a bold arraignment of King George for his failure to keep the promises made to his subjects at the time of his accession, that " on his part they might be assured of a regular and becoming economy," [44] and the next division is a fearless exposure of Lord North's blunders and mismanagement as a financier and as a war administrator. " The present Treasury," it is asserted, " instead of profiting by the expense of the last war, (though Lord North had a place at that Board all the time) has set out in this unnatural war with a design not to check the public expenditure, but to increase the *Influence* of the *Crown* by the most unexampled extension of profusion, dissipation and bad economy." [45] The futility of the various expenditures and extravagances listed in the pamphlet is emphasized in the conclusion:

It has been stated in Parliament and has not been denied, that (notwithstanding all these enormous expenses) we had not in our great arsenal (the Tower of London) *fifteen thousand* stand of serviceable arms in May, 1778; which was two months after the French rescript of war had been presented to our court. This has been attempted to be in some measure accounted for; but in a very awkward manner; for it has been said to arise from the great quantities of arms which have been exported to America: thus proving (besides the improvidence of

[43] *Facts addressed to Landholders, Stockholders,* etc., Third Edition, London, p. 20.

[44] *Ibid.,* p. 30.   [45] *Ibid.,* pp. 46–47.

the measure) that we have been, absurdly as inhumanly, employing our *best* arms against our *friends,* and have now left only the *worst* to cope with our enemies.[46]

In his opening speech as candidate for Westminster, in 1796, Horne observed that during the reign of George III England had been involved in two wars and that in both, the principles advocated by the Administration were against Liberty, in the one case, against Liberty in France and in the other, against Liberty in America. He reminded his audience that for his disapproval of the American war he had paid a heavy fine and spent twelve months in the King's Bench Prison, and that for his disapproval of the French war, he had spent six months under rigid custody in the Tower and a month in Newgate.

It is gratifying to discover that this honest reformer, who paid so dearly for fidelity to his principles, has had his services in behalf of the American Colonists appropriately recognized by their descendants. On June 17, 1919, the New England Society of Brooklyn, New York, unveiled in old St. Mary's Church, Ealing, England, a memorial tablet to Horne " As a recognition of his actions in raising a fund for widows and orphans of American soldiers, killed on April 19, 1775, at Lexington and Concord, Massachusetts, at the outbreak of the struggle for American Independence, and further to commemorate the alliance in 1917 of American and British Arms in a war for Freedom and the Rights of all nations to self government." [47] The decision to honor this pioneer radical for his open and fearless support of the struggling Colonies was made two years prior to the actual ceremony, his grave in the meantime having been repaired at the expense of the society.

[46] *Ibid.,* p. 93.
[47] *Horne Tooke Memorial,* published by New England Society of Brooklyn, June, 1920, p. 9.

The bronze memorial tablet on a small base is the work of Lieutenant L. F. Roslyn of the Royal Air Force, a member of the Royal Society of British Sculptors, and the medallion of Horne which ornaments the top of the tablet was copied from the portrait in the National Gallery. The memorial exercises, which were attended by the members of the English-Speaking Union and many Americans in London, were, in the unavoidable absence of Ambassador Davis, conducted by the Hon. Robert P. Skinner, United States Consul-General. After the unveiling of the tablet, Mr. Lafayette Hoyt de Friese, President of the New England Society of Brooklyn, gave in behalf of that organization, a check for a sum corresponding to the amount raised by Horne for the Colonists,[48] to be used for the relief of the widows, the orphans, and the aged parents of the English soldiers who had lost their lives in the Great War. An impressive and formal procession around Horne's grave, while Lowell's famous stanza, beginning " Once to every man and nation," was sung, concluded the appropriate ceremony.

Mr. John W. Davis, in the speech that he had composed for the occasion, summarized the achievements of the patriot to whom his country was paying homage and spoke of the far-reaching consequences of the struggle in which he had participated. Many notable newspapers on both sides of the Atlantic commented on the significance of the memorial, the *Brooklyn Eagle* paying the following tribute to Horne:

So in the green church yard of Ealing with the rays of the June sun falling like a benediction on grass blade and clinging vine, amid the song of birds, the blood that stained the common at Lexington was wiped away as sons of nations once at strife

[48] At Lexington in the Hancock-Clarke House there is a tablet which records Horne's efforts in behalf of the Colonists.

clasped hands in amity and peace over the grave of one who dared to stand for a principle. And men thought that no better symbol could be desired as a herald of the day when the brotherhood of man shall be the human race.[49]

[49] Quoted in the Memorial Article by Edward V. Riis in the *Horne Tooke Memorial,* published by the New England Society of Brooklyn, New York, June, 1920.

CHAPTER V

" THE DIVERSIONS OF PURLEY "

A PERSON of Horne's energy could not be idle even in prison. Debarred for a time from exercising his talents as a reformer, he turned his attention once more to the study of language, which had occupied him prior to his activities in behalf of the Colonists. He now employed " the leisure which imprisonment afforded " [1] him to write to his friend Dunning a remarkable letter, which was occasioned by a question that had come up in connection with his motion in arrest of judgment, as to the grammatical interpretation to be placed upon the conjunction *that* in one of the precedents advanced against him. As the *Quarterly Review* for June, 1812, reminds us, " He comes hot from the court of King's Bench to discuss the nature of particles, of which, it seems, a shameful ignorance, on the part of the judges, had just been manifested in a verdict against him." [2]

Dr. Johnson, who had denounced Horne for his criticism of the Government in the American crisis, and had even expressed the wish that he might suffer the humiliation of being placed in the pillory, a mode of punishment, by the way, which the Attorney-General had strongly advocated, relented toward him, after reading the *Letter to Dunning*. When he had perused it, says Boswell, " though not treated in it with sufficient respect, he had candour enough to say to Mr. Seward, ' Were I to make a new edition of my

[1] Taylor Edition of *The Diversions of Purley*, London, 1857, p. 686.

[2] Vol. VII, p. 324.

103

Dictionary, I would adopt several of Mr. Horne's etymologies; I hope they did not put the dog in the pillory for his libel; he has too much literature for that.' "[3]

It is to be regretted that Dr. Johnson and Tooke, who thoroughly despised each other, never met. An encounter between them would have been almost as dramatic as the famous meeting between Johnson and Wilkes. Professor Lounsbury, finding little that was genuinely characteristic of either Johnson or Tooke in Landor's imaginary description of a meeting between the two linguists, says: " If ever a conversation had a right to be termed imaginary, this one is entitled to the distinction. It is not worth while to spend much time upon the numerous glaring anachronisms contained in it throughout. In the very opening of the dialogue, Tooke is represented as congratulating Johnson upon the completion of his great undertaking. It had been sent him the moment it came from the press, and he had been engaged ever since in its perusal. Now the Dictionary was published in 1755, when Tooke, or Horne, as was his name then, was but nineteen years old. In the lie which is represented as coming soon after from his mouth, that he had read almost all the old English authors that were printed or extant, the matter of age is of little consequence. It would have been a lie, different in degree but the same

[3] Birrell Edition of Boswell's *Life of Johnson*, Vol. V, London, 1906, p. 58.

Horne " mentions this compliment," in *The Diversions of Purley*, Boswell adds in a footnote, " as if Dr. Johnson, instead of *several* of his etymologies, had said *all*. His recollection having thus magnified it, shows how ambitious he was of the approbation of so great a man."

In the passage to which Boswell refers, Horne quotes Seward as confiding to him Dr. Johnson's assertion " that if he lived to give a new edition of his dictionary, he should certainly adopt my derivations." (*Diversions of Purley*, Part I, p. 128.)

in kind, had he been ninety instead of nineteen. But the
unreality of the conversation is due to the part severally
played by the two speakers in the dialogue. Tooke does
practically all the talking. Johnson is represented as be-
having in a way he was incapable of doing. He listens
most of the time in submissive silence, occasionally emitting
a growl at the personal character or beliefs of his inter-
locutor, but accepting with assent or without contradiction
some of his most preposterous statements, and at intervals
contributing to the discussion some observations of his own
almost as absurd. To any one knowing about the men the
part that Johnson is made to play is more than imaginary:
it is inconceivable." [4]

Shortly after his release from prison in 1779, Horne,
anxious to establish himself in the calling for which he was
preparing himself at the time of his prosecution, applied
for admission to the bar. Since he had kept the requisite
number of terms, he believed that he had only " to order
his wig and gown, pay the usual fees into the hands of the
treasurer of the Inner Temple, and invite his companions
to an entertainment on the occasion." [5] The Benchers, who
might use their discretion in cases of admission, subject of
course to the final decision of the judges, refused, however,
to accept his application. They had only a short time before refused to admit Murphy because he was a comedian,
a decision which was later reversed, and they now rejected
Horne because he had been a priest, " though," as we are
reminded by an early editor of *The Diversions of Purley,*
" it is notorious that all lawyers in England before the
reformation were clergymen." [6]

[4] Lounsbury: *The Standard of Usage in English,* New York and
London, 1908, pp. 41–42.
[5] Stephens: *Memoirs of John Horne Tooke,* Vol. II, p. 13.
[6] *Diversions of Purley,* Philadelphia, 1806, Part I, p. 60.

Since the decision against him was not final, however, Horne presented a second application to the authorities in 1782. He inquired of his examiners " whether the injunction of an ecclesiastical tribunal directing clerks to abstain from secular employment, were legally binding? whether since the Reformation such a question had ever been raised? whether they would raise it against any other applicant than himself? whether the profession of a clergyman was indelible? whether a clergyman in full orders cannot be secularized? and lastly whether he, by giving up his preferment, did not actually become a layman? "[7] In spite of the strong arguments in his favor, he lost his case by one vote, and believing that appeal to the judges and to Parliament would be futile, he was forced to resign himself to the verdict of the Benchers. As late as 1794 his name appeared on a list of applicants for admission to the bar, but none of the examiners interested themselves in his behalf. His exclusion from a profession which his talents and his training had qualified him to enter was a cruel disappointment to him. The experience, according to Stephens, made him bitter and cynical.

Shortly after he was first rejected by the Benchers, Horne decided to try his success at farming, a legacy from his father and the sale of his living enabling him to buy and improve a small estate at Witton, near Huntingdon. In all probability he would very soon have sunk his small fortune in his new enterprise had it not been that before he was fairly well established in his recently purchased country home, his health necessitated a removal from the neighborhood.

After being so fortunate as to return the property to its former owner, he decided to take up his residence in Lon-

[7] Thorold Rogers: *Historical Gleanings,* Second Series, London, 1870, p. 223.

don, where he rented and furnished a house in Richmond Buildings, Dean Street, Soho. Here he was the agreeable host to numerous friends and acquaintances, in whose company he delighted, and here, too, for the first time, he entertained during the holidays, when she had a vacation from boarding school, his daughter, Mary, and later her sister, Charlotte. The two girls, who were known as the Misses Harte, made their home afterwards with their father, who made no secret of their relation to him. In his address to the freeholders of Middlesex in 1770, Horne asserted that he had neither wife nor children to consider when he risked his life to bring the murderers of young Allen to justice. If we attach any importance to this statement, his daughters must have been born after the events described in his speech. Since his eldest child was old enough, however, to be in attendance upon a boarding school at the time her father went to London to live, she was probably born before he resigned his living.

It is a commentary on the morals of the eighteenth century that a former clergyman could introduce his illegitimate children [8] to his friends and acquaintances without, apparently, provoking any very general condemnation of his character. In this age of profligacy and vice the irregularity of his private conduct excited comparatively little criticism even from his enemies. Horne, who would have been utterly indifferent to any opinion, however censorious, that the world might have entertained of his defiance of conventionality, felt, nevertheless, the responsibility of rearing his daughters properly and giving them every educational advantage. William Sharpe was employed to teach

[8] Horne also had a son, who went by the name of Montague. The latter was sent to India, where he entered the service of the East India Company. (See Stephens: *Memoirs of John Horne Tooke,* Vol. II, p. 501.)

them drawing and engraving, and they were encouraged by
their father to vie with each other in these arts. Horne,
who himself carefully supervised their study of the classics,
declared that his daughter Charlotte knew as much Latin
as most of the bishops, and Samuel Rogers was astounded
at the facility with which one of the Misses Harte read
Greek. Both of the daughters were so well trained that
they frequently served as secretaries and amanuenses to
their father.

In the city, Horne found an interest in political discussions with his guests and in an attendance upon the meetings of the new Society for Constitutional Information,
founded in 1780 by Major Cartwright, as a successor of the
former society of that name. The two public events of
paramount interest to him in the year 1782 were Pitt's first
attempt at Parliamentary reform, an effort in which Horne,
who himself addressed a letter to Lord Ashburton on the
subject, heartily supported him, and the conclusion of the
war with America, which was confirmed by vote of the
House of Commons. In the same year that was made
memorable for him by the political occurrences just mentioned, he assumed the name of his benefactor, William
Tooke, whose heir he presumably became. After his removal to London, he had resumed his friendship with this
early acquaintance, and he now spent much of his time at
Purley Lodge, the latter's country home, which was particularly attractive to Horne for having been the residence
a century earlier of the Judge Bradshaw who had presided
at the trial of Charles I. The latest master of the estate
and his guests enjoyed the natural beauty of the spot and
entertained themselves with horseback riding, piquet, and
other sports.

During this period when Horne Tooke, as we shall now
call him, was apparently dividing his time between city
politics and the pleasures of the country, he was giving

serious attention to the study of language. The results of
his scholarly investigations were at last given to the public
in 1786 when Part I of *The Diversions of Purley,* his
treatise on philology, appeared. While the title of the
masterpiece compliments the author's patron, it is a mistake to suppose that even a part of the book was actually
written at Purley. The term *Diversions,* moreover, which
suggests Tooke's delight in his subject, must ever remain,
except to those few who are initiated into the pleasures of
etymology, an equally misleading part of the title. According to Hazlitt, some had mistaken Tooke's masterpiece
for a game; others, for a novel. A reviewer for *Blackwood's*
thus describes his " boyish disappointment " upon opening
the famous treatise: " From the attraction of its title and
frontispiece we had selected it as a sure source of entertainment for Christmas week and dire was our dismay when
we found that *The Diversions of Purley* consisted in discussions upon prepositions, pronouns, and past participles,
even duller and drier than those to which our school studies
condemned us." [9]

The zeal with which Tooke was pursuing his philological
studies in 1794 when he was called upon to answer to a
charge of treason, led his counsel, Erskine, to state that he
was " painfully bestowing a greater portion of his time to
the advancement of learning than the rudest health could
with safety bring to it "; that he was " intensely devoted to
researches which will hereafter astonish, and will not be
soon forgotten by the world "; and that he was indeed " *at
that very moment,* engaged in a work such as the labor of
man never before undertook, nor perhaps his ingenuity ever
accomplished." [10]

Before completing another division of his work, however,

---

[9] *Blackwood's,* Vol. 47, p. 484.

[10] Gurney: *Trial of John Horne Tooke for Treason,* London, 1795,
Vol. I, p. 406.

Tooke met, in 1798, the demand for a new edition of his first volume. It was not until 1805 that he published the second part of his treatise. To this latter volume, as well as to the second edition of Part I, his friends subscribed liberally. Samuel Rogers, who greatly admired the philologist and his work, was a generous subscriber to the volume of 1805. It was largely through the interest and exertion of such acquaintances as Rogers and Sir Francis Burdett, perhaps, that Tooke realized in all from the sale of his masterpiece a sum totalling four or five thousand pounds. This amount, moreover, was clear gain, for no book could have been advertised less than was *The Diversions of Purley.* Ten pounds, we are told, would have covered the cost of advertisement. During the earlier part of his life, Tooke had received small remuneration for his literary efforts. " Of all the things I ever wrote in my life," he stated in one of his letters to Wilkes, " the profits amount to £66. 4s. 1½d., not sufficient to furnish you with two months claret." [11]   It is gratifying to discover, therefore, that although he was denied the privilege of engaging in a vocation which would have assured his financial success, he was rewarded so richly in later years for his scholarly labors.

The Diversions of Purley was, moreover, the means of introducing him to many prominent persons of his day, for men of letters and others interested in the subject of language sought his acquaintance. Even his former implacable enemy and prosecutor, Lord Thurlow, fearing that he would not live to read the last part of his treatise, requested an interview with him to learn the content of that division. Tooke received his guest with cordiality and the two ancient foes became eventually congenial companions, their mutual detestation of William Pitt, the powerful minister of the

[11] *Controversial Letters of John Wilkes, the Rev. John Horne and Their Principal Adherents,* London, 1771, pp. 23–24.

day, who had aroused Tooke's distrust after he had deserted the cause of reform, going a long way, no doubt, to make them forget old scores.

To understand the reputation which Tooke enjoyed as a linguist we must recall how unique a book *The Diversions of Purley* was at the time of its appearance. Only in comparatively modern times, it must be remembered, has there been any decided progress in the study of language. Not until 1786 when Sir William Jones introduced Sanskrit to Europe and suggested the idea of a family relationship among languages, was fruitful investigation possible. Earlier etymologists had been directed in their researches by mere surface resemblances between words. Little effort had been made to study language on a comparative basis. The results obtained by generations of scholars had been, for want of a sufficient body of knowledge and a scientific method of study, fragmentary and unsatisfactory. Linguists had been occupied with speculating on how language came into existence and with building up highly artificial systems to account for its vagaries. Their conclusions had been based upon assumption rather than upon fact.

When Tooke entered upon his linguistic studies, Latin was still generally regarded as a dialect of Greek, and both Greek and Latin were supposed to have been derived from the Hebrew. The northern languages were just beginning to receive serious attention, and Tooke, more than any of his contemporaries, called attention to the necessity for studying them. He regretted that the parent tongue had not been introduced into the seminaries, and he flattered himself that as a result of his investigations the study of the Teutonic languages would be stressed in the future. The time usually devoted to Latin and Greek was " amply sufficient," he insisted, " for the acquirement also of French,

Italian, Anglo-Saxon, Dutch, German, Danish, and Swed-
ish," [12] since the five languages last named were hardly
more than varying dialects of one tongue. Tooke's acquaintance with Anglo-Saxon and the other northern languages makes his etymology far more reliable than that of
his contemporaries. His derivations, for example, were
more trustworthy than those of Johnson, who, like most of
the earlier linguists, was more concerned with the purity
of the language than with a scientific knowledge of its
history.

The eighteenth century opened the way for a profitable
study of language by the compiling of dictionaries, the
writing of grammars, and the translating of Anglo-Saxon
and Oriental literatures. Even in this scholarly period,
however, little was known of the real life and development
of language. Between the publication of the Port Royal
Grammar of the seventeenth century, generally regarded as
the first practical approach to anything like a philosophy
of language, and Tooke's treatise, there were scant contributions to a definite system of language study. The
Hermes of John Harris, which Bishop Lowth considered
" the most beautiful example of analysis that had been
exhibited since the days of Aristotle," [13] embodied the ele-
mental principles of a philosophy of language, but it dealt
with questions of a grammatical rather than of a philological nature, and was largely a restatement of the opinions
of Greek philosophers. That Tooke was aware of the need
of such a study as he himself undertook, and that he wished
to differentiate his task from that of the mere lexicographer,
is clear from his assertion: "I am not here writing a
dictionary (*which yet ought to be done, and of a very different kind from anything ever yet attempted anywhere*)

[12] *Diversions of Purley*, Part I, p. 82.
[13] Quoted in the *Works* of James Harris, Vol. II, p. xvi.

but only laying a foundation of a new theory of language." [14]

Tooke's predecessors had never conceived of so unified and complete a theory of language as did he. Before his time the subject had been treated, on the whole, as an abstraction; it had been explained in pedantic and obscure technical terms. Tooke, however, as Tuckerman observes, " approached the subject as if it had never been subjected to this complex treatment. He undertook to examine it as the botanist does plants, or the geologist fossils. Regarding language as a branch of natural history, he treated words with the cool and systematic analysis that a physiologist treats animal life, tracing back the quadruped to the animalculae. In this way he soon satisfied himself that the only absolute and natural parts of speech are nouns and verbs, others so called being nothing more than abbreviations, rendered formidible by elaborate grammarians. Davy reducing a gas into its elementary forms, or Audubon gathering specimens of birds and arranging them in species, did not more completely follow the inductive method than Tooke, in distributing words into families and genera, and tracing their lineage to a primal expression." [15] In demonstrating the relation to the verb of all the indeclinable parts of speech, Tooke was, says Murray, the first philologist to apply inductive principles to the history of language.

At first thought it seems rather odd that a political agitator like Tooke should have made so unique a contribution to the study of language. Political reformers, however, have not infrequently turned grammarians or etymologists. Cobbett and Hazlitt, for example, both radicals, wrote

[14] *Diversions of Purley,* Philadelphia, 1806, Part I, p. 326.
[15] Tuckerman: *Characteristics of Literature,* Second Series, Philadelphia, 1851, pp. 112–113.

grammars, the latter, a disciple of Tooke, incorporating in his treatise the theories of his master. Many public figures besides the Philologer of Purley have distinguished themselves as linguists. More than one of the writers, indeed, with whom Tooke disagreed, held office under the Crown. With the exception of Cobbett, however, who gave a political coloring to his grammar by dedicating the work to Queen Caroline, and by adding to his conclusions " Six lessons, intended to prevent statesmen from using false grammar, and from writing in an awkward manner," these authorities did not, like Tooke, mix politics with grammar or philology. The author of *The Diversions of Purley* could not, as we shall see, cast aside political prejudices or forget the wrongs that he had endured, even when he assumed the rôle of a scholar. " When employed in his great work," said Samuel Rogers, " Horne Tooke amuses himself with thinking how posterity will feel when they read it, and reflect on the persecutions he has suffered." [16]   *The Diversions of Purley* is, therefore, not merely a treatise on language. It is a book on the pages of which the author's personal animosities are boldly inscribed.

Attributing his political martyrdom to an erroneous interpretation of words, Tooke connected his personal experiences with his theory of language, and actually " contrived to graft his great philological inquiry upon a legal squabble." [17]   Rankling under the injustice that had subjected him to twelve months' imprisonment, he reviewed in the 1798 edition of *The Diversions of Purley*, the circumstances that had provoked his *Letter to Dunning* and the publication of his more extended study of language. " The substance of that Letter," he states, " and of all that I have

[16] Quoted in Clayden's *Rogers and His Contemporaries*, London, 1889, Vol. I, p. 80.

[17] *Quarterly Review*, June, 1812, Vol. 7, p. 324.

further to communicate on the subject of Language, has
been amongst the loose papers in my closet now upwards
of thirty years; and would probably have remained there
some years longer, and have been finally consigned with
myself to oblivion if I had not been made the miserable
victim of — *Two Prepositions and a Conjunction.*

" The officiating priests were themselves of rank and
eminence sufficient to dignify and grace my fall. But that
the conjunction *that* and the prepositions *of* and *concerning*
(words which have hitherto been held to have *no* meaning)
should be made the abject instruments of my *civil extinc-
tion,* (for such was the intention, and such has been the
consequence of my prosecution) appeared to me to make
my exit from civil life as degrading as if I had been brained
by a lady's fan." [18]

To understand how three particles could have decided
Tooke's fate, we must recall that he was found guilty of
writing and publishing " a certain false, wicked, malicious,
scandalous and seditious libel *of* and *concerning* his Majesty's Government," [19] and that when his trial was reopened, he objected to the interpretation placed upon the
conjunction *that,* in one of the precedents advanced against
him. Maintaining that the information against him really
charged him with no crime, he had made a motion in
arrest of judgment, since nothing could be urged against
him, he had protested, but what was expressed in the
record.

Upon Tooke's motion, Lord Mansfield adjourned the
decision, " and instead of arguments on the merits of my
objection (which however by a side wind were falsely

[18] *Diversions of Purley,* First American Edition, Philadelphia,
1806 and 1807 (this edition is referred to throughout the chapter),
Vol. I, p. 61.
[19] *State Trials,* Vol. 20, p. 653.

represented by him as merely *literal* flaws) desired," Tooke informs his readers, "that *precedents* might be brought by the Attorney-General on a future day. None were however adduced, but by the Chief Justice himself; who indeed produced two. (Thereby depriving me of the opportunity of combating the precedents and their application, which I should have had, if they had been produced by the Attorney-General.) And on the strength of these two precedents alone, (forgetting his own description and distinction of the crime to the jury) he decided against me." [20]

One of the precedents advanced against him, Tooke adds, was "merely *imagined* by the Chief Justice, but never really existed," and the other, owing to a misconception as to the meaning of the conjunction *that,* "had never been truly understood; neither by the counsel who originally took the exception, nor perhaps by the judges who made the decision, nor by the reporter of it, nor by the present Chief Justice who quoted and misapplied it." [21] An argument had arisen in court, it should be stated, in explanation of the preceding quotation, as to whether the words " She knowing *that* Crooke had been indicted for forgery, did so and so," should be construed as an averment that Crooke had been indicted, Tooke contending that the expression must be regarded as the equivalent of two propositions; namely, " Crooke had been indicted for forgery," and " She knowing *that,* did so and so." [22]

" Mr. Dunning undertook to prove (and did actually prove in the house of Lords) the *non-existence* of the main

---

[20] *Diversions of Purley,* Part I, p. 62.

[21] *Ibid.,* p. 65.

[22] *Letter to Dunning.* Tooke thus attempts to prove that the averment said, by the Judge, to be omitted in this information, quoted as a precedent against him, was " not only substantially, but *literally* made."

precedent; " said Tooke, in concluding his account of the
decision against him, " and I undertook, in that letter to
Mr. Dunning, to shew the real merits and foundation, and
consequently, Lord Mansfield's misapplication of the other:
and I undertook this, because it afforded a very striking
instance of the importance of the meaning of words; not
only (as has been too lightly supposed) to metaphysicians
and schoolmen, but to the rights and happiness of mankind
in their dearest concerns — the decisions of courts of
justice.

" In the house of lords these two precedents (the foundation of the judgment in the king's bench) were abandoned;
and the description of my crime against government was
adjudged to be sufficiently set forth by the prepositions *of*
and *concerning.*" [23]

The subject of language had fascinated Tooke, as we
have noted, ever since his Cambridge days, and after his
resignation from the Church he had devoted much of his
time to his studies. In the course of his trial for seditious
libel he had intimated that he was engaged in a scholarly
undertaking that might one day benefit the public. Undoubtedly, therefore, he would eventually have published
his speculations on language had he not been offered up as
a victim of the specified parts of speech. His prosecution,
however, provided him with a strong motive for acquainting the public with the results of his investigations.

The unprecedented freedom, however, with which he thus
united politics with etymology provoked adverse criticism
of Tooke in his lifetime and aroused prejudice against him
for more than a generation after his death. In Coleridge's
opinion, it showed " a base and unpoetical mind to convert
so beautiful, so divine a subject as language, into the

[23] *The Diversions of Purley,* Part I, p. 65.

vehicle or make weight of political squibs," [24] and Dugald
Stewart, who objected to Tooke's unusual methods of presenting and illustrating his theories, expressed the hope
that in the third volume which he had promised the public,
he " would condescend to adopt the usual style of didactic
writing, without availing himself of a form of composition
which eludes the most obvious and the most insuperable
difficulties by means of a personal sarcasm, or of a political
epigram." [25]   Even so devoted a disciple of Tooke as Richardson regretted that the violent passions " excited in the
hotbed of politics, should be carried into the retreats of
literary life." [26]   Tooke's masterpiece, as DeVere complains,
is " unfortunately so filled with an animosity, for which his
political martyrdom is hardly sufficient excuse, and such
fanciful vagaries, that his pregnant views on formative
words have seldom obtained that credit for themselves and
that honor for their author, which his genius and even his
caustic humor certainly deserved." [27]

The advantage which the philologist took of his readers
by instructing them in politics, as well as in language, is
illustrated by numerous passages from his treatise.   To
emphasize the imperative need of a reform in the House of
Commons, for example, he adds to his explanation of the
word *nether* the following illustration of its former use:

" The word *nether* is indeed at present fallen into great
contempt, and is rarely used but in ridicule and with scorn:
and this may possibly have arisen from its former application to the House of Commons, antiently called (by Henry
8) ' The Nether house of parliament.'   That the word
should thus have fallen into disgrace is nothing wonderful:

---

[24] *Specimens of the Table Talk of the Late Samuel Taylor Coleridge*, New York, 1856, p. 308.

[25] *Philosophical Essays*, Philadelphia, 1811, p. 210.

[26] *On the Study of Language*, London, 1854, Preface, p. ix.

[27] *Outlines of Comparative Philology*, New York, 1853, p. 56.

for in truth, this *nether* end of our parliament has for a long time past been a mere show and mockery of representation, but is now become an impudent and bare faced usurpation of the rights of the people." [28]

From a discussion of the possibility of reforming abuses in the language, he digresses to comment ironically on the impossibility of effecting a reform in the Government: " Reform. God forbid. I tremble at the very name of *reform*. The Scotch and the English lawyers in conjunction (*Pitt* and *Dundas*), with both the Indies in their patronage point to the *Ecce Homo* with a sneer; and insultingly bid us — ' behold the fate of a reformer! ' " [29]

The following definition, with its timely application, is another characteristic illustration of the political tone of Tooke's book:

Bread is the past participle of the verb *to bray* (French broyer) *i.e.* to pound or to beat to pieces: and the *subauditum* (in our present use of the word *Bread*) is *corn,* or *grain,* or any other similar substances such as *chestnuts, acorns,* etc., or any other *substitutes* which our blessed ministers may appoint for us in this blessed reign.[30]

In a lengthy passage such as the following, the philologist, in defining the term *right*, airs his political creed:

The Right I revere is not the Right adored by sycophants; the *jus vagum,* the capricious *command* of princes or ministers. I follow the law of God (what is *laid down* by Him for the rule of my conduct) when I follow the *laws* of *human nature:* which without any human testimony, we know must proceed from God: and upon these are founded the *Rights* of man, or what is *ordered* for man. I revere the Constitution and Constitutional Laws of England; because they are in conformity with the laws of God and nature: and upon these are founded the rational *Rights* of English-

[28] *Diversions of Purley,* Part I, p. 330.
[29] *Ibid.,* Part II, p. 438.
[30] *Ibid.,* p. 38.

men. If princes or ministers or the corrupted sham representatives of the people, *order, command,* or *lay down* anything contrary to that which is so *ordered, commanded* or *laid down* by
God, human nature, or the Constitution of this government, I will
still hold fast by the higher authorities. If the meaner authorities
are offended they can only destroy the body of the individual, but
never can effect the *Right* or that which is ordered by their
superiors.[31]

Tooke's political beliefs found their way into many illustrations of the meaning of words. After asserting, for
example, that *Lord* means " high-born or of an exalted
origin," he observes significantly:

You will perceive that Kings can no more make a *Lord* than they
can make a traitor. They may indeed place a thief and a traitor
amongst Lords; and destroy an innocent and meritorious man as a
traitor. But the *theft* and *treachery* of the one, and the innocence
and merits of the other, together with the infamy of thus mal-
assorting them, are far beyond the power of any kings to do
away.[32]

In addition to political allusions of the preceding type,
Tooke indulged freely in witticisms and sarcasm at the
expense of his enemies. Indeed, judging by the bitter temper of the passages in which he refers to Windham and
Pitt, one might almost conclude that his chief purpose in
publishing a second edition of his masterpiece was to acquaint his readers with the shortcomings of his foes. Certainly, the bold commentaries on these statesmen are the
distinguishing features of the new volume.

Tooke's sensitiveness to criticism which he could impute
to an enemy is proved by his wrath against the Reverend
J. Bruckner of Norwich, who signed himself " J. Cassander " in a letter addressed to the author of *The Diversions
of Purley*. Very probably Tooke would have ignored this
attack, which was slight enough to be overlooked by the
public, had he not attributed its instigation to Windham,

<hr>

[31] *Ibid.*, p. 11.   [32] *Ibid.*, p. 126.

at that time a member for Norwich. In replying to Cassander, who had credited Professor Schultens with the discovery that all particles were nouns and verbs, he denounced to posterity the critics who would question the originality of his theory of language:

The enemies of the *established* civil liberties of my country have hunted me through life without a single personal charge against me through the whole course of my life; but barely because I early descried their conspiracy, and foresaw and foretold the coming storm, and have to the utmost of my power *leally* resisted their corrupt, tyrannical and fatal innovations and usurpations: they have destroyed my fortune: they have illegally barred and interdicted my usefulness to myself, my family, my friends, and my country: they have tortured my body: they have aimed at my life and honor. Can you wonder that, whilst one of these critics takes a cowardly advantage (where I could make no defense) to brand me as an *acquitted felon,*[33] I am unwilling (where I can make a defense) that he should, in conjunction with his anonymous associate, exhibit me as a convicted plagiary and impostor? But no more of these cowardly assassins. I consign them to the lasting contempt they have well earned, and which no future *title* will ever be able to obliterate from the name of Windham.[34]

Not content with the arraignment of Windham in the preceding paragraph, Tooke resurrects for that statesman an ancestor whose undesirable qualities have presumably been transmitted to his descendant. To illustrate the etymology of the word *coward,* for instance, he quotes from Hakluyt, a passage from the *Voyage to Benin* by Thomas Windham, to which he adds the following note: " This Thomas Windham was a Norfolk gentleman: and a curious account is given in this voyage, of his usurping and cruel conduct, and of his mean, violent, selfish, and tyrannical character." [35] Into a discussion of the unchangeable gram-

[33] Windham had referred to Tooke and his companions who were tried for treason as " acquitted felons."

[34] *Ibid.,* Part I, pp. 201–202. [35] *Ibid.,* Part II, p. 36.

matical character of words, he introduces adroitly and humorously another reference to his accuser: "It is with words as with men; call this squire, my lord; then he will be comparative: call him by the new fangled marquis, or call him duke; then he will be superlative: and yet whosoever shall trust him or have to do with him will find to their cost that it is the same individual squire Windham still." [36]

On Pitt, as on Windham, but for different reasons, fell Tooke's maledictions. In the first volume of *The Diversions of Purley,* which was published in 1786, Tooke, who at that time was a strong supporter of Pitt, prophesied that upon the head of the latter, because of his important relation to parliamentary reform, would descend " the blessings or execrations of all posterity forever.[37] In 1798, after Pitt had not only deserted the cause of reform, but had instigated the famous State Trials, in which he himself had figured so prominently, Tooke disclosed the infidelity of this " lost leader " to a cause which he had once championed. By publishing in his treatise a letter which he had received from Pitt in 1782, pledging his influence to the cause of reform, after Tooke as a representative of a delegation from Westminster had waited upon him, he made the perfidy of his former idol complete. " This letter," he observes, " was produced by me upon my trial at the Old Bailey, in the year 1794: when fidelity to the sentiments it contains was seriously and unblushingly imputed to me as high treason. The original of this letter, Mr. Pitt, upon his oath, to my astonishment, acknowledged to be in his own handwriting, although every trace of Delegation was totally effaced from his memory." [38]

The name of this brilliant statesman was boldly introduced into the following illustrations of grammatical usage:

[36] *Ibid.,* Part I, p. 214. [37] *Ibid.,* p. 167.
[38] *Ibid.,* p. 168.

Thanks to Pitt, it is *along* of him that we not only keep our boroughs, but get peerages into the bargain.

Curses on Pitt: It is along of him that the free constitution of this country is destroyed.

" I suppose," Tooke adds satirically, " that Lord Lonsdale, Lord Elliott, and the father of Lady Bath, would not mean to impute any *fault* to the minister in the former of these sentences: though the people of England do certainly impute an inexpiable crime and treachery to him in the latter." [39]

Tooke, who had frequented the hustings and been arraigned in the law courts, drew freely for grammatical illustration, as the preceding quotations suggest, upon the public situation and his own political misfortunes. The violent partisanship which he displays, his exposition of his theory through the medium of dialogue,[40] and his ingenious etymological explanations, relieve his discourse from tediousness, and make it, in parts at least, anything but dull. In the opinion of Lord Brougham, " he has made one of the driest subjects in the whole range of literature or science, one of the mosts amusing and even lively of books." [41]

In presenting his theory of language, Tooke exhibits no modesty or scholarly reserve. He " triumphs," says Sir James Mackintosh, " over the blindness of the whole human race who left him the discovery." [42] Convinced of the

---

[39] *Ibid.*, pp. 348–349.

[40] The initials " B," " T," and " H " are employed in Part I to indicate the speakers, Dr. Beadon, William Tooke, and the author, respectively. In Part II, in which the conversation is restricted to Sir Francis Burdett and the author, the initials " F " and " H " are employed.

[41] *Statesmen of the Time of George III*, Second Series, Philadelphia, 1839, Vol. I, p. 146.

[42] Robert James Mackintosh: *The Life of Sir James Mackintosh,* London, 1835, Vol. II, p. 232.

priority of his conclusions, he asserts at the outset that he differs from all preceding grammarians. "Their systems and their difficulties vanish together," [43] he declares. For the most influential linguists of his day he expresses contempt. He observes, for example, that a safe rule to adopt in regard to the opinions of Lord Monboddo is to take always the opposite view. Far from joining, moreover, with the popular grammarian, Bishop Lowth, in his praise of Harris, the author of *Hermes*, or with Harris in his compliments to the Bishop, he vigorously attacks both of these learned contemporaries. With Harris, who has mistaken "fustian for philosophy," he particularly disagrees. "A little more reflection and a great deal less reading, a little more attention to common sense, and less blind prejudice for his Greek commentators would have made him," says Tooke, " a much better grammarian, if not perhaps a philosopher." [44]

The following criticism reveals Tooke's attitude toward the literary dictator of his age:

Johnson's merit ought not to be denied to him; but his dictionary is the most imperfect and faulty, and the least valuable of any of his productions: and that share of merit which it possesses makes it so much the more hurtful. I rejoice, however, that though the least valuable, he found it the most profitable: for I could never read his preface without shedding a tear. And yet it must be confessed, that his *grammar* and *history* and dictionary of what he calls the English language, are in all respects (except the hulls of the latter) most truly contemptible performances: and a reproach to the learning and industry of a nation which could receive them with the slightest approbation.

Nearly one third of this dictionary is as much the language of the Hottentots as of the English: and it would be no difficult matter so to translate any one of the plainest and most popular

---

[43] *Letter to Dunning.* (See Taylor's Edition of *The Diversions of Purley,* London, 1857, p. 694.)

[44] *Ibid.,* p. 722.

numbers of the *Spectator* into the language of that dictionary, that no mere Englishman, though well read in his own language, would be able to comprehend one sentence of it.

It appears to be a work of labor, and yet it is in truth one of the most idle performances ever offered to the public: compiled by an author who possessed not one single requisite for the undertaking and (being a production of a set of book sellers) owing its success to that very circumstance which alone must make it impossible that it should deserve success.[45]

Tooke never lost an opportunity to ridicule the great lexicographer. He accuses him of " making a bulky book without trouble," [46] and he observes ironically that " S. Johnson in point of etymology and the meaning of words, is always himself." [47]

The mistakes of his predecessors may be attributed, says Tooke, to their supposing " all words to be *immediately* either the signs of things or the signs of ideas: whereas in fact many words are merely *abbreviations* employed for despatch and are the signs of other words." [48] In reminding his readers that " words have been called winged," [49] he emphasizes the " winged " character of words of the second class. These abbreviations, which have served as wings to conversation, are used, he says, in three ways — in terms, in sorts of words, and in construction. To the second of these functions Tooke proposes to devote his attention, Locke, whose conclusions are a starting point for his speculations, having treated the first in a masterly way, and numerous authors, the last.

The old grammarians, holding the opinion that the

---

[45] *Diversions of Purley,* Part I, pp. 182–183.

[46] *Ibid.,* p. 288.

[47] *Ibid.,* p. 362.

[48] *Ibid.,* p. 21.

[49] *Ibid.,* p. 22. The complete title of Tooke's treatise is *Epea Ptereonta* (Winged Words) or *The Diversions of Purley.*

primary object of language was to convey thought, failed
to see, Tooke points out, that the object of language is not
only to convey thought, but to convey thought rapidly.
Abbreviations, which are the signs of other words, facilitate
speech, and are therefore, he says, " the *wheels* of language,
the wings of Mercury. And though we might be dragged
along without them, it would be with much difficulty, very
heavily and tediously." [50] The superiority of a language, it
is obvious from Tooke's classification, depends upon its
" *abbreviations of terms,* and abbreviations in the *manner*
of *signification* of words," [51] all other differences being of
no importance.

Commenting upon the character of our language, Tooke
states that " at the dawn of learning in this country, those
who became acquainted with the Latin and French authors
perceived (and especially when they came to translate them
or to repeat anything after them) a convenient short
method of expression in those languages, with which their
own could not furnish them. Finding therefore this pe-
culiarity, and not knowing whence it arose; as they proceeded to be more familiar with those languages, they
borrowed the whole Latin and French words in which the
abbreviation they wanted was contained: instead of using
their own periphrastic idiom as formerly, or forming (as
they should have done) a correspondent abbreviation in
words of their own language. And thus, by incorporating
those words, they obtained partially (for it extended no
further than the very words adopted) that sort of abbreviation to our language which it had not before." [52]

Most of the arguments that have been set forth by linguists for or against what has been termed by some, the

[50] *Ibid.,* p. 20.
[51] *Ibid.,* p. 40.
[52] *Ibid.,* Part II, p. 443.

" enriching," and by others, the " deforming " of the early
language, have been confined, says Tooke, to a consideration of *complex terms,* and never to " the abbreviation in
the *manner* of *signification* of words," [53] although the latter
class was more in need of new terms than the former. In
Tooke's judgment, practically all of the complex terms
borrowed from other lands were better expressed in Old
English, because they were in harmony with the language.
For this reason, those who have produced our present English speech, by borrowing, " deserve from us, but in a very
different degree, both thanks and censure," he observes.
" *Great* thanks, in that they have introduced into the English some most useful *abbreviations in manner of signification:* which the Anglo-Saxon, as well as all the other
northern languages wanted: and *some censure,* in that they
have done this incompleatly, and in an improper manner.
The fact certainly is, that our predecessors did not themselves know what they were doing: any more than their
successors seem to have known hitherto the real importance
and benefit of what has been done. And of this the grammars and philosophy both of antients and moderns are a
sufficient proof. An oversight much to be deplored: for
I am strongly persuaded (and I think I have good reason
to be) that had the Greek and Latin grammarians known
and explained the nature and intrinsic value of the riches
of their own language, neither would their descendants have
lost any of those advantages, nor would the languages of
Europe have been at this day in the corrupt and deficient
state in which we, more or less, find them. For those languages which have borrowed these abbreviations, would
have avoided the partiality and patchwork as well as the
corruption and improprieties with which they now abound;
and those living languages of Europe which still want these

[53] *Ibid.,* p. 459.

advantages wholly, would long ere this have entirely supplied their defects." [54]

Tooke was at one with Swift, we may note at this point, in his condemnation of foreign idioms, and his sentences seem oftentimes to have been modeled after the vigorous style of that prose giant. His neatness and precision as a writer were the accompaniments, he himself would have informed us, of clear thinking. " Now whenever any man finds the difficulty to express himself in a language with which he is well acquainted," he reminds his readers, " let him be persuaded that his thoughts are not clear enough: for, as Swift (I think) has somewhere observed: ' When the water is clear you will easily see to the bottom.' " [55]

The importance of those terms which he classifies as abbreviations cannot, in Tooke's opinion, be exaggerated, inasmuch as " a short, close method of speech answers the purpose of a map upon a reduced scale: it assists greatly the comprehension of our understanding; and, in general reasoning, frequently enables us at one glance, to take in very numerous and distinct important relations and conclusions, which will other-wise totally escape us." [56] With the exception of nouns and verbs, which are the only kinds of words essential to the communication of thoughts, all the so-called parts of speech are, according to Tooke's theory of language, merely abbreviations. In other words, verbs and nouns are the immediate signs of ideas or objects, and all other words are the signs of *signs*.

" The business of the mind, as far as it concerns language, appears to me to be very simple," says Tooke. " It extends no further than to receive impressions, that is to have sensa-

[54] *Ibid.*, p. 460.

[55] *Ibid.*, Part I, p. 33.

[56] *Ibid.*, Part II, p. 461.

tions or feelings. What are called its operations are merely
the operations of language. A consideration of *ideas* or of
the *mind*, or of *things* (relative to the parts of speech) will
lead us no further than to the noun," [57] which may be
defined as " the *simple* or *complex*, the *particular* or *general sign*, or *name*, of *one* or *more ideas*." [58] The verb,
the other part of speech, " must be accounted for," it is
explained, " from the necessary use of it in communication.
It is in fact the communication itself." [59]

The fundamental principles of Tooke's system of language were announced in his *Letter to Dunning*. Indeed
most critics agree with Coleridge that Tooke made practically no progress as a philologist beyond these conclusions
of 1778. Certainly all of his radical statements concerning the conjunction were, as he himself admits, set forth at
that time.

Rejecting all previous expositions of the conjunction,
which his own experiences in a court of law had determined
him to explain, he came to a satisfactory definition, on the
basis of which he erected his theory of language. An examination of numerous illustrations of this so-called part
of speech led him to conclude that there was " not such a
thing as a Conjunction in *any* language, which may not
by a skilful herald, be traced home to its own family and
origin; without having recourse to contradiction and
mystery, with Mr. Harris, or with Mr. Locke, cleaving
open the head of man, to give it such a birth as Minerva's
from the brain of Jupiter." [60]

By pointing out that such connectives as *if* and *an* were

[57] *Ibid.*, Part I, p. 41.

[58] *Ibid.*, p. 42.

[59] *Ibid.*, p. 41.

[60] *Letter to Dunning*. (See Taylor's Edition of *The Diversions
of Purley*, London, 1857, p. 695.)

originally the imperative forms of the verbs to *give* and to *grant,* he indicates the derivative origin of conjunctions, and suggests the error of classifying them as separate parts of speech. " I hope it will be acknowledged," he observes in commendation of his own interpretation, "that this is coming to the point, and is fairer than shuffling them over as all philosophers and grammarians have hitherto done; or than repeating after others that they are not themselves any part of language, but only such *Accessories as Salt* is to *Meat,* or *Water* to *Bread:* or that they are the mere *Edging,* or *Sauce* of language: or that they are like the *Handles* to *Cups,* or the *Plumes* to *Helmets,* or the *Binding* to *Books,* or *Harness* for *Horses:* or that they are *Pegs* and *Nails,* and *Nerves* and *Joints,* and *Ligaments* and *Lime* and *Mortar,* and so forth." [61]

In Part I of *The Diversions of Purley,* the explanation of conjunctions presented in the *Letter to Dunning* is re-stated and amplified. The extended study of these terms, upon which, as we have learned, Tooke based his theory of language, is, indeed, the outstanding and unifying division of the whole vŏlume. The conclusion to which his con-sideration of conjunctions leads him, is that the gram-marians will find themselves without this part of speech, for all of those words classified by them as conjunctions are sometimes used "without connecting sentences." [62] The word *that,* for example, whether regarded as article, or pronoun, or conjunction, retains always, he says, one sig-nificance only. Unobserved abbreviations in construction have produced an appearance of change and led gram-marians of every language into making the same mistakes. An examination of the language of any nation will reveal the use of a "supposed *conjunction,* which they employ as

[61] *Ibid.,* p. 697.
[62] *Diversions of Purley,* Part I, p. 181.

we do *That:* and which is also the same word as their supposed article or pronoun." [63]

" The whole of Tooke's reasoning," as Hazlitt points out,
" turns upon showing that the conjunction *That* is the
pronoun *That,* which is itself the particle of a verb, and in
like manner, that all the other mystical and hitherto unin-
telligible parts of speech are derived from the only two
intelligible ones, the Verb and the Noun." [64] In other
words, believing that there was no term in any language
that had not its own full meaning and significance, he
concluded that conjunctions, prepositions, and the other
indeclinable parts of speech had distinct significations
easily discovered. Even if it be granted that he was
anticipated in this conjecture by Schultens, Lennep, or
others, as some of his critics have contended, the theory
which he advanced " was never," we may agree with the
Annual Review, " applied before on so grand a scale, and in
so instructive a manner." [65]

Tooke tells us that he evolved his theory of language by
an *a priori* process of reasoning, that he was outrageously
ignorant of etymology at the time that he conceived his
opinions, and that to defend his system on etymological
grounds did not occur to him until long after his beliefs
were settled. Then it suddenly became obvious to him
that if his conclusions concerning the conjunction were true,
" there must be in the original language from which the
English (and so of all other languages) is derived, literally
such and *such* words bearing precisely *such* and *such*
significations." [66] He was the more delighted with his sup-
positions because he was unacquainted at this time with

[63] *Ibid.,* p. 71.
[64] *Works,* Vol. IV, p. 238.
[65] *Annual Review* for 1805, p. 676.
[66] *Diversions of Purley,* Part I, p. 108.

the " Anglo-Saxon and Gothic characters," and his experi-
ment, therefore, offered him a means, he informs us, either
of disabusing his mind of error or of obtaining a confirmation strong enough to prove to him that he had really made
a discovery. " For, if upon trial," he asserts, " I should
find in an unknown language precisely those very words,
both in sound and signification, and application, which in
my perfect ignorance I had foretold: what must I conclude,
but either that some demon had maliciously inspired me
with the spirit of true prophecy in order the more deeply to
deceive me: or that my reasoning on the nature of language
was not fantastical." [67]

Future etymologists, Tooke boasts, will acknowledge
their debt to him for his discoveries in regard to the conjunction. " They shall no more," he says, " expose themselves by unnatural forced conceits, to derive the English
and all other languages from the Greek, or the Hebrew; or
some imaginary primeval tongue. The particles of every
language shall teach them whither to direct and where to
stop their inquiries: for wherever the evident meaning and
origin of the particles of any language can be found there
is a certain source of the whole." [68]

In considering those terms which, unlike the noun and
the verb, cannot be classed as parts of speech, Tooke comes
to the conclusion that the fate of the article " has been most
singularly hard and unfortunate." [69]   It deserves more
prominence than the " brutish, inarticulate interjection,
which has nothing to do with speech, and is only the miserable refuge of the speechless." [70]   The article, moreover,
although it must be considered a *substitute*, may be distinguished from other substitutes classified as abbreviations, inasmuch as " it is *necessary* for the communication

[67] *Ibid.*, p. 109.   [69] *Ibid.*, p. 49.
[68] *Ibid.*, p. 121.   [70] *Ibid.*

of our thoughts, and supplies the place of words which *are not* in the language; whereas *abbreviations* are *not* necessary for communication: and supply the place of words which *are* in the language." [71]

To emphasize the absurdity of classifying the interjection as a part of speech, Tooke says wittily: " The dominion of speech is erected upon the downfall of interjections. Without the artful contrivance of language, mankind would have nothing but interjections with which to communicate *orally*, any of their feelings. The neighing of a horse, the lowing of a cow, the barking of a dog, the purring of a cat, sneezing, coughing, groaning, shrieking, and every other involuntary convulsion, with oral sounds, have almost as good a title to be called parts of speech as interjections have." [72]

Upon applying his principle to the preposition, Tooke finds that this form, like the conjunction, has its origin in the other parts of speech. "The same sort of corruption, from the same cause, has distinguished both," he declares, " and ignorance of their true origin has betrayed grammarians and philosophers into the mysterious and contradictory language which they have held concerning them." He derives real entertainment, he confesses, from observing " the various shifts used by those who are too sharp-witted and too ingenuous to repeat the unsatisfactory accounts of these prepositions handed down by others; and yet not ingenuous enough to acknowledge their own total ignorance on the subject." [73]

Such prepositions as *before, behind, below, beside,* and *besides* are, Tooke asserts, " merely the imperative *be* compounded with the nouns *fore, hind, low, side,* which remaining still in constant and common use in the language as — the *fore part,* the *hind part,* a *low place, the side,* require

[71] *Ibid.,* p. 57.   [72] *Ibid.,* p. 51.   [73] *Ibid.,* pp. 250–251.

no explanation." [74] The assumption, therefore, that prepositions are to be regarded as "'*little words invented to put before nouns, and to which all languages have had recourse,*'" [75] is erroneous. This class of words is absolutely necessary, says Tooke, since they take the place of the complex terms which are lacking in a language.

With some observations on the nature of adverbs, which he excludes from a class to which he admits only nouns and verbs, Tooke closes Part I of his treatise. In Part II, which was not published until 1805, almost twenty years after the appearance of the earlier volume, he sets forth his philosophical views, for words, he declares, bear a close relation to metaphysics, a term under which he classifies "all general reasoning, all politics, law, morality, and divinity." [76]

With the purpose of making a philosophical inquiry into the essential nature of that process which is known as abstraction, he first examines the derivation and the meaning of such words as *right, just,* and *law,* each of which is discovered to be the past participle of a verb. *Right,* for example, is "no other than *Rect-um* (regitum), the past participle of the Latin verb *regere.*" On the basis of this etymology, Tooke concludes that "when a man demands his Rights he asks only that which it is *ordered* he shall have," [77] that "to have *right* or law on one's side is to have in one's favor that which is ordered or laid down," and finally, that "a *right* and *just* action" is "such a one as is *ordered* and *commanded.*[78] Consistent with this explanation of terms, is the paradoxical assertion: "Not he who demands rights, but he who abjures them is an anarchist." [79] Proceeding a step further with his etymological

[74] *Ibid.,* p. 329.
[75] *Ibid.,* Part I, p. 260.
[76] *Ibid.,* Part II, p. 94.

[77] *Ibid.,* p. 7.
[78] *Ibid.*
[79] *Ibid.,* p. 12.

deductions, Tooke argues that "before there can be anything *Rect-um* there must be *reg-en's, reg's, rex, i.e.* qui or
quod *regit.*"[80] By a recourse to etymology he finds an
immediate means of deciding disputes concerning questions
of right, "for," says he, "if *Right* and *Just* mean *ordered*
and *commanded,* we must at once refer to the *order* and
command; and to the authority which *ordered* and *commanded.*"[81]

His study of such words as *right, just,* and *law,* suggests
to Tooke a means of accounting for what is called *abstraction* and so-called *abstract ideas,* terms which, regardless
of their denomination and construction, are, as a rule, he
says, participles or adjectives employed with no substantives to which they can be joined, and which are consequently to be regarded, in construction, as substantives.
Of such words the great body of language is really made
up. "These participles and adjectives, not understood as
such," he adds, "have caused a metaphysical jargon, and a
false morality, which can only be dissipated by etymology:
and, when they come to be examined, you will find that
the ridicule which Dr. Conyers Middleton has justly bestowed upon the papists for their absurd coinage of saints,
is equally applicable to ourselves, and to all other metaphysicians: whose moral deities, moral causes, and moral
qualities are not less ridiculously coined and imposed upon
their followers."[82] Words, for example, such as *Fate,
Chance, Luck, Saint, Providence, Hell,* and *Heaven* are all
"merely participles poetically embodied, and substantiated
by those who use them."[83]

Under the inspiration of his master, Locke, Tooke thus
attempts to prove that adjectives and all abstract substantives have their origin in words which represent

[80] *Ibid.*
[81] *Ibid.,* p. 13.
[82] *Ibid.,* p. 14.
[83] *Ibid.,* p. 15.

sensible ideas. Being a Nominalist, he derided the Aristotelian reasoning of Harris and Lord Monboddo, and definitely connected his philosophy with the study of words. After citing illustrations of his theory concerning abstractions in, as he himself calculated, " about a thousand words," the number of which might readily be augmented, he expresses the hope that he has disillusioned his readers as to " that imagined *operation of the mind,* which has been termed abstraction," [84] but which is, in truth, only a device of language for conveying thought more speedily.

The final chapter of *The Diversions of Purley* is devoted to a consideration of the claims of adjectives and participles to be ranked as parts of speech. In the case of the adjective, which he defines first, Tooke, setting aside the authority of Harris and Lowth, says that " an adjective is the *name of a thing* which is directed to be joined to some other *name of a thing* — And the substantive and adjective so joined are frequently convertible, without the smallest change of meaning: as we may say — a perverse nature, or, a natural perversity." [85] The adjective is, therefore, just as truly the name of a thing as is the noun. Those adjectives, for example, ending in *ous, ly, ful, some,* etc., are, in reality, compound words, the terminations of which were originally words added to the other words of which they are at present only endings. These terminations are found more frequently in our language now, it is pointed out, than formerly, since our writers, not satisfied with borrowing only those adjectives needed in our tongue, have also borrowed numerous " *adjective terminations* which we did not want, being before in possession of correspondent terminations of our own, which answered the same purpose with those which they have unnecessarily adopted." [86]

In Tooke's opinion, this borrowing, as has already been

[84] *Ibid.,* p. 332.   [85] *Ibid.,* p. 362.   [86] *Ibid.,* p. 410.

emphasized, has been " of advantage to the variety and harmony of the language, but is unphilosophical and unnecessary." [87]   While admitting, for instance, that the adoption of such foreign adjectives as *infantine, puerile, virile,* and *female,* in relation to *child, boy, man,* and *woman,* has improved our language, he maintains that the same result could have been more properly obtained by an *adjectiving* of native words.   As matters are now, he says, the unfortunate foreigner must learn not only the names of things in the English language, but must go to other tongues for a host of *adjectived* names of the same things, and an uneducated Englishman can never comprehend the meaning of a fourth of what is termed his native language.

His study of adjectives leads Tooke to conclude that such terms, however convenient as abbreviations, are not essential to language, and that they are not, therefore, to be classified as parts of speech.   To support his theory he quotes Jonathan Edwards, as stating, in his discussion of the language of the Indians, that " the *Mohegans* have no *adjectives* in all their language." [88]

The last abbreviation to which Tooke gives his attention is the participle, a term to which he objects, this improper designation being responsible, in his judgment, for the faulty definition popularly given to participles. For the word *participle,* he would substitute the name *verb adjective,* a term suggestive of its function.   The appropriateness of the name *verb adjective* is obvious, he insists, inasmuch as we find it necessary to *adjective* the verb just as we do the noun.   " By means of a distinguishing termination, not only the simple *verb,* itself, but every *mood* and every *tense* of the verb, may be made *adjective* as well as the *noun,*" he says.   " And accordingly, some languages have *adjectived* more, and some languages have

[87] *Ibid.*   [88] *Ibid.,* p. 413.

adjectived fewer of these moods and tenses." [89]   In accordance with Tooke's terminology, the present participle is "merely the simple verb *adjectived,* without any adsignification of manner or time," [90] and the past participle is "merely the past tense *adjective,*" [91] having the meaning of the past tense only.

Having discussed under the classification of abbreviations all of the so-called parts of speech but nouns and verbs, Tooke concludes his study of language by offering several definitions of the verb, all of which he ridicules. With the promise to the public of a third volume devoted to an explanation of this part of speech, he ends his labors. "We will leave off here for the present," he says. "It is true that my evening has now fully come, and the night fast approaching; yet, if we shall have a tolerably lengthened twilight, we may still perhaps find time enough for a farther conversation on the subject: and finally, (if the times will bear it) to apply this system of language to all the different systems of metaphysical (*i.e.* verbal) imposture." [92]

Tooke's failure to satisfy the curiosity of his readers by discoursing on the verb led Hazlitt to observe humorously: "This extraordinary man was in the habit of tantalizing his guests on Sunday afternoons with sundry abstruse speculations, and putting them off to the following week for a satisfaction of their doubts; but why should he treat posterity in the same scurvy manner, or leave the world without quitting scores with it?" [93]   Upon the appearance, in 1829, of Richard Taylor's enlarged edition of *The Diversions of Purley,* a reviewer for *Fraser's Magazine,* it may be added, suggested that the editor might have presented some-

[89] *Ibid.,* p. 417.
[90] *Ibid.,* p. 423.
[91] *Ibid.,* p. 425.

[92] *Ibid.,* p. 463.
[93] *Collected Works,* Vol. IV, p. 240.

thing worth while if he had been able to ascertain from Tooke's notes what he really knew about the verb.

Though his theories were openly attacked by many of his contemporaries, Tooke was generally recognized in his lifetime as an authority on his subject. The popularity of his system was attested to by John Fearn, who, in his *Anti-Tooke*, a treatise, as the name implies, written in direct opposition to the theories of Tooke, complains that " all men have bowed the knee to the Graven Image which the Philologer of Purley hath set up." [94] Fearn even refers to " the School of Tooke," which he admits is " no inconsiderable School of Language," [95] all subsequent grammarians having quoted Tooke and paid deference to his discoveries. Harris's once popular theory of language has, to Fearn's regret, been eclipsed by the more popular scheme of the " Lynx-eyed Philologer of Purley." [96]

According to Tooke, as we have seen, every word meant a thing, and the art of reasoning consisted in combining words. Commentators erred, he maintained, in defining a word simply by examining the selection in which it occurred. By adopting this method, they associated with the unknown word the meaning of other words in the passage. " A little regard to the individual etymology of the word whose meaning is sought would secure them from this perpetually repeated error," he said, and conduct them to the *intrinsic* meaning of the word." [97] He repudiated, furthermore, the idea that words so changed their nature as to belong at different times to different parts of speech. " Let them," he declared," give the rule who thus confound together the *manner* of signification of words, and the *ab-*

[94] *Anti-Tooke,* Vol. II, London, 1827, p. 4.
[95] *Ibid.,* p. 338.
[96] *Ibid.,* Vol. I, London, 1824, p. 88.
[97] *Diversions of Purley,* Part II, p. 214.

breviation in their *construction:* than which no two things
in language are more distinct, or ought to be more carefully distinguished. I do not allow that *any* words change
their nature in this manner, so as to belong sometimes to
one part of speech, and sometimes to another, from the
different ways of using them. I never could perceive any
such fluctuation in any word whatever: though I know it is
a general charge brought erroneously against words of
almost every denomination. But it appears to me to be
all error; arising from the false measure which has been
taken of almost every sort of words: whilst the words, themselves, appear to me to continue faithfully and steadily
attached, each to the standard under which it was originally
enlisted." [98]

In the opinion of Fearn, who contended that the meaning
of words, when grouped, was almost altogether dependent
upon the order of their arrangement, Tooke's belief in " the
absoluteness of words in their grammatical character," [99]
was ridiculous, and his supposition had led him to elevate
etymology " into an authority of *paramount* and *exclusive*
worship." [100] The author of *Anti-Tooke,* whose avowed
purpose was to insist upon a separation of the work of the
" Inductive Etymologist " and the " Universal Grammarian," would " awake Philologists and all the higher classes
of readers in the Department of Language, from that sleep
of security in which they have enveloped themselves, in
cherishing the opinion that the Philosophy of Language
had begun to see the light in the speculation of Etymologists." [101]

From the significance which Tooke attached to etymology, his readers might infer that in accordance with his
teachings, the meaning of a word must first and always be

[98] *Ibid.,* Part I, pp. 68–69.

[99] *Anti-Tooke,* Vol. I, p. 175.

[100] *Ibid.,* Vol. II, p. 4.

[101] *Anti-Tooke,* Vol. II, p. 146.

the same which it or its root possessed originally. That it was not the intention of Tooke to convey such an impression, however, was pointed out by Richardson, who devoted a volume to an exposition of *The Diversions of Purley*. According to Richardson, Tooke meant to imply only that the essential, intrinsic significance of a word was once and forever the same. It did not follow that the way in which we use the term must be entirely in the original radical sense. " The meaning or intention of the speaker in using the word," says Richardson, " may be very different from the meaning of the word itself: but there must be some inference or deduction in the mind of the speaker, known to the hearer, which will warrant the usage. And such is the clear and decided doctrine of Horne Tooke." [102]

Adverse criticism of *The Diversions of Purley* was provoked, however, by the importance which the author assigned to etymology in formulating his philosophical system. Hazlitt, who found the philological divisions of the book excellent and the grammatical parts unimportant, considered the metaphysical passages " down-right, unqualified, unredeemed nonsense." Tooke's philosophical speculations were, he declared, " mere midsummer madness." [103] In contradiction, for example, to the philologist's assertion that we have neither complex nor abstract ideas, Hazlitt contended that we have no other. " If our ideas," he said, " were absolutely simple and individual, we could have no idea of any of those objects which in this erring, half-thinking philosophy are called individual, as a table or a chair, a blade of grass, or a grain of sand. For every one of these includes a certain configuration, hardness, color, etc. — *i.e.* ideas of different things, and received by different senses, which must be put together by the understanding before

[102] *On the Study of Language,* London, 1854, p. 193.
[103] *Complete Works,* Vol. XI, p. 119.

they can be referred to any particular thing, or form one idea. Without the cementing power of the mind all our ideas would be necessarily decomposed and crumbled down into their original elements and flexional parts." [104]

Like Hazlitt, Sir James Mackintosh, as the following quotation from his *Memoirs* makes clear, recognized the importance of Tooke's philological discoveries, but objected to his metaphysical reasoning:

Horne Tooke's is certainly a wonderful book, but the great merit was the original thought. The light which shines through such impenetrable words as articles and pronouns, is admirable — " the " and " it." No single book, perhaps, ever so much illustrated language; yet, how much more might he have done had he known the collateral languages! Adelung's Dictionary alone would have yielded great assistance. The author will not be content with mere philological praise: his object is philosophical; it is to prove the system of the Nominalists by an almost complete enumeration of all the words in one language; it is to show that, as all words are found ultimately to represent sensations, we can have no ideas but those of individual objects conveyed through the senses. The farther inferences which he intends to make from this position are evident enough; the word " metaphysics," and all systems of it, he is to prove to be nonsense. It is clear that he uses the word in its etymological sense, for " what is above or beyond nature," and that by " nature " he means, " that which is the object of our senses." But is the first position proved? All words do, or rather did, denote sensible objects; therefore there exist only sensible objects — this is the first step. All words seem to represent, originally, *visible* objects; would it be just to conclude that there are neither impressions of touch, smell, sound, nor taste in the human mind? The argument seems to be the same.

But, supposing the first proposition granted, would the annihilation of metaphysics follow? This seems to be no consequence. Why should not the words " necessity," " identity," etc., and a thousand others, be the subject of operations — of translation, and retranslation, as much, and with a degree of the same success, as algebraic signs? Because all numeration may be traced to sensible

[104] *Ibid.*, p. 128.

perception, it does not follow that we must count by the fingers instead of resorting to the rules of arithmetic. This is to confound a science with its practical methods. Though Nominalism should universally prevail, a system of logic and metaphysics, more extensive than those of Aristotle and Kant may, and if human understanding proceeds, must be erected on a nominal basis.[105]

Dugald Stewart, who detected the materialistic tendency of Tooke's scattered philosophical speculations, became an outspoken critic of *The Diversions of Purley*. Tooke, he said, had confused " the historical progress of an art with its theoretical principles when advanced to maturity," and regarded " language as a much more exact and complete picture of thought, than it is in any state of society, whether barbarous or refined." [106] Coleridge, whose comments on Tooke's theories were not very different from the Scotch critic's, complained that the philologist had affected " to explain the origin and whole philosophy of language by what is, in fact, only a mere accident of its history." His judgment of Harris was, therefore, superficial and unjust, said the poet, since Harris " was dealing — not very profoundly, it is true — with the philosophy, the moral and metaphysical causes of it, etc.," while Tooke, in discussing the formation of words only, " thought he was explaining the philosophy of language, which is a very different thing." [107]

The Diversions of Purley is, as Leslie Stephen describes it, " a premature attempt to apply philological inquiries to the history of thought." [108] Modern discoveries in Sanskrit

[105] Robert James Mackintosh: *Life of Sir James Mackintosh,* London, 1835, Vol. II, pp. 230–232.

[106] *Philosophical Essays,* Philadelphia, 1811, p. 202.

[107] *Specimens of the Table Talk of Coleridge,* New York, 1856, p. 308.

[108] *English Thought in the Eighteenth Century,* London, 1902, Vol. I, pp. 58–59.

and an increasing knowledge of Anglo-Saxon, which Tooke, apparently, ranked as a primitive tongue, have, of course, revealed the fallaciousness of many of his conclusions. His definition of *true*, for example, as " that which is *trowed* " suggests little, it has been pointed out by Müller, inasmuch as *trow* is only a derivative verb, which means " to hold a thing true." An acquaintance with the Sanskrit origin of the word *true*, which is *dhruva*, meaning " firm, solid, anything that will hold; from *dhar*, to hold," [109] would, moreover, have modified Tooke's deductions on the basis of his etymology. " Truth," says he, " supposes mankind: for *whom* and *by whom* alone the word is formed, and *to whom* only it is applicable. If no man, no truth. There is therefore no such thing as eternal, immutable, everlasting truth; unless mankind, such as they are *at present*, be also eternal, immutable and everlasting. Two persons may contradict each other, and yet both speak truth: for the Truth of one person may be opposite to the Truth of another. To speak Truth may be a vice as well as a virtue: for there are many occasions when it ought not to be spoken." [110]

Tooke's extraordinary conclusions provoked criticism, as we might expect, of his philosophy. Barclay, the author of *A Sequel to the Diversions of Purley*, finds the etymology of *Truth* and *True* probable, but makes the following strictures on its application: " True is simply and merely what is trowed, is no superior to this, that danger is simply and merely what is feared; or that a sick man's complaint is merely his cries and groans; South merely seething, what seeths or is seethed." [111] In accordance with

---

[109] Müller: *Science of Language,* Second Series, New York, 1870, p. 361.

[110] *Diversions of Purley,* Part II, p. 339.

[111] *Sequel to the Diversions of Purley,* London, 1826, Part II, p. 87.

Tooke's reasoning, says Barclay, " Mrs. Croaker might tell her husband his hat was on his head, and his friend Honeywood contradict her, and say it was off; and yet both might be speaking truth." [112]

The principles which Tooke advanced were sound and suggestive, but a deficiency of knowledge led him to erroneous assertions. His work was completed just before the dawn of the new era in philological research. By the middle of the nineteenth century the investigations of Bopp, Grimm, and Pott had raised the study of language to the rank of a science. Had Tooke been familiar with the fundamentals of Modern Comparative Philology, his theories would have undergone some radical changes. His discoveries, however, were far in advance of his predecessors'. As the originator of an ingenious system of language study, he occupies a unique position in the history of philology.

[112] *Ibid.*, p. 89.

CHAPTER VI

TRIAL FOR TREASON

THE period of leisure and study in which Tooke completed the first part of his treatise on language came to an end in 1790, when, not satisfied with merely arraigning apostates to the cause of reform, he decided to enter the political lists himself as a candidate for Westminster against Lord Hood and Fox. Though defeated in the campaign, he so ingratiated himself with the electors that he polled 1679 votes without having solicited a single name. After the returns he made an address to the electors, in the course of which he expressed satisfaction at the manner in which his campaign had been conducted. Criticizing the system of elections then in vogue, he declared:

Gentlemen, I do not consider what has been passing before us as any real election. As things at present are managed, it is impossible that the real electors of Westminster should enjoy even that pitiful share of representation which is nominally left them. I trust I shall be the means of doing away for ever the infamies of what is called a Westminster election.

The sacrifice which I have already made is, personally, very important to me; but, I will go further, I will present a petition against the return of Mr. Fox and Lord Hood to parliament. And I will endeavour to extort, by shame, from those whom no engagements, no honour, no sense of public justice, or of public decency can move; I will endeavor, by shame to extort redress, and a peaceable, quiet election in future, without perjury or bloodshed, for the real electors of Westminster.[1]

In accordance with his promise to the electors, Tooke sought redress for these grievances by appealing to the

[1] Stephens: *Memoirs of John Horne Tooke*, Vol. II, pp. 91–92.

146

House of Commons. His petition, which was regarded as
very irregular by the Speaker, was finally read at the
table, and a day was set for its discussion. The committee
appointed to look into this singular plea for justice and
reform reported in due time that it was "frivolous and
vexatious," a decision which entitled the successful candidates, by a recent act of Parliament, to damages against
the petitioner. An unsuccessful candidate for election to
the House, in 1780, had aired his grievances against his
rival by petitioning Parliament, and the committee selected
to report on the case had found it "frivolous and vexatious." From this precedent an act was passed in 1789,
making petitioners responsible for the costs whenever
their complaints were found to be "frivolous and vexatious."

Lord Hood did not press his claims against Tooke, but
Fox at length brought suit against him in the Court of
King's Bench, for the sum of £198 2s. 2d., the taxed costs
of the petition which had been presented to the House.
Tooke objected to the Parliamentary Act of 1789 because
it deprived the petitioner of the right of appeal to a jury.
He rejoiced, therefore, in Fox's action against him, since it
gave him an opportunity to appear in a court of justice,
where he might, in the course of the proceedings against
him, expose the corrupt election practices of the period.

At the trial, which was opened on April 30, 1792, Lord
Kenyon, Tooke's former associate in the study of law,
presided, and the defendant conducted his own case. After
listening to the charges against him, Tooke arose, and with
his usual complacency and air of assurance, addressed himself to the jury in the following terms:

"Gentlemen of the Jury, we are called upon this day —
both you and I — to perform a very important business of
great national concern: the memory of which, I will venture

to foretell will not be buried with ourselves; nor will its consequences finish with your verdict.

" In the performance of this duty to our country, I must beg you to observe, and carefully to remember it to the end, that there are only three efficient and necessary parties, — Mr. Fox, the Plaintiff; myself, the Defendant; and you, gentlemen, the Jury. The judge and the cryer of the court attend alike in their respective situations; and they are paid by us for their attendance; we pay them well; they are hired to be the assistants and reporters, but they are not, and they never were intended to be the controulers of our conduct. For the whole of this business is comprised in Mr. Fox's action, in my defence, and in your verdict." [2]

In pleading his case, Tooke reminded the court that " a great and important national right " was in the balance. " The last and only security," he said, " which the full-grown corruption and iniquity of the times have left to the people of this land for their lives, their liberties, and their property, this last and only security — a *real* Tryal by a Jury of our country — is now attempted to be wrested from us." [3] The plaintiff, Tooke was almost certain, shared his sentiments on this grave question. It should be mentioned in this connection, that Fox, who in his earlier years had scoffed at the rights of jurors, had only a few months before, on February 20, 1791, introduced a bill into Parliament, giving to the jury the right to deliver a general verdict in a case of libel. The object of Fox and of those who favored the new Libel Bill was to uphold the rights of jurors and to guarantee to the subject a fair trial by his

[2] *Proceedings in an Action for Debt between the Right Hon. Charles James Fox, Plaintiff, and John Horne Tooke, Defendant, Published by the Defendant*, J. Johnson, London, 1792, pp. 4–5.

[3] *Ibid.*, p. 5.

peers. The Bill, which was strongly supported by Erskine and Pitt, was passed in 1792, soon after Fox's case against Tooke had been decided.

Tooke may have had the recently proposed statute in mind when he referred to the legal situation of the time. He must certainly have been keenly interested in the passage of a bill which was designed for the express purpose of superseding the rulings of Lord Mansfield, who had ignored the rights of jurors by maintaining that the court had power to decide on the criminality of a libel. An information for libel under Lord Mansfield's interpretation of the law, was equivalent, Tooke had complained in 1777, to an accusation. In defending himself before Lord Kenyon, Tooke reminded the jury that they were not only to give a verdict but to decide on the justice of the case. " A jury not entitled to inquire into the merits of the question brought before them, nor into any thing that relates to the merits, is no Jury at all," he declared; " nor can in any respect answer the object of their appointment: and any Jury that shall give a verdict against any defendant, without having first, according to the oaths of the Jurors, *well* and *truly Tried* the question at issue between the parties, is a perjured Jury."[4] The Act of Parliament upon which Fox's action against him was based was " a *penal* statute and very penal," Tooke asserted, " giving to a Committee of the House of Commons the power of inflicting very heavy punishment, absolute ruin if they please, without any intervention of a Jury; and that too in a case where they are themselves the interested parties." [5]

After an attempt, which was none too convincing, perhaps, to persuade the jury that he had committed himself in the first place to a political campaign only that he might combat a corrupt election system, Horne complained of the

[4] *Ibid.*, p. 14.　　　　　[5] *Ibid.*, p. 37.

futility of his sacrifice, by adding: "If you represent to the House of Commons and offer proof of a continued series and regular system of bribery, perjury, riot, and murder, at an election, together with the utter impossibility of any decision of the Return; no fine, no punishment, no ruin is sufficient for such *frivolous* and *vexatious* charges." [6]   In entering the campaign for patriotic motives he had been sure of but one vote — his own — "and on that vote," he declared, "I should equally have petitioned the House, well aware before hand that whatever my petition should contain, it would be voted *frivolous* and *vexatious*." [7]

Notwithstanding Tooke's efforts to justify his action, the jury after adjourning once because they could not agree, at last handed in a verdict in favor of the plaintiff. The defendant, however, had thoroughly enjoyed the situation in which he had found himself despite the decision against him. He had derived enough pleasure from displaying his knowledge of the law and tormenting the judge to console him for the loss of his case. "The report of his trial before Lord Kenyon," says Hazlitt, "is a masterpiece of acuteness, dexterity, modest assurance, and legal effect." [8]   Kenyon, who lacked dignity and self-control, was powerless to curb his insolence. He is said to have shed tears during the trial.

Tooke now gave up his home in Richmond Buildings and took up his residence at Wimbledon, in the suburbs of London. Settled on his new estate, he occupied himself with his garden and the improvement of his house and grounds, and entertained numerous friends and acquaintances from the metropolis and elsewhere. Two years after he had removed to Wimbledon, however, the pleasant life upon which he had entered was rudely interrupted by his apprehension on a charge of treason. To understand the reasons

[6] *Ibid.*, p. 13.   [7] *Ibid.*, p. 17.   [8] *Works,* Vol. IV, p. 236.

for the action of the Government against him, we must
review briefly the political history of the period.

The French Revolution, which during its first stages was
hailed with delight by most English patriots, eventually
came to retard reform in Great Britain. The exultation
which all lovers of liberty had experienced at the fall of the
Bastille was followed by a feeling of revulsion on the part
of many at the atrocities that characterized the later course
of events in France, and the more conservative members of
radical societies, frightened at the length to which certain
of the clubs were going in an approval of the Revolution,
withdrew from them. The Government, which, at the same
time, began to look with distrust upon all political organizations, gave itself up finally, after the execution of Louis
XVI and the fall of the French monarchy, to a policy of
prosecution that is a blot on the administration of the
period. The authorities, panic-stricken at the turn of
events in France, failed to distinguish between violent
revolutionists and moderate reformers.

Among the latter class no one was more conspicuous as
a member of political societies than was Horne Tooke, who
in the past had won such notoriety for his championship of
the Colonists. His previous struggles in the popular cause
made him the obvious leader of those patriots who were
working in organized groups for legitimate reforms. Associated formerly with him in one of these societies that
had fallen under the suspicion of the Administration, the
Society for Constitutional Information, were such distinguished patriots as Pitt, Fox, Sheridan, Lord John Rus-
sell, Earl Stanhope, and the Duke of Richmond, who was
at one time chairman of the organization. Encouraged by
this liberal group, Pitt had presented before the House of
Commons three times, in 1782, 1783, and 1785, respectively,
the question of Parliamentary reform. In a letter dated

May 10, 1782, Tooke, who strongly favored Pitt's plan,
had addressed Lord Ashburton, as we have noted, on the
questions of a reform in the House. " The voice of the
people in the present reign," he wrote, " has not been heard
till lately (and then heard but once) within the walls of the
House of Commons nor will it ever be heard there again;
fresh errors and fresh misleadings will again take place; the
voice of contractors, of pensioners, of jobbers, together with
the proprietors of a few decayed burgage tenures, will again
be called the only voice of the people, unless the honesty,
or the good sense of Administration afford the remedy by
reforming substantially the vices of representation." [9]

As long as Pitt led the cause of Parliamentary reform,
Tooke was his staunch supporter. On the occasion of his
trial for treason, when he was examining Pitt as a witness,
Tooke reminded the court that he himself had never advocated any one scheme for securing a fair representation in
the House. " The whole of my efforts have been directed
to Reforms," he boasted, " and what I am brought here for
is, the having been friendly to any sort of Reform that
should alter the present situation of the representation in
the House of Commons, thinking none could be for the
worse; not having been a favourer of any particular plan
more than of the plan of this gentleman, which they cannot
say I followed, because I was in it before he was born; he,
in a high situation, I followed in his steps, having always
done as that right honourable gentleman has done; assuring
the committee that my exertion should never be wanting in
support of a measure, which I agreed with him in thinking
essentially necessary to the independence of Parliament,
and the liberty of the people." [10]

[9] *A Letter on Parliamentary Reform Containing the Sketch of a
Plan*, Second Edition, London, 1782, pp. 34–35.
[10] Gurney: *Trial of Horne Tooke for Treason*, London, 1795, Vol.
II, p. 67.

One by one, patriots who had been active, as well as Tooke, in the liberal cause, renounced their earlier principles. The Duke of Richmond, after becoming Master of the Ordnance, forsook his former platform of reform, and other influential members of the Society for Constitutional Information followed the Duke in deserting that organization. The thinning of the ranks, however, did not discourage Tooke, who continued through his association with political groups to promote every effort looking to a reform in the House of Commons.

In the following letter, which was produced in court as damaging evidence against him when he was standing trial for treason, he not only urges the society to assist their representative but describes the faithlessness of Pitt to a cause which he had once advocated:

I am directed by the Society for Constitutional Information, to write to all the members of the Society requesting their contribution towards the support of Mr. Sinclair.

When the Delegates from the different Constitutional Societies in Scotland, lately met at Edinburgh, for the purpose of consulting together, and concerting of measures which might be proper to be pursued, in order to obtain a fair representation of the people of Great Britain, in Parliament, Mr. Sinclair attended, as Delegate, from the Society for Constitutional Information, and behaved, upon that occasion with a moderation and temper, which have not only been highly approved, but have much endeared him to this Society.

For that conduct, which we highly approve, Mr. Sinclair was indicted in Scotland, and returned to London upon bail; since that time Mr. Skirving and Mr. Margarot have been sentenced in Scotland (for the same conduct as Mr. Sinclair) to *fourteen* years of transportation: with the fate of Messrs. Palmer, Muir, Skirving, and Margarot before his eye, Mr. Sinclair has returned to Scotland, and in discharge of his faith, as a private man, towards his bail, and in discharge of his duty towards an oppressed and insulted public; he has returned, not to take a fair trial, but, as he is well persuaded, to a settled conviction and sentence. These sentences of transportation are *novelties* both to England and to Scotland and exceed, in cruelty and impudence, anything practiced in the odious and abhorred reigns of the Stuarts; and these sentences are to be carried into execution under the administration of Mr. Pitt; and by him who formerly (though hypocritically and treacherously) professed himself a strenuous advocate for Parliamentary Reform, and himself met the Delegates throughout England, assembled in Convention, at the Thatched House Tavern for the same purpose as that for which the late Convention met in Scotland.

Should it one day be the fate of this Mr. Pitt to be tried by the people of this insulted and oppressed Country, for his treachery to the cause of Parliamentary Reform, we trust they will never consent to send him to Botany Bay; in the meantime we earnestly solicit your assistance to alleviate the sufferings of Mr. Sinclair's situation, and to afford him every comfort in our power, under this his honourable and meritorious martyrdom; in which, and in worse (if there be worse), we declare ourselves ready to follow him in pursuit of the same object, videlicet a fair representation of the people in Parliament.[11]

After the resignation of the Duke of Richmond, Tooke acted as chairman of the Society for Constitutional Information, and in 1792 he drew up the constitution for the London Corresponding Society, an organization which became very popular since, as Stephens reminds us, it " excluded none but females, and such males only as were rendered unfit either by infancy or mental incapacity, from exercising the elective franchise." [12] The enthusiastic response with which one of Tooke's witticisms was received at a celebration of the Revolution Society, at the London Tavern, on November 5, 1792, is suggested by the following quotation from a letter written by John Hall:

It happened that a company of Aristocratic French and Spanish merchants were met in the very room under, and Horne Tooke

---

[11] *Ibid.*, Vol. I, pp. 280–281.
[12] *Memoirs of John Horne Tooke*, Vol. II, p. 83.

got up and sarcastically requested the company not to wound the tender feelings of the gentlemen by too much festivity. This sarcasm was followed by such a burst of applause as I never before heard.[13]

Besides taking an active interest in the political societies of the period, Tooke welcomed to his home the friends of reform. At these gatherings all were admitted who could bring letters of introduction from any prominent man of the Radical party. The intentions of the host and his guests were far from revolutionary, but after John Wharton, a government spy, became a member of the political faction that enjoyed the hospitality of Wimbledon, Tooke and eleven other members of the Constitutional Society were arrested and held on a charge of treason. Although Tooke had soon discovered the duplicity of his guest, he had determined not to expose him but to outwit him if possible. For the purpose, then, of foiling Wharton at his own game, he had adopted the perilous device of deliberately misleading him as to the power, size, and intentions of the Radical organization. Under the pretence of taking him into his confidence, he had conveyed the astounding information that the nation was actually on the verge of a revolution. " After a number of interviews, he at length affected to own," says Stephens, " that he himself was at the head of the conspiracy, and boasted like Pompey of old, ' that he could raise legions, merely by stamping on the ground with his foot.' " [14]

Tooke was in the habit, we are told, of uttering heresies which might easily have rendered him liable to prosecution but for the saving clause which usually concluded his bold declarations. " He was a man cautious and even timid in

[13] Conway: *Life of Thomas Paine,* New York and London, 1909, Vol. II (Appendix), pp. 471–472.
[14] Stephens: *Memoirs of John Horne Tooke,* Vol. II, p. 117.

action," says Brailsford, "but there was a vanity in him which led him to say 'hanging matters' when he had an inflammable audience in front of him within the four walls of a room." [15] In explanation of his conduct just prior to his apprehension, it has been suggested that he thought he could embarrass the Government by enticing them into a prosecution which could not be sustained by the facts in the case. "It is unquestionable," says one of his critics, "that his language, his officious zeal, and his bustling in all matters which offered the shadow of suspicion were to be accounted for on no other principle, than that he either was a conspirator or wished to be thought one." [16]

As a matter of fact, however, Tooke was too busy in his garden and in his library to be plotting revolutions. Beadon, who was summoned as a witness at his trial, described him as studious and scholarly, and affirmed that he was obviously more interested in reading and in research than in dethroning the King. William Sharpe, who taught Tooke's daughters engraving, testified, when questioned as to how his patron spent his time, that indoors he was usually employed in poring over old books, as Sharpe supposed, in preparation for his grammatical work. Notwithstanding his peaceful pursuits and his conservatism as a reformer, his propensity for joking and his pretences led him, as we shall see, to the very foot of the gallows.

Thomas Hardy, secretary of the Constitutional Association, was the first of the State prisoners to be arrested. Immediately after his apprehension, Jeremiah Joyce dispatched to Tooke the following enigmatical letter:

Dear Citizen, — This morning at six o'clock, Citizen Hardy was taken away by an order from the Secretary of State's office. They

[15] *Shelley, Godwin and Their Circle*, p. 34.
[16] *Blackwood's*, Vol. 34, p 223.

seized everything they could lay their hands on. Query: Is it possible to get ready by Thursday? [17]

The letter was intercepted by the authorities, whose suspicions having been aroused by reports of the Wimbledon gatherings, read into it revolutionary plans for a universal uprising. It would not have been surprising, indeed, to discover that, in accordance with his obvious intention of deceiving Wharton, Tooke had actually induced Joyce to write the ambiguous letter and that he himself had contrived to have it intercepted. While he had not devised this means of misleading his guest, he was certainly highly amused, as the following passages from his cross-examination of William Sharpe reveal, by the misinterpretation which the Government put upon the letter and by their precautionary measures after its seizure:

Q. Can you recollect on the 15th of May, the day before I was apprehended, where you dined?

A. Yes, in Spital Square.

Q. Can you recollect any particular circumstance that passed there at dinner?

A. Yes, there was a conversation about a letter from Mr. Joyce to you, which I understood was intercepted.

Q. Do you know that I ever received any letter from Mr. Joyce, in my life?

A. You said you had not received any.

Q. You do not know that I had?

A. I do not know that you ever did.

Q. Do you know that I ever wrote him one in my life?

A. You are very backward at writing letters, I should suppose not.

Q. Were you informed of the subject of that letter?

A. Yes, that letter was alluding to the red book — there were to be extracts made from the red book, of the sinecures and pensions which Mr. Pitt and his family received from the public —

---

[17] Stephens: *Memoirs of John Horne Tooke,* Vol. II, p. 119.

Mr. Joyce called upon me the day Hardy was taken up, and told me he had sent a letter to you, to acquaint you that Hardy was taken up, and desired you to be ready at Spitalfields on Thursday next, with those extracts.

Q. Do you recollect the story being mentioned at the dinner, and considerably laughed at?

A. It was.

Q. Do you remember one expression in that letter was — " Is it possible to be ready by Thursday? "

A. I remember that was talked of at dinner.

Q. You recollect the interception of this letter being much talked of at that dinner?

A. Yes.

Q. Which contained the horrible plot of taking from the Court Calendar a list of large sinecure places and pensions enjoyed by Mr. Pitt, his family and creatures?

A. Yes.

Mr. Tooke. I ask these questions, because I believe it was for this plot — I was apprehended the next day — if the intercepted letter is in Court have I a right to ask for its production?

Lord Chief Justice Eyre. If there is a letter which is in the hands of the Officers of the Crown that appears to you to be necessary for your defence, to be sure you may call upon them to produce it.

Mr. Tooke. I mean for the purpose of this cross-examination?

Lord Chief Justice Eyre. To be sure, if they have it, they will produce it — Is it a letter from Mr. Joyce, supposed to be intercepted?

Mr. Tooke. A letter from Mr. Joyce to me, which was intercepted.

Lord Chief Justice Eyre. That is, there was a conversation that such a thing had happened.

Mr. Tooke. A great deal more than that — I am informed, from pretty good authority, that a letter was intercepted, which should have come by the post to me, on the Wednesday previous to my apprehension — that it was produced before the Privy Council, and made the subject of very serious examination; that great alarm, and great apprehensions, were entertained from the particular way of wording that letter — and it is for the purpose of this cross-examination that I wish to have that letter produced.

The letter was at once produced and read in court, after which the cross-examination of Sharpe was continued.

Mr. Tooke. Do you know, by conversation with Mr. Joyce, what it was I was to be ready with by Thursday?

A. The extract from the redbook, of the emoluments that Mr. Pitt and his family derived from the public.

Chief Justice Eyre. Who was to make those extracts?

A. Mr. Tooke was to make the extracts.

Mr. Tooke. In your passage to dine at Mr. Pearson's, in Spital-square, did you see any light horse?

A. Yes, I saw the last pass the window; I was saying there were some light horse; I looked through and saw the last.

Q. Was it understood, or had you any reason to suppose, that these light horse were sent in consequence of the interception of this letter containing this horrid treason?

A. I understood, that the army was out.

Lord Chief Justice Eyre. What reason had you to understand that?

A. A person came and told me, that there went to Spitalfields some light horse that day. I enquired of a military gentleman, a day or two after, and he said there was an order came the night before, for them to be there.[16]

Although Tooke implied in the course of his trial that the Joyce letter was the occasion of his arrest, he makes no allusion to it in the following account of his apprehension:

Tuesday, May 20, 1794, I began to mark this translation of Boethius in the Tower, with my pencil, being denied the use of pen and ink. I was apprehended at Wimbledon, May 16, conducted to the Tower, Monday, May 19, 1794, without any charge; nor can I conjecture their pretense of charge. Mr. Dundas, Secretary of State, told me in the Privy Council, that " It was *conceived* that I was guilty of treasonable practices." He refused to tell me *by whom* it was conceived. I offered to be examined, *to any extent*, if the Chancellor or Dundas would declare that there was *any* treason. The Chancellor said that I seemed to object to

[16] Gurney: *Trial of Horne Tooke for Treason,* London, 1795, Vol. I, pp. 348–351.

the legality of the *warrant;* but that I might object to that here-after in another " place." [19]

Tooke later ascertained that at this very time a bill was introduced into the House to make the warrant legal and to justify the authorities in issuing it.

On the pages of a copy of *The Diversions of Purley* [20] which was sent to him very probably along with three volumes which, we are told, were found on his table at Wimbledon, namely, the Boethius just referred to, Locke, and Bishop Wilkins's essay on language, he kept a daily record of his prison experiences. On May 24, for example, he notes that he has received, by order of the Privy Council, paper, ink, tea, sugar, and lozenges for his cough. In other entries he complains of the strictness of his custody and of the unnecessary humiliation to which he is exposed. He frequently expresses his anxiety for the safety of his daughters during his enforced absence from them. On July 14, for instance, he writes:

I read this day in all the papers " Yesterday Mr. Pitt with a party of his friends dined with several members of both houses of

[19] Samuel Rogers: *Recollections,* Boston, 1859, p. 164.

[20] The history of this valuable volume, which is now in the Library of the British Museum, is related by a contributor to *Notes and Queries,* who signs himself " G. J. W." " I lately had intrusted to me," he writes, " an interleaved copy of the first edition of *The Diversions of Purley,* with notes and emendations for the second edition in the author's handwriting. The most interesting feature in the book, however, lay in a rough diary, kept by Horne Tooke from May to October, 1794, whilst he was a prisoner in the Tower, awaiting his trial for high treason, extracts from which I now give for the readers of ' N. and Q.' Since the author's death the volume remained continuously in the possession of his descendants or kinsmen till some fifteen years ago, when it passed by will to the late owner, whose executor kindly lent it to me. The writing is in places somewhat crabbed and difficult to decipher." (*Notes and Queries,* Eighth Series, Vol. XI, January 9, 1897, p. 21.)

parliament at Mr. Dundas's villa at Wimbledon." The air no doubt blew fresher on them, from the consideration that his next door neighbor was sent to spend his summer a close prisoner in the Tower; and they might contemplate with luxury the forlorn condition of my poor disconsolate girls. " For thee fair freedom, welcome all the past! " [21]

He asserts in several passages that he is unable to understand the motive for his arrest. On July 4 he writes:

I have been this day seven weeks in close custody without any charge of accusation, and all I know or can conjecture of the cause which is to be pretended, is that Mr. Dundas told me " It was *conceived* (he would not say by whom or why) that I was an active and leading member of the Corresponding and Constitutional Societies; and had been guilty of treasonable practices." I sent fruit and vegetables to each of the prisoners; *i.e.*, to Bonny, Kyd, Joyce, Martin, Richter, Hardy, Thelwall, Loveit.[22]

In his entry for July 25 he makes a boast which he repeated almost word for word at his trial four months later:

I have this day been *ten* weeks in close custody. In this so close custody I have had time to review my life that is passed; and I cannot find any one action that I have committed, any word that I have written, any syllable that I have uttered, or any single thought that I have entertained, of a political nature, which I wish either to conceal or to recall.[23]

While the real cause of his apprehension was at first unknown to Tooke, as the preceding quotations prove, it was later revealed to him, we are informed by a writer for *Tait's Edinburgh Magazine,* in a way which prevented its being made public during the life of the person who made the disclosure. After the death, about the year 1806, of

[21] *Notes and Queries,* Eighth Series, Vol. XI, p. 103.
[22] *Ibid.*
[23] *Ibid.*

this individual, the secret was divulged to several persons, among them the writer just mentioned, to whom it was told " by an eminent divine." The correctness of the story was confirmed in the year 1820 by John Thelwall, one of Tooke's associates, who was imprisoned with him, on the same charge of treason. The contributor to *Tait's*, therefore, vouches for the authenticity of the following account of the manner in which Tooke learned definitely of the use that Wharton had made of the information against him:

One evening after Tooke's nephew,[24] who usually visited him every day, had left him, a stranger was announced by the turnkey. Tooke desired he might be shown in, when a tall man, muffled up in a wrapping cloak, and with his hat slouched over his face, entered the room, and saluted him courteously. When the turnkey had retired, the stranger addressed Mr. Tooke to this effect: " You are no doubt surprised at my visit, but I beg to say that it is a perfectly friendly one, in proof of which I am about to put my life in your hands in order to save yours. I am a member of his Majesty's Privy Council, and my object in coming is to inform you of the real cause of your arrest, and of the danger to which you are exposed. It will be in your recollection that at your dinner party on Sunday last, a motion was proposed, to be brought before Parliament, for increasing the pay of the navy; and that when it was objected by one of the company that this would breed a mutiny, you remarked, *'that's exactly what we want.'* This observation was carried to the Minister by Wharton, the member for Beverley, who was of the party, and your arrest was the consequence.

" In the Privy Council held today, Wharton has been examined, and it was afterward debated in what way his evidence should be adduced against you; whether the informer should be called by the Crown, or whether they should allow you to call him, and so convict you out of the mouth of your witness? The Council broke up without deciding this question, which will be brought

[24] In his Diary Tooke states that his nephew, John Wildman, received permission on October 8 to visit him. It was some time after this date, therefore, that Tooke learned the immediate cause of his arrest.

before it again to-morrow. I will, therefore, be here again to-morrow evening, to let you know their decision."

"The scoundrel," said Tooke, when the stranger had concluded: "I always suspected him of not being over hearty in the cause, but I could not have believed him guilty of so atrocious a breach of confidence. However, we must endeavor to out-manoeuvre them yet." After a short conversation the stranger took his leave.

Tooke, who, as we have observed, had not been entirely deceived as to Wharton's intentions, could not have been so surprised at the preceding revelation as he pretended to be. But, to continue the story. "The next morning," says the narrator, "Tooke sent for his solicitor, and in confidence communicated to him what he had learned, but without divulging the way in which he obtained his information. He then directed him to go to Wharton and serve him with a subpoena and to beg of him not to absent himself from the court at the trial; that he considered him the most important witness in his favour; and, in short, that he depended on him more than all the rest; and it was, therefore, of the utmost consequence to him that he should be present on the occasion.

"This was done the same day; and in the evening, Tooke's incognito visitor again made his appearance, and stated that Wharton had detailed to the Privy Council what had passed with the solicitor. Upon which it was unanimously agreed, that Tooke should be allowed to call him as a witness, and that then the council for the Crown should obtain the most direct and unequivocal evidence against the prisoner by a cross-examination.

"Tooke now felt completely at ease and began making his arrangements for his defense. It is said that he had determined to defend himself; but his solicitor, after a long argument with him on the subject concluded by saying, 'Well, Sir, you must act as you please: but if you do, you

will certainly be hanged.' ' Then,' replied Tooke instantly,
' I'll be hanged if I do,' and directed him to give the brief
to Henry Erskine." [25]

In October, about a month before his trial, Tooke was
transferred, as the law required, to Newgate. Upon his arrival at the city jail, however, he found himself in a curious
predicament. The jailer refused to admit him, as no warrant could be produced for his commitment. His nephew,
therefore, returned to the Tower to secure the necessary
papers, while his uncle sat in a comfortable room before a
blazing fire, enjoying his delayed entrance to a prison notorious for its dampness and unhealthfulness.

The state trials of 1794 were preceded by two occurrences
that were very fortunate for the prisoners. In the first
place, Thomas Holcroft surrendered himself to the authorities to be tried on the same charge of treason, and in the
second place, there appeared in the *Morning Chronicle* for
October 21, a bold arraignment of Lord Chief Justice Eyre
for his definition of treason, a reply which was unsigned
but which, it was discovered later, was written by William
Godwin. " Having fully revolved the subject, and examined the doctrine of the Lord Chief Justice's charge to
the grand jury," Godwin states in his diary, " I locked
myself up on Friday and Saturday and wrote my strictures
on that composition, which appeared at full length in the
Morning Chronicle of Monday, and were transcribed from
thence into other papers." [26] " Was it necessary," asked

[25] *Tait's Magazine,* September, 1853, Vol. 20, p. 530. In the *Life
of Thelwall* (p. 258) we read that when Thelwall expressed a desire
to plead his own case, Erskine retorted, " If you do, you'll be
hanged," whereupon Thelwall replied, " I'll be hanged if I do! "
The writer for *Tait's* has, it seems, attributed to Tooke the witty
rejoinder of Thelwall.

[26] Paul: *William Godwin. His Friends and Contemporaries,*
London, 1876, Vol. I, pp. 118–119.

this daring pamphleteer, " for the destruction of twelve
private and untitled men, to create all this confusion, to
produce all this ruin, to overturn everything that is valuable
in English liberty, and place us for time coming under the
most atrocious and inexplicable despotism that the world
ever saw? " [27]   Godwin, it may be added, was present every
day at the trials of both Hardy and Tooke.

The trial of the latter was finally opened in the Sessions
House of the Old Bailey on Monday, November 17, 1794.
Samuel Rogers, who with Boddington paid five guineas for
a seat in the court room, mentions the following incident
in connection with the prisoner's conduct on first entering
the hall: " It was the custom in those days (and perhaps
is so still) to place bunches of strong smelling plants of different sorts at the bar where the criminal was to sit (I
suppose, to purify the air from the contagion of his presence!).   This was done at Tooke's trial; but, as soon as he
was brought in, he indignantly swept them away with his
handkerchief." [28]

Unperturbed, apparently, by the seriousness of his situation, Tooke produced the effect of taking personal charge
of the proceedings.   " Cool and prompt, ready at repartee,
and fond of notoriety, he trod the boards of the Old Bailey,"
says Townsend, " like some amateur actor pleased with his
part and resolved to make the most of it, even though the
catastrophe should terminate in his death.   After the acquittal of Hardy, the reverend agitator would have depre-
cated his not being brought to trial as a personal misfortune.
It is impossible to read this grave state prosecution without
frequently indulging in an involuntary smile.   From the

[27] Godwin: *Cursory Strictures on the Charge Delivered by Lord
Chief Justice Eyre to the Grand Jury,* London, 1794, p. 20.

[28] Dyce: *Table Talk of Samuel Rogers,* New York, 1856, pp.
125–126.

constant merriment which rewarded his sallies it might be guessed that a madder wag never stood at the bar; and yet he rarely laughed himself, but glanced around from his keen and arch eyes a satirical look of triumph." [29] As soon as he was placed in the dock, he glanced up critically at the ventilator of the room and informed his judges that he hoped they would be so kind as to settle the case quickly since he feared he might take cold. Upon being arraigned and questioned by the officer of the court as to how he would be tried, he replied: "'I *would* be tried by God and my country — but ' — and looked sarcastically round the court." [30] He soon asked to be allowed to sit by his counsel, engaging in a witty dispute with Lord Chief Justice Eyre, who was presiding at the trial, as to whether his request ought to be granted as a favor or as a right. He was finally permitted by the indulgence of the Court to sit by his defender, Erskine.

While the audience were enjoying the pleasantries of the defendant, the case was opened for the State, the prisoner being charged "with the crime of High Treason in compassing the death of the King." [31] Sir John Scott, afterwards Lord Eldon, assisted by the Solicitor General, represented the Crown. Since no overt acts could be ascribed to the prisoner, the prosecution had to make the most of the pile of doubtful writings in their possession and of all the damaging information that had been zealously and thoroughly collected to expose the functions and revolutionary intentions of the radical organizations to which Tooke belonged. "The whole power of the Court of the King, and of the Judges of the King's Court," says Stan-

[29] *Twelve Eminent Judges,* London, 1846, Vol. II, p. 24.

[30] Massey: *History of England,* Vol. IV, p. 111.

[31] Gurney: *Trial of Horne Tooke for Treason,* London, 1795, Vol. I, p. 22.

ton in his summary of the proceedings against both Hardy and Tooke, " was brought to bear upon the doomed prisoners, aided by the multifarious lore and subtle reasoning of the Attorney-General. Every doubtful word was distorted, every ambiguous look transformed into lurking treason. The rules of evidence were put to the rack, to admit bits of letters and conversations, written and uttered by others than the accused, and to hold them responsible for all that had been said and done by every man who, at any time and anywhere, had belonged to the societies or taken part in their discussions." [32] The accusations made by the State and the evidence produced to sustain them, says Godwin, could not be " exceeded in vagueness and incoherence by anything in the annals of tyranny." [33]

Shrewd and resourceful, Tooke ridiculed his prosecutors by exposing the fallacies in the arguments advanced against him. When, for example, the Crown attempted to prove that a society to which he belonged was Republican, since it had approved certain measures of the National Assembly, he observed ironically that it was well the Society had not expressed approval of some things in the Koran, as it might, by so doing, have laid itself liable to accusations of having Mohammedan inclinations. In similar manner, when the question of the validity of private letters as evidence was raised in court, he declared that if he were to be judged by his letters, he might be accused not only of treason, but of blasphemy as well. " I do not answer common letters of civility," he said, " but I have received and kept many curious letters. I received some letters from a man whose name is Oliver Overall, and he

[32] *Reforms and Reformers of Great Britain and Ireland,* New York, 1850, p. 37.

[33] Paul: *William Godwin. His Friends and Contemporaries,* Vol. I, p. 117.

endeavored to prove to me that he was God the Father, Son, and Holy Ghost. (I kept the letters out of curiosity, and it is probable they may be produced against me.) He proved it from the Old Testament; in the first place because God is *Over*-all; that is, God over all. He proved he was God the Son, from the New Testament — verily, verily, I am he; that is *Veral I, Veral I,* I am he. Now, if these letters, written to me, which I, from curiosity, have preserved, but upon which I have taken no step, and to which I have given no answers are produced against me, I do not know what may become of me." [34]

After the verdict had been delivered, Tooke admitted that his own caution had led to his arraignment on a false charge. The confusion of the Court in the deciphering of his writings might be attributed, he said, to his having corrected the wording of papers of the Constitutional Society brought to him before their publication, when the original wording might have led to the prosecution of the writers. To this practice of his might be traced all of the uneasiness and suspicion of his prosecutors. He had been in the habit of correcting the writings of any persons who came to him for advice or criticism. He had even corrected a book written against himself. Not foreseeing the consequences of his services in these matters, he had, to save others from prosecution for libel, subjected himself to a trial for treason.

Tooke had an eloquent defender in Erskine, whose championship of the cause of Hardy and the other state prisoners and his masterly efforts to prove their innocence cannot be too highly commended. Enraptured by the great lawyer's plea for Hardy, Tooke had declared that the speech would live forever. In defending Tooke, Erskine " showed himself not only a great orator," says Samuel Rogers, " but a

[34] Gurney: *Trial of Horne Tooke for Treason,* Vol. I, p. 157.

great actor; for, on the fifth day, when the Attorney-General Eldon was addressing the jury and was using a line of argument which Erskine had not expected and could not reply to (the pleading for the prisoner being closed), I well remember how Erskine the whole time kept turning towards the jury, and by a series of significant looks, shrugs, and shakings of his head, did all he could to destroy the effect of what the Attorney-General was saying." [35]

The defence produced evidence to prove that the prisoner, in spite of his approval of the French Revolution, had no desire to see the movement extended to England, that for two years preceding his apprehension he had been averse to any strong measures being introduced into the Society for Constitutional Information, and that he had even been criticized for favoring long adjournments. One witness testified that he remembered Tooke's expressing the desire that an act of Parliament might be passed making it death for him to leave home.

The Duke of Richmond, Pitt, Sheridan, Earl Stanhope, and other important persons, who had been subpoenaed by Tooke as witnesses, were called upon to give accounts of their activities as reformers. The principles which they had advocated were altogether as radical, the defence clearly proved by their testimony, as were those that had been advanced at any time by Horne Tooke. The chief crimes that the prosecution had succeeded in fastening upon the prisoner were that he was a member of the Society for Constitutional Information and of the Corresponding Society, the former of which had raised a subscription for Tom Paine's benefit, and that he had been present at a meeting of delegates from liberal organizations, an offence of which the Prime Minister himself had been guilty. " At first," says Jesse, " Pitt's memory conveniently failed him

[35] Dyce: *Table Talk of Samuel Rogers,* New York, 1856, p. 125.

during the searching interrogation to which he was subjected; but having apparently had it refreshed by the
straight-forward evidence of Sheridan, who was the next
witness examined, it was solicited from him, on his being
allowed to revise his evidence, that at least on one occasion,
he had assisted counties to take measures for procuring parliamentary reform." [36] When Tooke had concluded his examination of the Premier, his nephew observed that he had
got the better of Pitt and might have embarrassed him still
further. "Yes, I might, John," replied Tooke, "but never
in my life did I choose to trample on a fallen foe." [37]

The absurdity of prosecuting Tooke for treason was
clearly demonstrated by his trial. His attitude toward the
motions adopted by English Radicals at the Anniversary
dinner held on July 14, 1790, at the Crown and Anchor, was
so cautious that even Burke, who regarded the celebration
as inimical, might have applauded the sentiments which he
expressed. "I remember very distinctly," said Richard
Brinsley Sheridan, who was called upon to describe Tooke's
behavior at the meeting, "his stating that an unqualified
approbation of the French Revolution, in the terms in which
I had moved it, might produce an ill effect out of doors;
that it might induce a disposition to revolution in this
Country, or if it did not produce that effect, at least, it was
capable of being misrepresented so as to be stated to have
that object and intention. — I think, I recollect perfectly
Mr. Tooke's adverting in his speech to the circumstance of
all the gentlemen at the meeting, having national cockades
in their hats, which we all had — he argued the necessity of
qualifying our approbation of the French Revolution, and
the establishment of liberty in France, with a declaration
of our attachment to the principles of our own Constitution.

[36] *Celebrated Etonians,* Edition de Luxe, Vol. II, p. 328.
[37] Stephens: *Memoirs of John Horne Tooke,* Vol. II, p. 152.

I remember, perfectly, his speaking in a figurative manner, and describing the former government of France, as a vessel so foul and decayed, that repair merely could not save it from destruction — I cannot be positive to the words, I am positive to the purport of those words, I am going to state now — I am quite positive to the very terms, that in contrasting our state, he said, thank God, the main timbers of our Constitution are sound, having before observed that some reforms were essentially necessary; I remember the conversation, or debate, the more accurately from the circumstance of those sentiments of Mr. Horne Tooke having been received by some violent people, or by people who mistook his intention, with great disapprobation, and with very rude interruption, inasmuch that, I believe Lord Stanhope, the chairman, interfered to preserve order." [38]

The witnesses for the defence were all agreed as to the moderation of the prisoner's political activities, which, they testified, were uniformly directed towards Parliamentary reform. The following rather humorous testimony to the singleness of his aims was furnished by one of them:

I have found him both when he had drank a great deal of wine and when perfectly sober in the morning, uniformly consistent with the same principles. I have heard him reprobate the introduction of Paine's principles here, saying that this country was not fit for a Republic; that the only thing he wanted was a Parliamentary Reform; and he also told me that he refused being a Delegate to the Scotch Convention. [39]

Major Cartwright referred in his testimony for Tooke to an illustration which the latter had employed on two or three occasions to define the bounds of his radicalism:

[38] Gurney: *Trial of Horne Tooke for Treason*, London, 1795, Vol. II, pp. 78–79.
[39] *Ibid.*, p. 145.

He said, men may get into the same stage coach with an intention of traveling to a certain distance; one man chooses to get out at one stage, another at another; some men may want something more — a Reform in the House of Commons is what I want. And, still pursuing his simile of the stage and coach, he said — When I find myself at Hounslow I get out, those that want to go further may go to Windsor, or where they like; but when I get to Hounslow (applying it to the House of Commons), then I get out, no further will I go, by God.[40]

This famous illustration, it may be noted, provoked unfavorable comments from both Coleridge and Hazlitt, the former of whom raises the question: " Suppose you know, or suspect, that a man is about to commit a robbery at Slough, though you do not mean to be his accomplice, have you a moral right to walk arm in arm with him to Hounslow, and, by thus giving him your countenance, prevent his being taken up? " in answer to which he says: " The history of all the world tells us, that immoral means will ever intercept good ends." [41]

Hazlitt, who objected to Tooke's cautious attitude as a reformer, made the following criticism of his comparison:

In the case of the State Trials, in 1794, Mr. Tooke compromised his friends to screen himself. He kept repeating that " others might have gone on to Windsor, but he had stopped at Hounslow," as if to go farther might have been dangerous and unwarrantable. It was not the question how far he or others had actually gone, but how far they had a right to go, according to the law. His conduct was not the limit of the law, nor did treasonable excess begin when prudence or principle taught him to stop short, though this was the oblique inference liable to be drawn from his line of defence.[42]

[40] *Ibid.*, Vol. I, p. 458.

[41] *Specimens of the Table Talk of the Late Samuel Taylor Coleridge,* New York, 1856, p. 309.

[42] Hazlitt: *Works,* Vol. IV, p. 236.

The trial was a prolonged one, lasting six days, but the jury came to a decision in approximately eight minutes after their withdrawal from the room. Major Cartwright, Tooke's loyal friend and colleague, " who would not but have been an evidence on this trial for the world," [43] described in a letter to his wife the enthusiasm with which the verdict of the jury was received, and the final scenes in the court room:

On the words " not guilty," the air was rent with joyful shouts and Felix trembled. As soon as the shouting subsided, Tooke addressed the court, in a very few words, thanking them for their conduct on the trial, and then said, " I hope, Mr. Attorney-General, that this verdict will be a warning to you not to attempt to shed men's blood upon lame suspicions and doubtful inferences," or words to that effect. He then turned round to the jury and thanked them for his life. Every man of them shed tears. This brought tears to the eyes of Tooke, who, during a six days' battle, while the advocates of power were thirsting for his life, stood as dauntless as a lion, giving a stroke to one and a gripe to another, as if he were at play.[44]

His calmness and fearlessness had provoked the admiration even of his enemies. When it 'was falsely rumored that upon his commitment to the Tower he had burst into tears, Wilkes is reported to have said that he knew he was a knave but that he never thought he was a coward. The perilousness of his situation, as we have seen, merely sharpened his wit. In excellent spirits throughout the trial, he relieved the seriousness of the occasion by timely and humorous commentaries. To a lady admirer, for example, who threw a silk handkerchief about his neck to prevent his taking cold, as he was walking one evening from the courtroom to the jail, he remarked admonishingly: " Pray

[43] F. D. Cartwright: *Life and Correspondence of Major Cartwright,* London, 1826, Vol. I, p. 209.

[44] *Ibid.*, pp. 208–209.

be careful, Madam, I am rather ticklish at present, about that particular place." [45]

One of the most amusing of his observations was provoked by the emotion of his joint accusers, when the Attorney-General in concluding his charges addressed himself with pathos to his conscience and referred tearfully to the inheritance of integrity and public virtue which he expected to leave his children. At this point, to quote Lord Campbell, " the Solicitor-General, who was not generally of the *melting mood,* to the surprise of the beholders sobbed violently in sympathy and some one exclaiming ' Just look at Mitford: What on earth is *he* crying for? ' Horne Tooke sarcastically answered ' At the thought of the *little inheritance* that poor Scott ls likely to leave his children.' " [46] Immediately after the verdict of " not guilty " was delivered, Tooke declared that if he should ever be indicted for treason again, he should plead guilty at the outset, hanging or beheading being preferable to the Attorney-General's long speeches.

To Lord Chief Justice Eyre, who corrected him in the course of his trial for introducing an improper subject into cross-examination, Tooke replied: " I have been but forty years a student, when I shall come to be called to the bar, I hope I shall know better." [47] To the resourcefulness of this mere " student " of the law, however, there was apparently no limit. The records of his several appearances before courts of justice, to answer charges of libel or treason, furnish us, as we have seen, with choice illustrations of his wit and ingenuity. In dealing with such an extraordinary prisoner, " all that the Mansfields and the Bullers

[45] Thorold Rogers: *Historical Gleanings,* London, 1870, Second Series, p. 229.

[46] *Lives of the Lord Chancellors,* Vol. IX, p. 198.

[47] Gurney: *Trial of Horne Tooke for Treason,* Vol. I, p. 150.

could ever effect," says Lord Brougham, " was to occasion a repetition, with aggravating variation, of the offensive passages; all that Attorney-Generals could obtain was some new laughter from the audience at their expense." [48]

When the trial was concluded, Samuel Rogers tells us, " a daughter of one of the jurymen was anxious to be introduced to Tooke; who, shaking her by the hand, said very prettily, ' I must call you sister, for you are the daughter of one of those to whom I owe my life.' " [49] Rogers was convinced that if Tooke had been convicted, he would most certainly have been hanged. " We lived then," he said, " under a reign of terror." [50]

Before retiring from the court room, Tooke, who had come near paying dearly for his entertainment of a government spy, turned to Wharton, on whom he had, no doubt, cast accusing and significant looks throughout the trial, and reproached him for his double-dealing. " Thou base scoundrel," he said, " go home to your Yorkshire den, and hide your head there, for you are unfit to mix in the world with honest men." [51] Wharton had not been called upon to testify, for after ten or fifteen witnesses had been examined, Tooke, satisfied that the verdict would be in his favor, had expressed his desire to his counsel that the defence might be closed. The prosecution had objected, of course, since their only hope of a conviction then depended upon the testimony of Wharton, who had been subpoenaed by Tooke, but the defendant had been insistent, and the Crown had lost its chance to condemn Tooke by a cross-examination of its representative.

[48] *Statesmen of the Time of George III*, Second Series, Philadelphia, 1839, Vol. I, p. 142.

[49] Dyce: *Table Talk of Samuel Rogers*, New York, 1856, p. 127.

[50] *Ibid.*

[51] *Tait's*, Vol. 20, p. 532.

Upon leaving the Old Bailey, Tooke and his daughters went directly to the home of Dr. Cline, Tooke's physician, who was their host for the night. Among the approximately twenty guests that had gathered at Cline's to celebrate Tooke's victory was Major Cartwright, who had written to his wife that if Tooke escaped the "bloodhounds,"[52] he expected to dine with him.

With the acquittal of John Thelwall, the third of the state prisoners to be prosecuted, the trials came to an end, and there was rejoicing throughout the nation. "The perusal of my Journal for the year 1794," says Crabb Robinson, "has brought a few facts to my recollection that deserve to be briefly mentioned. The chief of these are the famous State Trials of Hardy, Horne Tooke, and Thelwall. I felt an intense interest in them. During the first trial, I was in a state of agitation that rendered me unfit for business. I used to beset the post-office early, and one morning at six I obtained the London paper with 'Not Guilty' printed in letters an inch in height, recording the issue of Hardy's trial. I ran about the town knocking at people's doors, and screaming out the joyful words."[53]

Wordsworth, writing to William Mathews in January, 1795, expresses his delight at the acquittal of the prisoners, though he cannot entirely approve of the character of Tooke. "He seems to me," says the poet, "to be a man much swayed by personal consideration, one who has courted persecution, and that rather from a wish to vex powerful individuals, than to be an instrument of public good. Perhaps I am mistaken; if so, I could wish to have my opinion rectified; such he has appeared to me. I

[52] F. D. Cartwright: *Life and Correspondence of Major Cartwright,* London, 1826, Vol. II, p. 208.

[53] *Reminiscences of Crabb Robinson,* Boston, 1870, Vol. I, pp. 17–18.

must add that I have not taken up this idea from this last event, for in his share of it I see nothing to blame, but from the tenour of his political conduct previous to that period. The late occurrences in every point of view are interesting to humanity. They will abate the insolence and presumption of the aristocracy, by showing it that neither the violence nor the act of power can crush even an unfriended individual though engaged in the propagation of doctrines confessedly unpalatable to privilege; and they will force upon the most prejudiced this conclusion that there is some reason in the language of reformers. Furthermore, they will convince bigoted enemies to our present Constitution that it contains parts upon which too high a value cannot be set. To every class of men occupied in the correction of abuses it must be an animating reflection that their exertions, so long as they are temperate, will be countenanced and protected by the good sense of the country." [54]

At a citizens' meeting which was held on February 7, 1795, at the Crown and Anchor, commemorating the happy conclusion of the trials, Earl Stanhope made a lengthy protest against the irregular and unprecedented legal character of the proceedings against the prisoners. One of the alleged offences of the twelve, said the Earl, was that they were so revolutionary as to address one another as " citizen." Although impudence " did not go quite so far as to state that crime to amount to *High Treason*," he explained, " it was seriously termed ' *a kind of indication of an Evil Intent.*' " When the Earl heard " such contemptible and solemn nonsense," he was reminded of a story that was told of a certain Court Physician. " You must know, Citizens," he said, " that the Physician was sent for, by a Patient who was very ill, and who wished to know whether he had got

[54] Knight: *Letters of the Wordsworth Family from 1787–1855*, Boston and London, 1907, Vol. I, p. 81.

the measles: and the Doctor, being asked the Question, said '*I can find no measles.*' Upon which the Patient asked him whether he had any of the *Symptoms* of the Measles? To which this learned Doctor, with a very grave face, and in a very solemn tone of voice, replied, ' No, Sir, you have got *no such Symptoms;* but I will tell you what you have got; you *have* certainly very dangerous Indications of the Symptoms of the Symptoms of a Symptom.' " [55]

" To the credit of George III," says Lord Campbell in his sketch of the life of Lord Loughborough, one of the chief promulgators of the trials, "when the whole subject was understood by him he rejoiced in the acquittals, and, laying all the blame on the Chancellor, he said, ' You have got us into the wrong box, my Lord, you have got us into the wrong box. Constructive treason won't do, my Lord, constructive treason won't do.' " [56]

[55] *Substance of Earl Stanhope's Speech Delivered from the Chair at a Meeting of Citizens at the Crown and Anchor, on the 4th of February, 1795, etc.,* p. 7.

[56] *Lives of the Lord Chancellors of England,* Vol. VIII, p. 147.

CHAPTER VII

EXCLUSION FROM PARLIAMENT — SUMMARY OF PUBLIC CAREER

UNDAUNTED by a series of political vicissitudes which had reached a climax in his trial for treason, Tooke announced his candidacy for election to Parliament, in 1796, as a member for Westminster against Sir Allan Gardiner, who represented the interests of Pitt. Since he had gained tremendous notoriety and popularity by his conduct during his trial, when he had given proof of the honesty of his efforts as a reformer, it was not unreasonable that he should have expected a victory at the polls. While his trial was still in progress, Major Cartwright had prophesied that if acquitted, Tooke would probably become a member for the district which he now offered to represent.

The sheer delight of meeting his rivals at the hustings was compensation enough to Tooke for his habitual defeat. He was noted for his replies to members of the opposite faction. In the Westminster campaign of 1790 he ridiculed Fox, after the latter had persuaded Sheridan to plead his cause, by announcing that when the quack doctor withdrew, he left his merry Andrew behind him. To O'Brien, who during one of the Westminster campaigns ventured to observe: " I understand, Mr. Tooke, you have all the blackguards in London with you," he immediately rejoined: " I am happy to have it, Sir, on such good authority." [1] When his rival, Sir Allan Gardiner, objected to Fox because " he was always against the *minister, whether right or wrong,*"

[1] Rogers: *Recollections,* Boston, 1859, p. 170.

179

and Fox failed to note the inconsistency of this reasoning, Tooke, at once seeing a chance for a joke, remarked that " he thought it at least an equal objection to Sir Allan that he was always with the minister, whether right or wrong." [2] " He watched his competitors with a wary eye," says Hazlitt, " picked up the mistakes or absurdities that fell from them, and retorted them on their heads; told a story to the mob; and smiled and took snuff with a gentlemanly and becoming air, as if he was already seated in the House." [3]

The campaign of 1796, which proved expensive for all the candidates, would have imposed heavy financial burdens on Tooke, had his debts, amounting to approximately a thousand pounds, not been paid by an admirer of distinguished rank. Service of a more singular nature was rendered him by one who had formerly been his bitterest enemy. On the very first day of the voting, John Wilkes, then the chamberlain of London, arrived at the hustings, and after paying a public tribute to the powers of the veteran politician, cast his vote for him. Tooke, it should be noted, spoke of Wilkes during his last years with no ill feeling.

Tooke's failure, in spite of his popularity, to win the election, must be attributed solely to the corrupt elective system of the times. At the end of the campaign his followers, who were gratified at the approximately three thousand votes that he had received, gave a dinner at the Crown and Anchor to celebrate his defeating so far the enemies of the liberal cause. This expression of confidence became the subject of a poem by Coleridge, whose indignation had been aroused two years before by Tooke's arraignment on a charge of treason. The poet's verses were addressed " To J. Horne Tooke and the company who met on June 28th, 1796, to celebrate his Poll at the Westminster Election."

[2] Hazlitt: *Works*, Vol. IV, p. 232.   [3] *Ibid.*, p. 235.

After his health had been drunk, Tooke made an address, in the course of which he assured his friends that " the Reign of Corruption " [4] was drawing to a close. " A very little knowledge of our History will show," he declared, " that *Terror* was the engine principally employed for the Despotism of the Stuarts: That Government attempted to be absolute by Terror: they proceeded as Tyrants always do — using Power as their right hand, and Reason only as their left. A little more than a hundred years ago, they were shipwrecked in that attempt to govern by Terror. They succeeded in *murdering* those whom they pleased, and were *murdered themselves* for the *murders* which they had committed. A different era and a different system followed; and those who did not dare to pursue the system of Terror, followed the System of Corruption: and this has drained the people almost to the dregs; for the conduct of Lord North was such that when Mr. Pitt came into office, he did not find money enough to corrupt with — barely enough for *himself* and his *family;* and he was compelled to have recourse to the Corruption of Vanity. New titles were employed. We had but one Marquis then, and now we have them in great plenty. If I am not mistaken, this title of Marquis was first conferred in England by that weak Tyrant, Richard the Second. Englishmen would not bear it; and the man upon whom it was conferred, was compelled to make an apology to the House of Commons, and get rid of the title. Another of Mr. Pitt's methods was to increase the number of Knights of the Garter; it was determined that Princes of the Blood should not be reckoned among the established number. Another method was to establish the new Order of Saint

[4] *Speeches of John Horne Tooke during the Westminster Election, 1796, with his Two Addresses to the Electors of Westminster, etc.,* p. 38.

Patrick. Another method was to pretend, that to be a
Baronet was a necessary step to being a Baron, in order to
make that foolish title of Baronet desirable, for a number
of persons had said they were Gentlemen, and would not
degrade themselves to become Baronets. But the force of
Corruption being now almost dry, they proceed to the
system of Slaughter! They attempt our lives! They think
we are afraid to die — For they never resort to Terror
whilst they can go on with Corruption. But as Ribbons
are still desired, it is probable, indeed it is rumored, that
some fresh Orders will be created. And as we have this
one advantage by the tax upon houses, that we are able to
know how many there are in the land; so if Mr. Pitt will
but give a Ribbon to every one who is willing to wear it,
we shall be able to tell; exactly to a unit, how many fools
there are in the Country." [5]

Although Tooke failed in his efforts to secure a place
in the House through election, he finally entered Parliament in 1801 as the representative for Old Sarum, the property at that time of Lord Camelford, who had been so
attracted by his talents as to offer him his patronage. In
consenting to be returned for such a forsaken borough as
Old Sarum, Tooke was acting, it cannot be denied, inconsist-
ently with his former protests against such a system of representation. It was only after a conference of three days
and three nights with Lord Camelford that he had been
persuaded to accept that nobleman's proposition.

On the occasion of Tooke's taking his seat on February
16, a dramatic scene was enacted in the House, when he
went through the customary formality of shaking hands
with the Speaker, for the presiding officer was, at the time,
no other than the late solicitor-general, who, only a few
years before, had exhausted his eloquence in an effort to

[5] *Ibid.*, pp. 38–39.

convict the new member of treason. Tooke's self-possession and good breeding helped to relieve the embarrassment
of the situation in which both he and the Speaker, but
chiefly the Speaker, found themselves under these unusual
circumstances.

During the short time that he held his seat, Tooke participated freely in the discussions of the House and displayed his ability as a debater. His opinions on the " Poor
Relief Bill " revealed a keen insight into economic con-
ditions. " If you wish to promote the comfort of the poor,"
he wisely suggested, " raise as speedily as possible the
price of labour. It is far too low, and must soon rise in
spite of you. Though not young, I am not very old, and
within my recollection the price of labour has been trebled.
Effects will still follow causes and it must soon advance
much further." [6]

Though admirably qualified for service as a legislator,
Tooke was not privileged to remain long a member of
Parliament. He had formerly been refused admission to
the bar because he had once been a clergyman, and he
was now, for the same reason, denied the right to a seat
in the House of Commons. Thomas Robinson, in a letter
of March 9, 1801, addressed to his brother, Henry Crabb
Robinson, relates the following gossip connected with
Tooke's situation: " A very interesting debate is expected
to-morrow on a motion of Lord Temple to inquire into the
eligibility of a priest to a seat in Parliament. Lord Camelford, it is said, told Lord Grenville that if the black coat
were rejected, he would send a black *man,* referring to a
negro servant of his, born in England, whom he would
qualify to take a seat." [7]

The debate on the eligibility of a churchman to sit in

[6] Stephens: *Memoirs of John Horne Tooke,* Vol. II, p. 244.
[7] *Reminiscences of Crabb Robinson,* Boston, 1870, Vol. I, p. 53.

Parliament was opened, as it had been rumored that it would be, on March 10, when Lord Temple, who introduced the motion, called on Boucher, a notary public, to affirm that Tooke was actually an ordained priest. At this point, Fox, setting aside his personal enmity for Tooke, proposed that it first be decided whether a clergyman was eligible to take a seat in the House, after which the new member's priesthood might be investigated. A committee was shortly afterwards appointed to examine records and precedents of the House of Commons, respecting the rights of the clergy to hold seats in Parliament. When the report was finally presented and the debate resumed, Tooke, who spoke in his own behalf, described the opposition that he had encountered at every step of his career:

> I rise, Sir, on this occasion with the greatest reluctance. In the course of a long, and not an idle life, I have been engaged in many important struggles; but scarcely ever was I individually concerned. I fought with the enemies of law, of liberty, and of truth. It was of importance for me to succeed, but my failure was not of more consequence to myself than to the rest of mankind. The subjects in dispute were common as the elements air and water. Now, I am engaged in a personal struggle. This, however, is not exactly the first time that I have been in this unpleasant predicament.[8]

Tooke dwelt upon the exception that had been made of his case, first when he aspired to the degree of Master of Arts and later when he applied for admission to the bar. In concluding the list of his grievances against authorities who had so misused him, he declared: " Positively a stranger would imagine that I had been guilty of felony, or some infamous crime. I have been told to stand up and show myself. My eyes, indeed, Sir, are now very weak; but I am very much mistaken if the noble lord is

[8] *Parliamentary History,* Vol. XXXV, p. 1380.

such a terrible looking man that I should have been afraid to look him in the face without this admonition. Have I ever shown any symptoms of cowardice? " [9]

He inquired whether being in priest's orders constituted a " public delinquency " [10] or was at all infamous. The fact that he had been a churchman, he argued, indicated that he had been characterized by at least some degree of ability, morality, and religion. He contended, moreover, that " there have been gentlemen, not in holy orders, who held livings in the church, and continued members of this House," and he added ironically, that many who were listening to his words would gladly go into the Church for £1,500 or £2,000 a year if " they had the fair moral character " which he had possessed when he first took orders, " and the small pittance of learning necessary to qualify anyone for ordination." [11]

Tooke could not refrain in the course of his speech, it may be noted, from calling attention to the linguistic errors perpetrated by the reporter on his case, who had indulged in " a morsel of Old English," that had amused him not a little. " It was written no farther back than in the time of Henry 6th; " he said, " and, tho there are but twenty-one lines in all, the characters have been mistaken eleven times. Lest he should be directed to make a second search of this kind, I would inform him, that the letter he has mistaken so often for a *y* is the Saxon *theta;* and that instead of *yes, yat,* and *yese,* sounds not to be found in the English language at any period of history he should have wrote *this, that,* and *these.* Of the real Saxon *y* he is ignorant, and by mistaking it for *Z,* he has committed several blunders not less ridiculous." [12]

Upon reverting to a more direct argument in his favor,

[9] *Ibid.,* p. 1381.
[10] *Ibid.,* p. 1381.
[11] *Ibid.,* p. 1382.
[12] *Ibid.,* p. 1383.

Tooke reminded his audience that if he were a Jew, a Pagan, a Mahometan, a Jesuit, a Presbyterian or a Quaker, there would be no question as to his eligibility. All opposition against him, it seemed, rested on the fact that he had done nothing to be suspended or excluded from the Church. "Because," said he, "like a good subject, I chose to withdraw without stating my reasons and thus exciting scandal, I am forever ineligible."[13] His situation reminded him of an occurrence of a few years before. "A poor girl in very indigent circumstances, and quite destitute," he said, "went to a director of the Magdalen Hospital, and applied to be taken in. 'Why,' said he, ' 'tis true, there is now a vacancy, and I have no objection to admit you; but first let me hear something of your history.'" Upon discovering that the unfortunate young woman was poor but innocent, the director informed her: "You won't do for us then; if you wish admittance here, you must go and qualify."[14] Tooke's comparison, it is needless to say, completely demoralized the House.

By means of another humorous story, Tooke ridiculed his opponent, who denied holy orders to be a sacrament in the Protestant Church but maintained "the indelibility of the clerical character, by arguing that if it was not quite a sacrament, it was at least half a sacrament, as it had, like matrimony, the outward and visible signs of one." Tooke "had heard of casuists splitting hairs, but this was the first instance he ever heard of a casuist splitting sacraments; and he was sure the learned gentleman must have borrowed the idea from a learned casuist in divinity, of whose intense research and perspicacity he would relate an anecdote. The Divine alluded to wished to investigate the mystery related in the Scriptures of the legion of devils entering into a herd of swine; and, in order first to ascertain

[13] *Ibid.*, p. 1388.   [14] *Ibid.*

the numbers of devils composing a legion, he applied to the glossary, and found that a legion in the Roman army meant a certain number of men, more or less, in different reigns; but he took as his medium the number as it stood in the reign of Tiberius. He next set about inquiring into the number that composed a herd of swine; and for this purpose he directed his investigations into Syria, and other countries; and having taken the swineries of Mesopotamia as the most probable standard, he divided the number of a herd there by the number he had before ascertained of a legion, and the quotient proved to him that each hog was possessed by exactly a devil and a half, or somewhat less than a devil and three quarters. The name of the Divine was Dr. Smallwell, or Smallbridge, or Smallbrock; but ever after the learned casuist was called Dr. Split-Devil." [15]

Tooke, who never lost an opportunity for making an amusing comparison or indulging in an apropos rejoinder, thus enlivened every scene in which he acted a part. In concluding his speech, he assured his audience that though he desired to be out of the House, he felt it his duty to remain in it as long as he could and that he was prepared to contend for his rights. " I wish the House to proceed legally," he said; " I wish that an act should be passed, founded on the broad basis of general justice. Let the House save its character as much as possible, and try to preserve the confidence of the public. I sit down, Sir, in the full confidence that individual spleen will not be gratified; and that I shall not be punished for doing that which the noble lord, had he not the monopoly of the exchequer, would probably be glad to do himself." [16]

[15] *Parliamentary History,* Vol. XXXV, pp. 1419–1420.
[16] *Ibid.,* pp. 1389–1390. Lord Temple disliked Tooke for very good reasons. The ambiguously worded Joyce note that had aroused

The lengthy dispute as to Tooke's eligibility was at last settled by the new Premier, who introduced a bill making it illegal for any person in holy orders to hold a seat in the House. Tooke moved that for this bill of exclusion another bill be substituted, which would make it unlawful for clergymen elected to the House to hold a living and accept office. His proposed alteration was, of course, not accepted. In the House of Commons, Fox, who was opposed to the original motion of Lord Temple, sought to protect that body from a vote which he considered unconstitutional, and Erskine argued strongly for the eligibility of the clergy. In the House of Lords the bill was opposed by Tooke's former prosecutor, Lord Thurlow, who now sought to do justice to one whose ability he had at last come to admire. The proposed statute was, in his opinion, unprecedented and unprincipled. Notwithstanding this strong opposition the bill was passed and soon received the King's approval. The new ruling, however, did not prevent Tooke's holding his seat during the term upon which he had entered.

" It has been said that the House of Commons can do anything except reverse a law of nature," observes Thorold Rogers by way of commenting on Tooke's exclusion from Parliament. " It may be said, with equal truth, that no legislative body has ever before inflicted a disability on a whole profession, because it wished to avenge itself on one man, and that none has ever ventured on asserting, that because a person has entered on a profession, he shall not only while he follows it, but when he abandons it, be liable

---

the suspicions of the authorities in 1794, really referred to the lavish grants and gifts of which the Temples and the Granvilles were the recipients, and to Tooke's intention of exposing this prodigality on the part of the Administration.

to a perpetual civil disability; that no other representative body has ever written over the entrance to that occupation the stern warning of Dante's *Inferno* — ' Abandon hope, all ye who enter here.' " [17] In Part II of his treatise on language Tooke expresses astonishment that Parliament has not yet passed an act to make him conform to the liturgy, and to prohibit his " meddling with any words out of it." [18]

On the dissolution of Parliament Tooke retired to private life, his active participation in politics ceasing with his exclusion from the House. From his home at Wimbledon Common, however, he continued to watch with critical eye the course of public events. For forty years he had been an unwearied disturber of a blundering Administration. He had been an incorrigible reformer. Though pugnacious and conceited he had been an honest and courageous patriot who had not hesitated to face any public issue of his day. The trial of Warren Hastings was, it is singular to note, the one political occurrence of the period in which, aside from criticizing the length of the proceedings, he had seemed little concerned. In *The Diversions of Purley* he referred to Hastings as " that much injured man," who " was made the victim of all the corrupt parties in the kingdom." [19]

Fearn describes Tooke as " a *cultivated* man, a *clever* man, and a *party* man." [20] He was not, however, a party man in the sense of being attached to either of the conventional parties of the period. So anxious was he to preserve a complete independence of political character, that like many other patriots of the time, he refused to ally himself

[17] Thorold Rogers: *Historical Gleanings,* Second Series, pp. 240–241.

[18] P. 439.

[19] Part I, p. 238.

[20] *Anti-Tooke,* London, 1827, Vol. II, p. 6.

with either the Whigs or the Tories. He was unreservedly opposed to the principles of party affiliation. " Through-out the history of the world, down to the present moment," he declared in 1790, when he announced his candidacy for Westminster, " all personal parties and factions have been found dangerous to the liberties of every free people." [21] In one of his Westminster speeches of 1796, he reiterated his distrust of party organizations. *" I have never been,"* he asserted, *" and never shall be of any party.* Every man's honor ought to be in his own keeping. His own principles, and *the instructions, orders, and commands* of his *Constituents,* should always be the sole guides and directors of his conduct." [22]

However emphatic may have been their disapproval of party lines and party domination, both Tooke and his col-leagues, as Lord Brougham points out, were, nevertheless, " banded together in as regular and compact a body as ever flocked under the standards of the government or the oppo-sition; they acted together in concert; they gave up lesser differences of individual opinion for the purpose of joining to gain some greater advantage on grounds common to all; nay, they were as jealous of any Whig interference as the Whigs could be of them, and had a coterie of their own, with all the littleness of such assemblages, just as much as Devonshire House or Holland House." [23]

Although in his old age Tooke was prevailed upon, as we have just noted, to accept the patronage of Lord Camel-ford, he was throughout the greater part of his career under obligations to neither party nor patron. " My lords," he

[21] Stephens: *Memoirs of John Horne Tooke,* Vol. II, p. 86.

[22] *The Speeches of John Horne Tooke during the Westminster Election, 1796, with his Two Addresses to the Electors of West-minster,* etc., p. 8.

[23] *Statesmen of the Time of George III,* Second Series, Philadel-phia, 1839, Vol. I, p. 137.

said, addressing the Court on the occasion of his trial for seditious libel, " I never in my life solicited a favor: I never desire to meet with compassion." [24] Early in life, he affirmed, he had had the greatest of patrons, but he had renounced his patrons because he would not renounce his principles. Popularity, too, he affected to despise. " If popularity should offer itself to me," he declared, " I would speedily take care to kick it away." [25]

Of his disinterestedness in the popular cause there can be no question. He could hope for no personal reward for advocating reform and denouncing the Ministry. A passage from one of his speeches on the occasion of his trial for seditious libel describes the principles which uniformly directed his political conduct:

Gentlemen, I have been more concerned in my room than I have with the commerce of men in the world; and I read there, when I was very young, that when Solon was *asked* which was the best government, he answered — " Where those who are not personally injured, resent and pursue the injury or violence done to another, as they would do if done to themselves." That, he said, was the best government and he made a law empowering men to do so. Now, gentlemen, we are happier, we are under a better government, for our laws enjoin us to do what he only empowered man to do. By our laws the whole neighborhood is answerable for the conduct of each: our laws make it each man's duty and interest to watch over the conduct of all. This principle and motive has been represented in me as malice. It is the only malice they will ever find about me. They have in no part of my life found me in any court of justice, upon any personal contest or motive whatever, either for interest, or profit, or injury.[26]

Satisfied with the political privileges that the struggles of the past had made sacred, Tooke was a firm supporter of the Constitution. He and his friend Bosville had entered,

[24] Howell: *State Trials,* London, 1816–1828, Vol. 20, p. 78ə.
[25] *Ibid.*
[26] *Ibid.,* pp. 715–716.

he declared, " into a strict engagement to belong forever to the established government, to the established church, and to the established language " of their country, simply because they were " established." [27] It is ironical that with all of his respect for the existing order of things, Tooke should have been twice selected as a victim of governmental prosecution. As a reformer he was, as we have seen, more practical than visionary. " He was," says Leslie Stephen, " a type of the old-fashioned British radical who represented the solid tradesman's jealousy of the aristocratic patron rather than any democratic principle." [28] " He had," says Hazlitt, " none of the grand whirling movements of the French revolution — none of the tumultuous glow of rebellion in his head or in his heart." [29] He even disapproved of universal suffrage and annual parliaments. He was not a republican. Certainly he was no iconoclast.

With the more advanced reformers of the day, therefore, he was not in sympathy. Since he mingled freely, however, with even the most revolutionary of them, it is not surprising to find that he was popularly classed among them. " As for Talleyrand," wrote James Bland Burgess to Lord Auckland in 1792, after the arrival in England of the famous French diplomat, " he is intimate with Paine, Horne Tooke, Lord Lansdowne, and a few more of that stamp, and generally scouted by every one else." [30] With an extremist like Paine, who had no reverence at all for the Constitution, who was radically republican in his tenets, and who would build a new government on the wreck of the old, Tooke had, of course, little in common. With Cartwright, Jebb, and

[27] *Diversions of Purley,* Philadelphia, 1807, Part II, p. 438.

[28] *Horne Tooke* in the *Dictionary of National Biography.*

[29] *Works,* London, 1902, Vol. IV, p. 237.

[30] Quoted in Jesse's *Celebrated Etonians,* Edition de Luxe, Vol. II, pp. 226–227.

other such reformers, however, he met Paine frequently at the White Bear in Piccadilly, he entertained him at Wimbledon, and he was, it seems, on very intimate terms with him during the period immediately preceding the publications of the second part of *The Rights of Man*. A communication from Paine to his printer, Jordan, authorizing him to name the author and publisher of that treatise should any objections to it be raised, and mentioning the address at which a summons may reach him, concludes with the significant statement: " Send also to Mr. Horne Tooke." [31] In agreement with the preceding testimony as to Paine's reliance upon Tooke, is Cobbett's statement that when Paine was preparing to publish the second part of *The Rights of Man* he concealed himself in Fetter Lane and that no one knew where he was " except Mr. Horne Tooke, whose friendly care corrected the inaccuracies of his style, and Mr. Chapman, who was employed to print his book." [32]

The author of *The Rights of Man* was, in Tooke's judgment, not to be relied on too much. " No man can reason but from what he knows," he said. " Paine knew but little, and is therefore only to be trusted within his own sphere of observation." [33] Major Cartwright testified at Tooke's trial for treason that the defendant disapproved of certain parts of Paine's work but that he thought other parts might benefit England and other countries. Another witness stated that on one occasion after Tooke had received from Ireland an anonymous letter enclosing a letter to Paine he had consigned both communications to the flames.

Unlike Paine, Tooke preached no revolutionary doctrines.

[31] Conway: *Life of Thomas Paine,* New York and London, 1909, Vol. I, p. 336.

[32] *Life of Thomas Paine Interspersed with Remarks and Reflections,* by William Cobbett, p. 37.

[33] Rogers: *Recollections,* Boston, 1859, p. 152.

He advocated only those reforms that might be regarded as a ratification or an extension of the principles already recognized as the sacred rights of every Englishman. For the successive struggles by which his countrymen had wrested from their rulers a constitution that safeguarded their interests, no one, however, expressed more gratitude and enthusiasm than did he. He lauded " the glorious Revolution " of 1688 and wished that the event might be celebrated annually. Of James II he spoke with contempt. " That man," he said, " (for he never was for one moment a king) claimed the peculiar right, prerogative, and power of dispensing with the laws of the land." [34] " The right divine and sacredness of kings " was, said Tooke, " senseless jargon." He would go further, he wrote to Junius, than Cromwell, who declared that if he met the king on the battle field, " he would discharge his piece into his bosom as soon as into any other man's." " Had I lived in those days," declared Tooke, " I would not have waited for chance to give me an opportunity of doing my duty; I would have sought him through the ranks, and, without the least personal enmity, have discharged my piece into his bosom rather than into any other man's. The king whose actions justify rebellion to his government, deserves death from the hand of every subject. And should such a time arrive, I shall be as free to act as to say. But till then my attachment to the person and family of the sovereign shall ever be found more zealous and sincere than that of his flatterers." [35]

This pioneer reformer, who rejoiced in the passing of despotic kings, discovered, nevertheless, a tyranny yet to be defeated, in an arbitrary Ministry and a corrupt Parliament. " A King with the same designs and principles as

[34] Howell: *State Trials,* Vol. 20, p. 662.
[35] *Letters of Junius,* London, 1796, Vol. II, p. 160.

the Stuarts," he observed on one occasion, "would not, I apprehend, at this time of the day, ask, *Do I make the Judges? Do I make the Bishops?* No doubt they can do much; but they have been found inadequate to the task. That avenue to tyranny is now almost blocked up. His question at present I suppose would be, *Do I make the Parliament? Can I corrupt the Parliament?* If the answer was in the affirmative, the Parliament would soon become the grand instrument of oppression; and their votes would only serve as the index of a court dial to point out the hour of the day; directed by the ministerial wheels behind unseen, and moved by the weight of places and of pensions." [36]

"I love the King," he declared many years later, with his recent trial for treason obviously in mind, "according to Law; but I love my country better. A King may employ his time in hunting the harmless stag or timorous hare, while his ministers may enjoy the more sanguinary chase of running down his People: At present, therefore, I say, I love the King, according to Law; and whenever a King shall protect me and my fellow subjects from the murderous plots and conspiracies of his ministers, I will love him beyond the Law — beyond the letter of the bond." [37]

His loyalty to the Government, however, did not prevent his criticizing those officials who encroached upon the popular rights. Among political orators he belonged, says Hazlitt, to the class of "*trimmers.*" In one of his campaign speeches, for example, he declared ironically that the history of the country abundantly proved that many had "received a ribbon for services that deserved a halter." [38] Ever

---

[36] *Oration Delivered by the Rev. Mr. Horne at a Numerous Meeting of the Freeholders of Middlesex,* London, 1770, p. 35.

[37] *Speeches of Horne Tooke during the Westminster Election, 1796,* p. 9.   [38] *Ibid.*

on the lookout for some violation of Constitutional rights, he delighted, as we have seen, in tormenting and reproving his superiors when, in his opinion, they overstepped their authority. " He was," says Stanton, " the ablest pamphleteer and debater among the ultra-liberals, and was ever ready, with his keen pen and bold tongue to contend with the scribes of the Government through the press, or its orators on the rostrum, and he never gave cause to either to congratulate themselves on the results of the encounter." [39]

He enjoyed such a reputation, indeed, for writing lampoons and satires that on one occasion he was threatened with prosecution for writing a pamphlet for which he was not responsible. His *Letter to a Friend on the Reported Marriage of the Prince of Wales,* in which, strange to say, he took the position that the Parliamentary Marriage Acts were not to be regarded as binding, had advertised so keen an interest on his part in the question that another publication on the same subject, which was objectionable to the authorities, was also attributed to him. Only the striking difference in the style of the two pamphlets cleared him of the charge of authorship.

Conspicuous among the numerous political pamphlets by means of which Tooke angered or entertained the readers of his own day, is one of his later compositions entitled *Two Pair of Portraits.* The close relation between his literary activity and his politics is nowhere revealed more forcibly than in this extraordinary production, which, in his own time, was rivalled in popularity among his writings, only by *The Diversions of Purley.* The pamphlet, in which the author presents lengthy and sharp contrasts, first between Lord Chatham and Lord Holland, and next between

[39] Stanton: *Reforms and Reformers, of Great Britain and Ireland,* New York, 1850, p. 36.

Pitt and Fox, was provoked by the general election of 1788, when Fox, assisted by the aristocracy, succeeded in securing the return of Lord John Townshend, as his colleague. Tooke, who could not forgive Fox for his attitude toward the popular cause and for his later coalition with Lord North, associated this brilliant statesman with " Lord North and those men who persecuted and finally threw away America." [40] There is more than one allusion in the pamphlet to " Fox, North, and Co." [41]

After characterizing William Pitt the Elder and Henry Fox, " of diametrically opposite principles and practices," [42] both of whom began as Commoners and ended as Peers, the artist paints the portraits of William Pitt and Charles James Fox, the former of whom is distinguished by the virtues of Lord Chatham, the latter, by the vices of Lord Holland. This second pair of portraits " though not whole *lengths* and left for some younger hand hereafter to finish, have yet, (each of them respectively)," the writer insists, " a strong, family likeness to the former pair." [43] Had Tooke himself undertaken to complete his sketches only a short time afterwards, however, it is quite certain that the portraits would have undergone some decided alterations. His portrayal of the distinguished statesmen, in 1788, is concluded by two direct questions addressed to his readers:

Which two of them will you choose to hang up in your cabinets; the Pitts or the Foxes?
Where, on your consciences, should the other two be hanged? [44]

[40] *Two Pair of Portraits,* J. Johnson, London, 1788, p. 8.
[41] *Ibid.,* p. 14.
[42] *Ibid.,* p. 3.
[43] *Ibid.,* p. 7 (N. B.).
[44] *Ibid.,* p. 30. Fox, it is not surprising to discover, did not conceal his contempt for Tooke. Samuel Rogers recalled a dinner party given by William Smith in Westminster, when Fox ignored Horne Tooke

To the political standards which Tooke adopted at the very beginning of his public career he remained firmly attached throughout his life. In his case there was no renouncing of former principles. Nor was there, on the other hand, any steady growth of radical opinion. His politics, he boasted, would never be altered or " kept back on any occasion." [45] As Erskine reminded the Court in 1794, had been " the most uniform, firm, and inflexible in his political course," [46] and Major Cartwright, whose testimony agreed in every particular with the lawyer's characterization of the defendant, declared:

Of all men I ever knew Mr. Tooke appeared to me to be the steadiest and most invariable in his opinions from the time that I have known him, because I believe that they were formed prior to that period and his good sense never gave him occasion to alter them. [47]

" I have never," said Tooke in the Westminster campaign of 1796, " made any engagement except one — except that engagement which I entered into shortly after I was born, to oppose by all the means in my powers, Oppression and Tyranny, in whatever shape they presented themselves." [48] In his last political campaign the veteran politician, who had denounced the Administration in 1765,

---

and pretended not to hear any of the good things he said. " It was," declared Rogers, " the most painful scene of the kind I was ever witness to, except what occurred at my own house, when the Duke of Wellington treated Lord Holland much in the same way." (*Table Talk*, pp. 81–82.)

[45] *Diversions of Purley*, Philadelphia, 1806, Part I, p. 188.

[46] Gurney: *Trial of Horne Tooke for Treason*, London, 1795, Vol. I, p. 415.

[47] *Ibid.*, p. 457.

[48] *Speeches of John Horne Tooke during the Westminster Election, 1796*, p. 12.

described as a national curse " *the present incapable, tyrannical* and *detestable* ministry." [49]

It is to be deplored that circumstances relegated to a minor rôle in politics one whose services and abilities deserved recognition. As a politician he was " always below himself," says Lord Dudley, " always acting in subordination to his equals, or on a level with those whom nature and education had placed at an immeasurable distance beneath him. He began his career as an assistant in a struggle, from which the mock patriot Wilkes derived all the glory, and all the advantage; and he ended it by dividing the credit of turbulent, unsuccessful principles and lawful authority with Messrs. Hardy and Thelwall." [50]

In not a single instance, it may be said to his credit, did Tooke employ his talents and energies on the side of injustice and corruption. " At every successive crisis in our liberties," says Trevelyan, " when tyranny was so firmly in the ascendant that the hour demanded, not a champion, but a victim, all eyes were turned on the man who had braved the terrors of Privilege; and Horne Tooke always responded to the call, less eagerly and less boisterously as age and wisdom grew on him, but with the same constancy and self-possession as of old." [51] " Merely for attempting to prevent the final dismemberment of the empire," Tooke declared in his treatise on language, " I stand the single legal victim during the contest, and the single instance of proscription after it." [52.] His principles, however, needed no defence, he boasted, for " they have stood the test of

[49] *Ibid.*, p. 24.

[50] *Quarterly Review,* Vol. 7, p. 315.

[51] Trevelyan: *Early History of Charles James Fox,* New York, 1880, p. 448.

[52] Introduction to *Diversions of Purley,* Philadelphia, 1806, Part I, p. 1.

ages, and they will keep their ground in the general *commendation* of the world, till men forget to love themselves." [53]

William Cobbett, after reading the trial of Tooke for treason and the account of Fox's action against him, gave expression, in one of his letters, to his admiration for the veteran radical, who throughout a public career dedicated to the liberal cause had encountered nothing but opposition:

Really I do not wonder at Sir F's [54] attachment to him. Never did man show such courage and so much public virtue! What villains he had to deal with! His life is a history of the damned hypocritical tyrannies of this jubilee reign.[55]

[53] *Ibid.,* p. 2.
[54] Sir Francis Burdett.
[55] Melville: *Life and Letters of William Cobbett,* London, 1913, Vol. II, p. 38 (Letter to John Wright, 1810).

CHAPTER VIII

LAST YEARS AT WIMBLEDON

From the time that he resigned his living in 1773 until the end of the century Tooke lived upon a very moderate fortune. In 1799 he reported so small an income to the Government that the authorities questioned the accuracy of his statement. To the hasty observation, " Mr. Tooke, I do not understand you," ventured by one of the commissioners, who was not satisfied with his declaration, the insulted philologist is said to have replied: " Very possibly, but as you have not *half* the *understanding* of other men, you should have *double* the patience." [1] In answer to the officers who asked him to reconsider his statement that his income amounted to only sixty pounds a year, he addressed the following letter:

I have much more reason than the commissioners can have to be dissatisfied with the smallness of my income. I have never yet in my life disavowed, or had occasion to reconsider any declaration, which I have signed with my name. But the act of parliament has removed all the decencies which used to prevail between gentlemen, and has given the commissioners (shrouded under the signature of their clerk) a right by law to tell me that they have reason to believe I am a liar. They have also a right to demand from me, upon oath, the particular circumstances of my private situation. In obedience to the law, I am ready to attend them upon this degrading occasion so novel to Englishmen and to give them every explanation and satisfaction which they may be pleased to require.[2]

[1] Timbs: *English Eccentrics and Eccentricities,* London, 1866, Vol. II, p. 177.

[2] Stephens: *Memoirs of John Horne Tooke,* Vol. II, pp. 157–158.

Soon after Tooke had been forced by the law to disclose the state of his finances, his friends raised a subscription for him and bought an annuity of £600 for him
from Sir Francis Burdett. Among those who had interested
themselves in his behalf were Colonel Bosville and the poet
Samuel Rogers. Tooke's pension, " following Dr. Parr's
and Fox's " seemed to show, Crabb Robinson noted in his
Diary, that not all regard for public character was at an
end.[3]

The event of paramount interest to Tooke in the year
1802, was the death, at the age of eighty-three, of his benefactor, William Tooke. Although it had been understood
by the former when he took the name of his friend that
he was to become his heir, he received, on the settlement
of the Purley estate, only £500. By a provision of the
elder Tooke's will, however, a mortgage of £700, with
fourteen years' interest on the philologist's property at
Wimbledon, was cancelled. Tooke informed Stephens on
one occasion that he had resigned his living and taken up
the study of law at the earnest solicitation of his patron,
who had made him fair promises, every one of which he
had meant to keep but which he had failed to on account
of avarice. From the older Tooke he had received in all,
he calculated, a sum amounting to £8,900.

The eccentric master of Purley Lodge bequeathed the
greater part of his property to a grand-nephew by the
name of Beaseley, although he had threatened in the presence of Horne Tooke, with whom he had had a slight altercation, to leave all of his money to his nephew Colonel
Harwood. Tooke had immediately demanded that the new
heir should be summoned forthwith to Purley, and after his
request had been complied with and Harwood had actually

[3] *Diary, Reminiscences, and Correspondence of Henry Crabb
Robinson*, Boston, 1870, Vol. I, p. 39.

arrived on the scene, he and his rival had become congenial companions, the two eventually agreeing to be equal sharers in the estate. After the death of his patron, however, Horne Tooke experienced grave difficulty in persuading Harwood to give up a part of his interitance, and when the latter was finally induced to subscribe £4,000 — a sum at once invested by Sir Francis Burdett in annuities for Tooke's daughters and their mother — the transaction provoked a long suit in Chancery.

In his old age, Tooke, freed from all financial worries by the generosity of his friends, the settlement of his benefactor's estate, and the proceeds of his treatise on language, the 1798 edition and Part II of which, as we have noted, were subscribed to liberally, devoted himself to his garden and to his visitors.

The notoriety which he attained as a reformer and as a philologist was rivalled in his later years by the reputation which he enjoyed as a conversationalist and as a host. Though of humble origin, he had risen to the rank of a gentleman, and had become a prominent figure in the social life of the period. His aristocratic acquaintances were limited in number, it is true, but he was sought after by many of the influential politicians and writers of the day, who recognized in him the most cultivated person of his party. In his pleasant suburban home, where his doors were ever open to his many friends and associates from the metropolis and other quarters, " he sat like a king at his own table," says Hazlitt, " and gave laws to his guests — and to the world." [4]

Sunday was the day which Tooke set apart for receiving his visitors. During the week he might busy himself with his garden, pore over old volumes, apply himself to his studies, and play whist, but on Sunday he devoted himself

[4] Hazlitt: *Works,* London, 1902, Vol. IV, p. 233.

to his friends. The fame of his dinners, seasoned with political talk and enlivened by his delightful conversation and witticisms, was noised abroad, and the arrival of his guests became a feature of the Sabbath at Wimbledon Common. For years, Colonel Bosville, accompanied by a few friends, drove up in a coach-and-four to the veteran politician's door shortly before two o'clock on a Sunday afternoon, and a little later in the day visitors of varied rank and station made their appearance in the neighborhood. So insistent, indeed, was Tooke upon his friends availing themselves of his hospitality that he became offended if certain of his more intimate companions, who were expected to present themselves every week, failed to appear at the appointed hour. Samuel Rogers once unintentionally wounded Tooke's feelings by absenting himself for a brief time from his house.

Among the guests whom the philologist at one time or another received under his roof were many of his comrades in the popular cause, those who had supported him in the Westminster elections, those who, like himself, had been tried for treason, an officer of the guards who had formerly been his custodian, and, as we have already noted, even the attorney-general who, in the years gone by, had been his relentless prosecutor and bitter enemy. This genial host, moreover, entertained many others, who, though strangers to him personally, were welcomed at the Sunday gatherings when they arrived in the company of his friends. If he wished to compliment a guest particularly or to confer with him in private, he usually had to appoint a week day for a visit. In describing the mixed characters of the company that took advantage of Tooke's general invitation, Stephens says:

Here, at times, were to be seen men of rank and mechanics, sitting in social converse; persons of ample fortune, and those completely ruined by the prosecutions of the attorney-general. On one side was to be descried, perhaps, the learned professor of an university, replete with Greek and Latin, and panting to display his *learned lore,* indignant at being obliged to chatter with his neighbor, a member of the common council, about city politics. Next to these would sit a man of letters and a banker, between whom it was difficult to settle the precise *agio* of conversation, the one being full of the present state of the money market, and the other bursting to display his knowledge of all books — except those of *account* alone! A little further off, a baronet and a barrister could be heard discussing contested cases, both in the law and the constitution; the *suspected* atheist might be here seen, in amicable converse with a clergyman of acknowledged orthodoxy; while the trinitarian and the unitarian leaving difficult points to be settled by the controversies of former times, no longer argued with either the fierceness or intolerance of polemics.[5]

Most famous of the free-thinkers received at Wimbledon were Tom Paine and William Godwin, neither of whom their more conservative host admired unreservedly. Witnesses of the many debates between Tooke and Paine have testified to the unequalness of the contests, so superior were Tooke's controversial powers to those of his antagonist. Over Godwin, too, it appears, Tooke frequently triumphed in an argument. According to Coleridge, he "was always making a butt of Godwin,"[6] whose philosophy, the poet was persuaded, Tooke never could have comprehended. On one occasion, says Rogers, whose comments on Tooke's contempt for Godwin's philosophy agree with Coleridge's, the philologist, after inquiring critically just what Godwin meant by the "perfectibility" of man, added: "That limb is perfect which is fitted to perform all its functions, and that body is perfect which answers all

[5] Stephens: *Memoirs of John Horne Tooke,* Vol. II, pp. 296–297.
[6] *Specimens of the Table Talk of Coleridge,* New York, 1856, p. 310.

its purposes. He talks arrant nonsense." [7] The following
note of Godwin for the year 1795 makes it clear, however,
that he was not affected by Tooke's disagreement with him
on philosophical and political grounds, and that Tooke was
not unappreciative of the services which Godwin had rendered him on the eve of his trial for treason:

An incident worthy to be mentioned occurred to me on the 21st
of May in this year. I dined on that day with Mr. Horne Tooke
and a pretty numerous company at the home of a friend. The
great philologist had frequently rallied me in a good-humored way
upon the visionary nature of my politics — his own were of a different cast. It was a favourite notion with him that no happier
or more excellent government had ever existed than that of the
English nation in the reigns of George the First and George the
Second. From disparaging my philosophy he passed by a very
natural transition to the setting light, either really or in pretense,
by the abilities for which I had some credit. He often questioned
me with affected earnestness as to the truth of the report that I
was the author of the " Cursory Sketches on Chief Justice Eyre's
Charge to the Grand Jury," of which pamphlet he always declared
the highest admiration, and to which he repeatedly professed that
he held himself indebted for his life. The question was revived at
the dinner I have mentioned. I answered carelessly to his enquiry
that I believed I was the author of that pamphlet. He insisted
on a reply in precise terms to his question, and I complied. He
then requested that I would give him my hand. To do this I was
obliged to rise from my chair and go to the end of the table where
he sat. I had no sooner done this than he suddenly conveyed my
hand to his lips, vowing that he could do no less by the hand that
had given existence to that production. The suddenness of this
action filled me with confusion; yet I must confess that when I
looked back upon it, this homage thus expressed was more gratifying to me than all the applause I had received from any other
quarters.[8]

[7] Samuel Rogers: *Recollections,* Boston, 1859, p. 167.

[8] Paul: *William Godwin. His Friends and Contemporaries,* London, 1876, Vol. I, p. 147.

Several years after the occurrence of the incident just described, Godwin, who imagined, in an exaggerated state of sensitiveness, that he had been slighted by Tooke, received the following answer to his complaining letter:

My Dear Sir, — I this moment received your letter, and return an immediate answer, that you may not have an uneasy feeling one moment by my fault. What happened on Sunday to you may happen, and does happen to every one of my friends and acquaintances every day of my life. Bosville, his three friends, and Mr. Wood, came first, spoke to me in my study a very few minutes, and went away, leaving me to shift myself. W. Scott would have walked with them, but I called him back, having particular and important business to converse upon. Whilst we were importantly engaged, you arrived and sent up your name: to avoid interruption, I answered that I would come down speedily. I intended to finish my conversation, to dress myself, and then to ask you upstairs or myself to go down. I had not finished my business with W. Scott when the others returned; and they had not been in my room many minutes when they mentioned your being in the garden. I immediately begged them to call to you out of the window, at the same time telling them (what was very true) that I had quite forgot that you were there. You have the whole history, and ought to be ashamed of such womanish jealousy. You will consult your own happiness by driving such stuff from your thoughts. I know you do sometimes ask explanations from other persons, supposing that they fail in etiquette towards you: all compliments and explanations of the kind appear to me feeble and ridiculous. Every man can soon find out who is glad to see him or not, without compelling his friends to account for accidents of this kind, which must happen to every mortal.

Your jealousy, like all other jealousy, is its own punishment. I wish you punished a little for compelling me to write this letter, which is a great punishment to me; but I do not wish you to be tormented so much as this fractious habit will torment you if you indulge it. And besides, I should be very sorry that you missed any friends or valuable acquaintance by the apprehensions persons might entertain of your taking offense at trifles. You say Mr. Ward was a stranger. He is no stranger. He is Bosville's nephew, and a frequent visitor of mine. He did not act like a stranger: he went away in the middle of dinner; but I was not displeased at the liberty, but wish all my friends to accommodate themselves; and if I shall ever suspect (which I am not likely to do) that any of them slight me, I shall never seek an explanation, but leave it to him, and a repetition of slights to discover it to me.

Hang you and your weaknesses, or rather hang your weaknesses for making me write this stuff to you, upon such a foolish business. — I am, with great compassion for your nerves, very truly yours,

J. Horne Tooke.[9]

The letter just quoted, as well as the following, written two years later, on October 22, 1805, suggests the intimacy of the relation between Tooke and Godwin:

Dear Sir, — A letter from you, announcing a visit, is at all times pleasant to me; but the present is peculiarly so, because Mr. Jer. Joyce gave me much sorrow on Sunday last by informing me that Mrs. Godwin was ill.

I shall therefore see you on Friday with more pleasure than usual, and you may depend upon it, that if I was half so good at a leap as I am persuaded Mrs. Godwin is, I should often leap to Somers Town.

Mind, I do not say *at Somers Town;* for I am very careful how I employ the English particles, and am besides your most obedient servant,

J. Horne Tooke.[10]

Godwin, who had the highest respect for Tooke's literary abilities, consulted him when he was writing his *Life of Chaucer*. He found in him, no doubt, a helpful critic, for the philologist's understanding and appreciation of Chaucer, and his distrust of the poet's commentators, are apparent to every reader of *The Diversions of Purley*. Tooke objected, it may be noted here, to the principle upon which

---

[9] *Ibid.*, Vol. II, pp. 105–106. (The letter is dated December 6, 1803.)

[10] *Ibid.*, p. 144.

Tyrwhitt worked in his edition of Chaucer. " Had he given invariably the text of that manuscript which he judged to be the oldest," he says, " and thrown to the bottom the variorum readings with their authority; the obligation of his readers (at least of such as myself) would indeed have been great to him; and his industry, care, and fidelity would have been much more useful to inquirers, than any skill which he has shown in etymology or the northern languages; were it even much greater than it appears to me to have been." [11]

Tooke was so interested in one of his scholarly contemporaries, Sir James Mackintosh, as to wish to meet him, after he had come to know him as one of his supporters in the Westminster campaign of 1790, and after he had heard him speak in " The Speculative Society." Several years after he was introduced to Mackintosh, the latter became a frequent visitor at Wimbledon, where he engaged in animated debates with his host, who held opinions radically different in most instances from his own. Mackintosh, as the following paragraph from his *Memoirs* proves, was impressed by Tooke's violent prejudices against the writers of his day:

As to praise, he confines it to a few of his own sycophants; he praises nobody that deserves it, except Rogers. His invectives against his age, his country, and his literary contemporaries are not worthy of a wise or good man; his temper is soured, and his character corrupted by philology and disappointed ambition.[12]

Other notables who visited at Wimbledon were: Dr. Geddes, the erudite Roman Catholic priest, whose knowledge of Hebrew far excelled Tooke's; Richard Porson, the great classicist; Major James, the author of a Military

[11] *Diversions of Purley,* Philadelphia, 1806, Part I, p. 143.

[12] *Memoirs of Sir James Mackintosh,* London, 1835, Vol. II, p. 232.

Dictionary, to which Tooke contributed an article on Infantry; Sir Humphrey Davy, whose genius the philologist
was one of the first to recognize; Sir Philip Francis, who
was so impressed by Tooke's familiarity with the history
and constitution of the country that he consulted him several times when he himself was drawing up a plan for parliamentary reform; Lord Camelford, Tooke's combative
and eccentric patron; Major Cartwright, the reformer of
the period with whom Tooke was most closely associated;
Erskine, Tooke's able and eloquent defender; John Philpot
Curran, whose wit and conversational powers his host rated
high; Thomas Holcroft, the popular playwright and novelist; Jeremy Bentham, who made disparaging remarks about
Tooke's dinners and his library; Coleridge, who recorded
his impressions of Tooke; Samuel Rogers, to whom we are
indebted for many stories of the philologist and his friends;
Sir Francis Burdett, Tooke's most intimate and loyal friend
in his later years; and Alexander Stephens, the philologist's
biographer.

At Tooke's dinners Sir Francis Burdett usually occupied
the place of honor at the right hand of the host. After
their introduction in 1797 Tooke and Sir Francis [13] had discovered many interests in common. They even undertook
in the early period of their acquaintance the reading and
explanation of certain of the Latin classics. " We shall
never, I believe," said Tooke of Sir Francis, in *The Diversions of Purley*, " differ much in our actions, wishes, or

[13] Samuel Rogers indulged in the following bit of gossip at the
expense of Tooke's favorite caller:

" Burdett was, of course, a great deal with Tooke. In little
things, Burdett was a very inconsiderate person. One forenoon when
Tooke was extremely unwell, and a friend had sent him some fine
hot-house grapes, Burdett happening to call in ate up every one of
them." (Dyce: *Table Talk of Samuel Rogers*, New York, 1856,
p. 128.)

opinions." [14] The elder politician, who was always solicitous for the welfare and promotion of the younger man, did much no doubt to stimulate his ambition and to direct his conduct. " He was of great use to Burdett," said Bentham. " He gave him some degree of intellectuality." [15]

On one occasion, after the intimacy between the reformers had become the subject of criticism by their political foes, Tooke is said to have entertained Sir Francis by inviting him to listen to a satire riddling both himself and his visitor. The philosophically minded host not only read the most scathing passages aloud, but commented as he proceeded upon the merits of the verse, carefully improving the versification and the satire of any of the lines that seemed weak or ineffective. Tooke was in the habit, it may be mentioned, of securing all of the caricatures of himself and of his friends and hanging them in conspicuous places on the walls of his house.

Tooke's devotion to the interests of Sir Francis involved him just a few years before his death in a deplorable quarrel, which marred for a time the pleasantness of the social life at Wimbledon. Some account must be taken of this feud, which was occasioned by Tooke's entertainment of a politician by the name of Paull, who was introduced to the Sunday gatherings by Sir Francis. After the baronet and Paull had become enemies, however, and had fought a duel, Tooke was soon engaged in a newspaper controversy with Paull and his defenders.

Tooke became incensed on discovering in the *Times* of May 5, 1807, a reference to the fact that a certain speaker by the name of Power had, upon the authority of Paull, quoted him as being opposed to Sir Francis's having anything to do, at the time, with seats in Parliament, the

[14] Part II, Philadelphia, 1807, p. 2.
[15] *Works,* Vol. X, p. 404.

gossip indulged in by Paull, in this instance, having been gathered at one of Tooke's dinners. Tooke, angered by a disclosure of remarks made at his table, immediately dispatched to the *Times* a letter, in which he declared:

It is not very decorous, I believe, to bring before the public the free and unimportant conversation which passes in a mixed company at a dinner table: Mr. Paull and Mr. Power seem to think otherwise. Mr. Paull is very welcome to report anything he ever heard me say. But, for the sake of my friends, who may not be quite so indifferent as I am to tittle-tattle in the newspaper, neither Mr. Paull nor this Mr. Power (whoever he may be) shall ever with my consent hence forward dine at the same table with me.[16]

The writer added that he probably did make the assertion attributed to him. In any case, he was convinced that he should prevent, if possible, Sir Francis's being a candidate for Middlesex. " Of Mr. Paull," he continued, " I know nothing, but that he was introduced to me by Sir Francis Burdett; and that he afterwards invited himself to dine at my house on Sundays, when I receive my visitants. From the time of the election at Westminster, last November, he has missed dining with me only three Sundays." [17]

According to Tooke, Paull had determined to affiliate himself with Sir Francis, and had managed to carry his point on several occasions, in more than one instance, to the embarrassment of the baronet. Since his name had appeared in print in connection with Paull's, Tooke felt it his duty, he stated, to vindicate Sir Francis and at the same time to explain his own sentiments. Not satisfied, however, with ridiculing Paull in a public letter, he addressed " A Warning to the Electors of Westminster," which, besides disclosing Paull's further communications to

[16] *Letter to Editor of the Times,* London, 1807, p. 2.
[17] *Ibid.,* p. 3.

Sir Francis and the final reply of the latter to the effect that he would have no intercourse with his antagonist after his recovery from his wound, contained a violent denunciation of Paull's character.

The victim of Tooke's attack lost no time, of course, in refuting the " atrocious slanders " of his reviler. " I had, indeed, roused all the venom of his implacable heart," he informed the public, " by accusing him as the ' *dark and infernal adviser* ' of that foul and infamous procedure which caused the disastrous hostility which we have all so much lamented; not that I had charged him with an act which his feelings would disown, but that I had dared to speak, and in terms of just severity towards him, of what it would be high treason to his projects to disclose; namely, his influence over Sir Francis Burdett." [18]

In reply to the implication that he had been an obtrusive guest in Tooke's house, Paull described the pressing invitation he had received to attend the Wimbledon dinings. Astonished, therefore, at Tooke's denial of his former cordiality, he gave the public the following account of his first glimpse of the Sage of Wimbledon:

Sir Francis went up stairs to what is called the *study;* and, in a few minutes afterwards, *John Horne Tooke* entered the drawing room, so unseemly and so filthy that, as Murphy said of Johnson, " he appeared like Lungs the Alchymist, just having quitted making aether." [19]

Infuriated by his personal treatment at the hands of his former host, Paull also delivered himself on the subject of the philologist's dinners in the following terms:

[18] Paull: *A Refutation of the Calumnies of John Horne Tooke, Including a Complete Exposure of the Recent Occurrences between Sir Francis Burdett and Mr. Paull, In a Letter to the Electors of Westminster,* London, 1807, p. 8.

[19] *Ibid.,* p. 18.

Every body who knows any thing of these Wimbledon dinners, knows that they are social parties given for Sir Francis Burdett and his political friends; that they are supported chiefly at Sir Francis's expense; that Col. Bosville, and one or two others are considerable contributors, and that on the close of the year, it is customary for most of the visitors to make Mr. Tooke a present of wines or some other articles necessary for the supply of the table.[20]

Bentham's observations in regard to the philologist's dinings agree with Paull's: " Horne Tooke's dinners were pic-nic dinners. Every man sent something, and more than he took. Among the eaters Colonel Bosville was a republican. Humphreys was admitted on the strength of a bon mot." [21]

Very probably a few of Tooke's more intimate friends, realizing the expense which these weekly dinings incurred, may have made generous donations from time to time to the Sunday feasts. Colonel Bosville, it is certain, frequently brought with him from London contributions to the dinners. The statements of Paull and Bentham are misleading, however, for the financial burden as well as the elaborate preparation necessary for the liberal entertainments at Wimbledon devolved upon the master of ceremonies, who was so given to hospitality as to spend a large part of his income on his guests. That Tooke felt the financial strain of keeping an open house is proved by his decision at one period, when his funds were limited, to give up his large residence at Wimbledon for a cottage, in which he could not be expected to accommodate half so many guests as had been his wont. The subscription which was raised for him just at this time, however, and the legacies which he shortly afterwards received, enabled him to keep his fine house and to indulge more freely than ever in a lavish entertainment of his friends.

[20] *Ibid.*, p. 22.   [21] Bentham: *Works,* Vol. X, p. 404.

But, to conclude, as briefly as possible, the account of
the regrettable quarrel between Tooke and Paull, whom the
former obviously only pretended to have forgotten, it is
necessary only to add that Paull, after refuting the attacks on his personal character, instructed the public in
the former relation between himself and Sir Francis, with
the purpose of exposing Tooke's false representation of their
association, and that to vindicate Paull an author who
signed himself "Veritas" published several letters which
revealed a much more cordial relation between Paull and
Tooke than the latter's statements remotely suggested.
This uncalled-for controversy, it must be admitted, ended
rather ingloriously for Tooke, who could not disclaim the
actually produced written invitations that he had extended.

In contrast to this disagreeable episode of his last years,
there is abundant testimony to the pleasant relationship
between Tooke and the group of admirers that gathered
about him at Wimbledon. His satellites were, as a rule,
enthusiastic in their praise of his hospitality and talents.
Though not an aristocrat by birth, he was noted for the
elegance and distinction of his manner. He could be, in
turn, gracious, vivacious, or dignified. His deportment was
that of an urbane gentleman of the eighteenth century, who
set a high value upon good breeding and self-control. On
one occasion, he is said to have reminded a young scholar
who was violently disputing some classical point with
another, that good manners were better than good Greek.
It was only when he entered the political lists to engage in
a public contest with an opponent who had incurred his
dislike that he forgot all moderation and restraint. In his
home he was the genial and affable host, who sometimes
even astonished his guests, as we shall see, by his composure
under trying circumstances.

At approximately the same time that Sir Francis Burdett made the acquaintance of Horne Tooke, Alexander Stephens began to visit at Wimbledon. In the following passage he has recorded his first impressions of his host:

Instead of finding a man equally repulsive in his manners and appearance, as some had taught me to expect, I was most agreeably disappointed, at the first interview, to be received with the politeness of a well-bred gentleman, and entertained with all that ease, attention, and hospitality, which an intimate knowledge of the world added to liberal sentiments can alone confer.

When I first saw him he had already passed the meridian of life, and his dress, which savoured of the old school, seemed to add an air of dignity to his conversation. His coat, which consisted of a dark brown English broadcloth, was calculated for court, as it was destitute of the modern appendage of a collar; while his cuffs were adorned with a large row of steel buttons. His small-clothes exactly corresponded both in cut and colour; his waistcoat was handsomely tamboured; his stockings were of silk; he wore long ruffles at the wrist, while his hair was tied and powdered in the manner of former times. In the midst of conversation, he generally recurred to the contents of a large snuff-box containing rappee; and I thought I could perceive that he managed this in such a manner as to render it serviceable to his wit and repartee.[22]

" In point of stature," we are informed by his biographer, he " did not exceed the middle size; but nature had formed him strong and athletic. His limbs were well knit, compact and duly proportioned; and he might be said to have been comely, rather than handsome, in his youth. His features were regular, and his hair, towards the latter end of life, was generally combed loosely over the temples, and cut close behind. His eye was eminently expressive; it had something peculiarly keen, as well as arch in it; his look seemed to denote an union of wit and satire. When he first surveyed a stranger, he seemed to take *peep into his heart;* and in argument it was difficult to withstand the piercing

[22] Stephens: *Memoirs of John Horne Tooke,* Vol. II, p. 234.

sharpness of his vision, which appeared but to anticipate
the triumph of his tongue." [23]

The following lines from Shakespeare seemed to Stephens
to describe his subject:

> . . . He reads much;
> He is a great observer, and he looks
> Quite through the deeds of men —
> . . . .
> Seldom he smiles; and smiles in such a sort,
> As if he mock'd himself and scorn'd his spirit,
> That could be moved to smile at anything.

The fact that Tooke numbered among his acquaintances
and visitors so many distinguished men of his day, and
that he could maintain so complete a sovereignty over his
own particular circle, is a testimony not only to his reputation as a scholar and as a political leader but to his personal
magnetism as well. His long and unbroken friendships
with Beadon and Dunning, the companions of his younger
days, his intimacy with Sir Francis Burdett, Colonel Bosville, and Samuel Rogers, friends of his later years, and
his pleasant relations with many other striking personalities
among his contemporaries, are proof enough of his power, in
spite of his combativeness, to keep the affection and esteem
of his associates.

" There is no body of men with whom I am connected,"
declared Tooke in 1777. " There is no man or men from
whom I expect help or assistance or friendship, of any kind,
beyond that which my principles or services may deserve
from them individually. Private friendships I have, like
other men, but they are very few: however, that is recom-
pensed to me, for they are very worthy." [24] In a letter addressed to Colonel Bosville, he reflected again, toward the

[23] *Ibid.*, pp. 450–451.
[24] Howell: *State Trials*, Vol. 20, p. 786.

close of his career, on the blessings of friendship: " I have had all my life, and still have at the end of it, many very dear, deserving, and now long continued friends; amongst whom, no one has shown me more important and unearned affection and friendship than yourself, or has a better title to a disclosure from me, on every subject, of what I know, which is fit for me to tell." [25]   To those whom Tooke admitted to his confidence he was devotedly attached. Perhaps the greatest privation that he suffered during his imprisonment in the Tower was the separation from his afternoon callers. That he might miss their company the less he rearranged his schedule for rising and retiring.

In a letter written on December 1, 1794, Major Cartwright refers to " a joyous dinner and afternoon yesterday at Tooke's." On this occasion, obviously a celebration of the philologist's acquittal, the company drank a health to the King, "which I dare say," adds the Major, "was not suspected at the next door (Dundas's), where he had Pitt and a large party to dine." [26]   At an annual dinner commemorating the happy conclusion of his trial for treason, Tooke was the grateful host to Thomas Erskine, who even after his elevation to the peerage was a regular visitor at Wimbledon.

After he had been robbed of most of his silver by thieves, who apparently made their way into his house through the roof, the hospitable but eccentric Tooke, it is amusing to learn, decided to abolish all silver from his table. On the day following the theft, he made a special trip to London, carrying with him to be deposited in a bank, all of his silver that had not been appropriated by the robbers. Pewter spoons and china ware were thereafter substituted for

---

[25] Stephens: *Memoirs of John Horne Tooke*, Vol. II, p. 313.

[26] F. D. Cartwright: *Life and Correspondence of Major Cartwright*, London, 1826, Vol. I, p. 211.

silver spoons and plate at even the most pretentious of the Wimbledon dinings. Tooke's board, from which all silver was thus banished, literally groaned, however, under the weight of the rich and varied dishes that he served upon it. From all accounts of the hospitality which he dispensed,

It snewed in his hous of mete and drynke.

"The dinner, uniformly consisting of both white and brown meats, was always excellent because it was always substantial," says Stephens. "To such as had walked, and found their appetites sharpened by the keen and healthy air of the heath, it proved both refreshing and invigorating in no common degree. At the top, was to be found fish of the best kind and most delicate flavour — turbot, large soles, or cod, each in its respective season, and all accompanied with their appropriate sauces. This was generally followed by a fillet of veal. In the centre was usually to be seen a tureen of soup, and at the bottom, either a round of beef, or a sirloin. As side dishes, were to be found the produce of the garden, in great variety, and the highest possible degree of perfection, while pies and puddings, both excellent in respect to composition and flavour, were afterwards introduced." [27] Upon the removal of the cloth, wines of various kinds were placed before the guests, and a dessert consisting of delicious fruits grown in Tooke's garden was served.

The master of the house, although partaking heartily of the tempting food that came on his table, found time during the progress of the meal to amuse and fascinate his guests by a display of his talents as a wit and as a satirist. There were times, too, when he chose to divert himself at the expense of his visitors by engaging them in debate. "No one," says Stephens, "was ever better calculated for col-

[27] Stephens: *Memoirs of John Horne Tooke,* Vol. II, pp. 293–294.

loquial disputation; or that duel-like controversy, exhibited
by two disputants, when *pitted* together, with the breadth
of mahogany board only between them. On such an arena
he was invincible! wit, humour, learning, temper, genius —
all came in aid of argument, and when he made his most
deadly thrusts, it was with a smiling countenance and without any serious effort or emotion." [28]

Although he himself remained calm and unruffled in these
arguments, he not infrequently, it seems, infuriated his
antagonists. In such instances, however, his resourcefulness and self-command could almost immediately relieve
the embarrassment of the situation which he had created.
One stormy scene at his table has become famous. On this
memorable occasion he selected as a victim for his witticisms, Thomas Holcroft, who had no doubt been attracted
to Wimbledon, in the first place, by the political character
of the gatherings there. After Holcroft had been exhausted
and irritated beyond the limits of endurance by the raillery
of his host, he arose from the table in a towering rage and
exclaimed: "I am sorry, sir, to say to a gentleman in his
own house what I now tell you, that you are the greatest
rascal in the world." Tooke, realizing by this time that
he had carried his joking too far, calmly faced his guest
and without changing his countenance, inquired of him:
"Is it Friday or Saturday next, that I am to dine with
you?" "Saturday, Sir," said Holcroft. "Then," replied
Tooke, "you may depend upon it I shall be there at the
hour appointed." [29]

"It was delightful," says Hazlitt, after referring to the
preceding incident, "to see him sometimes turn from these
waspish or ludicrous altercations with over-weening antagonists to some old friend and veteran politician seated at
his elbow, to hear him recall the time of Wilkes and Liberty,

[28] *Ibid.*, p. 451.   [29] *Ibid.*, p. 477.

the conversation mellowing like the wine with the smack of age; assenting to all the old man said, bringing out his pleasant traits, and pampering him into childish self-importance, and sending him away thirty years younger than he came! " [30]

As might be expected, Tooke often lured his guests into a discussion of language. Nothing delighted him more than to introduce into a conversation with his scholarly friends a disputed point in etymology. He was accustomed to torment Fuseli, by inquiring as to the origin of Teutonic dialects; he was bold enough to interrogate the famous Dr. Parr concerning the origin of *Is;* and he engaged in at least one linguistic encounter with Coleridge, who gave an account of the incident.

" Horne Tooke was once holding forth on language," said the poet, " when, turning to me, he asked me if I knew what the meaning of the final *ive* was in English words. I said I thought I could tell what he, Horne Tooke himself, thought. 'Why, what?' said he. '*Vis*,' I replied; and he acknowledged I had guessed right." Upon Coleridge's informing the philologist that he disagreed with his, inasmuch as he believed the final *ive* to have been derived from *ick* or *vicus*, Tooke, to the poet's astonishment, made no reply. " I believe," Coleridge asserts triumphantly, " he found that he could not make a fool of me, as he did of Godwin and some other of his butts." [31]

In a letter written to Thomas Wedgwood in January, 1800, Coleridge suggests other distinctive traits of the popular host of Wimbledon Common: " He is a clear-headed old man as every man must needs be who attends to the real import of words, but there is a sort of charlan-

---

[30] Hazlitt: *Works,* London, 1904, Vol. IV, pp. 233–234.
[31] *Specimens of the Table Talk of Coleridge,* New York, 1856, pp. 477–478.

try in his manner that did not please me. He makes such a mystery out of plain and palpable things and never tells you anything without first exciting and detaining your curiosity. But it were a bad heart that could not pardon worse faults than these in the author of *The Diversions of Purley.*" [32]

Tooke's conversation, when not of an argumentative nature, was, as Coleridge complained, very often provokingly mystifying. He derived no little enjoyment, it seems, from bewildering his guests, or deliberately misleading them by some playful invention or mischievous allusion. The air of mystery, indeed, which he affected on occasion, and which he sometimes chose to assume when the popular question of the identity of Junius was introduced, was largely responsible for the opinion so firmly fixed in the minds of certain of his critics, that he and the great satirist were one and the same. His pleasantries, for example, completely deluded his American visitor, Dr. Graham, who conceived the idea in the summer of 1797, it seems, that his host was no other than Junius. In reply to certain questionings of Dr. Graham as to his controversy with Junius, Tooke had smilingly declared: "*Junius* is the best friend I ever had on earth," a statement which was regarded as strangely significant by his visitor. In further support of his theory, Dr. Graham records the following incident in his memoirs of Tooke:

On one occasion in my presence, a mutual and revered friend, in a similar conversation, put the question directly to Mr. Tooke — " Do you then know the author of *Junius?* " — " Yes," replied he, " I do know him better than any man in England! " — " Pray, Sir, is he now living? " — " Yes, my dear Sir, he is yet alive." — " He must then be an old man — do you know his age? " — Mr. Tooke

[32] Cottle: *Reminiscences of Coleridge and Southey,* New York, 1847, p. 320.

instantly replied, " *Strange as it may seem, I can assure you that Parson Horne and Junius were born on the same day in the city of Westminster.*" [33]

These extraordinary deliverances and similar assertions of an enigmatical nature at once suggested to Dr. Graham, as they did to others who took them seriously, that there was an intimate relationship between Tooke and Junius. Dr. Graham read into the following account by Stephens of Tooke's behavior when he was asked if he knew who Junius was, a corroboration of his theory:

On the question being put he immediately crossed his knife and fork on his plate, and assuming a stern look replied, " I do." His manner, tone, and attitude were all too formidable to admit of any further interrogation.[34]

For the sake of impressing his visitors Tooke frequently indulged in harmless equivocations. On one occasion, for example, he informed his callers that his eldest daughter brewed all the beer that was brewed in the house, when, as a matter of fact, no beer was brewed on the place. The elaborate fictitious account of the country on the eve of a revolution, with which in one fatal instance he entertained a guest, who happened to be a government spy, was, as we have seen, the immediate cause of his arrest on a charge of treason. Profiting by the experience of a trial for his life, Tooke became more cautious in his utterances thereafter, and although he did not discontinue his Sunday receptions, he excluded from his table several persons whose lack of moderation made them undesirable guests.

In more than one instance Tooke's good nature was put to a severe test by one of his most distinguished visitors, Richard Porson. Once, for example, he had good reasons

[33] Graham: *Memoirs of John Horne Tooke*, New York, 1828, p. 17.

[34] Stephens: *Memoirs of John Horne Tooke*, Vol. II, p. 358.

for repenting of his hospitable impulse to ask the scholar to dine with him at his home in London. Since the classicist had not been to bed for five nights, Tooke had thought he might be rid of him at a respectably early hour. Porson, however, being in no mood for slumber, did not retire at all, but kept his host up all night. The latter in desperation announced the next morning: " Mr. Porson, I am engaged to meet a friend at breakfast at a coffee-house, in Leicester Square." " Oh," replied Porson, " I will go with you," — and he kept his promise. Shortly after they reached the coffee-house Tooke effected an escape and ran home, commanding his servant not to let Porson in the house, even if he tried to knock down the door. " A man," said Tooke, " who could sit up four nights successively might have sat up forty." [35] Tooke's fears were not without foundation, for the scholar actually was accustomed to sit up all night over his cups, apparently feeling no debilitating effects at all from his dissipations. Tooke often declared that " Porson would drink ink rather than not drink at all." [36]

On another occasion, Tooke's hospitality was still more grossly abused by the Greek scholar, who in the course of a violent altercation with him at his table at Wimbledon announced his intention of kicking and cuffing his host. The philologist, in this critical situation, quieted his unruly visitor by offering him brandy until he was too drunk to be annoying, after which he himself drank a cup to the recovery of his guest lying prostrate on the floor, instructed his servants to take the proper care of the professor, and, as if nothing had happened, calmly repaired to the adjoining room where tea and coffee were served. Hazlitt said

[35] Dyce: *Table Talk of Samuel Rogers and Porsoniana*, New York, 1856, p. 298.
[36] *Ibid.*

that Porson, because of his wonderful memory and his knowledge of language, was the only person who inspired Tooke with any degree of awe. Rogers, on the contrary, maintained that the philologist did not share Dr. Parr's fear of Porson's intellectual powers. It was only the insults and the rudeness of Porson when he was drunk that he dreaded. Porson, it should be stated, recognized Tooke's abilities. " I have learned many valuable things from Tooke," he admitted; " yet I don't always believe Tooke's assertions." [37]

In still another instance, it may be noted, Tooke resorted to the bottle to win a triumph over his enemy, who, in this case, happened to be no other than the famous Scotch biographer. The latter and the philologist, who were dining one day at the same club, became engaged in a trivial dispute, in the progress of which Boswell is reported to have left the room upon Tooke's so far forgetting himself as to say " D—n it ! " " This, to be sure," observed Stephens, in his account of the incident, " was indecorous, but not an unpardonable offense, in the eyes of a man possessed of so much good humor. Accordingly, happening to meet at a gentleman's house, soon after, Mr. Boswell proposed to make up the breach — on the express condition, however, that they should drink a bottle of wine each between the toasts! Mr. Tooke would not give his assent, unless the liquor should be *brandy*. This was accordingly agreed to by both parties; and by the time a quart had been quaffed, the laird of Auchinleck was left sprawling on the floor." [38]

Foster's assertion that Tooke was easily one of the six best talkers of his generation is no exaggeration. Had he been so fortunate as to have a Boswell for his biographer,

[37] *Ibid.*, p. 314.
[38] Stephens: *Memoirs of John Horne Tooke*, Vol. II, p. 439.

his talents as a wit alone would have attracted the attention of posterity. Recognizing that his conversational powers were superior to his literary abilities, Tooke himself remarked on one occasion: " I converse better than I write; I write with labor." [39]   In an age in which pungent wit and clever repartee were cultivated to a rare degree, he had few rivals. Even Sheridan, it is said, could not compete with him in sustained witticism and pleasantry. He fascinated his companions and his audiences by the brilliancy of his discourse, enlivened, as it was, by fitting anecdote, apt comparison, pithy sayings, and charming word play. To George III, who asked him at a levee whether he played cards, he is reported to have replied that he did not know a king from a knave. " The repartee reads, however," as Townsend suggests, " like an *impromptu fait à loisir*, and, if ever made, was one of those *double entendres* in the use of which that shuffler in words prided himself, for he played with syllables, as at whist, an excellent rubber." [40]   Recollections of experiences that were varied and dramatic suggested to Tooke many of his delightful comparisons and satiric allusions. On one occasion, for example, he declared that all of the prophets might be classified as the dissatisfied in general, in particular " Jeremiah, who was notorious for complaining of *hard times;* in short, all these were libellers, and nearly all perished by violent deaths, except Daniel, who was thrown into the den of the attorney-general, and escaped by a miracle." [41]

Tooke's facetiousness was largely an accompaniment of his logical thinking. " His intellect," says Hazlitt, " was like a bow of polished steel, from which he shot sharp-pointed arrows, at his friends in private, at his enemies in

---

[39] Rogers: *Recollections,* p. 154.
[40] *Twelve Eminent Judges,* London, 1846, Vol. II, p. 27.
[41] Stephens: *Memoirs of John Horne Tooke,* Vol. II, p. 414.

public." [42] His " literal kind of wit set off, as tradition recounts, by a courteous manner and by an imperturbable coolness is not ill shown," observes Timbs, " in the following: ' " Power," said Lord —— to Tooke, " should follow property." " Very well," he replied, " then we will take the property from you, and the power shall follow it." ' " [43] To Judge Ashurst, who declared that the law was open to every one, he immediately retorted: " So is the London Tavern." [44]

To a member of his family, Tooke once remarked: " You and I have reversed the natural course of things; you have risen by your gravity; I have sunk by my levity." [45] This humorous confession of his lack of seriousness accords with the impression that he made upon one of his guests, whose observation Hazlitt has recorded: " I have heard a sensible and well-informed man say that he never was in company with Mr. Tooke without being delighted and surprised, or without feeling the conversation of every other person to be flat in comparison, but that he did not recollect having ever heard him make a remark that struck him as a sound and true one, or that he himself appeared to think so." [46]

In contradiction to the preceding statement, however, there is abundant testimony to the edification as well as to the pleasure which Tooke's companions derived from his delightful conversation. The large company of distinguished personages who sought his society were both instructed and entertained. Lord Camelford, for example, declared that he had received more information and enjoyment from his talk than he had from that of any other person of his ac-

[42] *Works*, Vol. IV, p. 231.
[43] *English Eccentrics and Eccentricities*, London, 1866, Vol. II, p. 178.
[44] Rogers: *Recollections*, Boston, 1859, p. 171.
[45] *Table Talk of Samuel Rogers*, New York, 1856, p. 123.
[46] Hazlitt: *Works*, Vol. IV, pp. 232–233.

quaintance. Of the many prominent men in literature and politics with whom John Philpot Curran associated, Tooke was his favorite and he yielded to him "the palm of conversational excellence." [47]

Tooke was enthusiastic in his praises of Curran's talents as a talker. After spending an evening in the company of both Curran and Sheridan for the first time, he observed on being asked for an opinion of the comparative merits of the wit displayed by each, that "Sheridan's was like steel highly polished and sharpened for display and use; that Curran's was a mine of virgin gold, incessantly crumbling away from its own richness." [48] On another occasion, he remarked in reply to a gentleman whose admiration of his own charms as a conversationalist had led him to state that he considered him the most felicitous companion in Great Britain: "Yes, I rather think I am, with the exception of one other gentleman, namely the Right Honorable John Philpot Curran." [49] We read of an amusing dinner party to which Mary Wollstonecraft, shortly after her marriage to Godwin, invited Fuseli, to meet Grattan, Curran, and Tooke, and we learn that the brilliant foreigner sank into such insignificance in the presence of the three wits that upon departing from the feast he upbraided his hostess for the decidedly unpleasant entertainment which she had offered him.

Samuel Rogers, who found in Tooke a stimulating and congenial companion and considered him the most gifted talker of the many brilliant persons that he had known, complimented him in the following verses from the early edition of his *Epistle to a Friend:*

[47] Philipps: *Recollections of Curran and Some of His Contemporaries,* New York, 1818, p. 195.

[48] William Henry Curran: *Life of John Philpot Curran,* New York, 1820, p. 405.

[49] William O'Regan: *Memoirs of the Legal, Literary and Political Life of John Philpot Curran,* London, 1817, p. 110.

> When He, who best interprets to mankind
> The " Winged Messengers " from mind to mind,
> Leans on his spade, and, playful as profound,
> His genius shed its evening sunshine round,
> Be mine to listen.

Happy in the admiration of a large circle of acquaintances and sincerely appreciative of the loyalty and devotion of his few intimate friends, Tooke approached the end of his life untroubled by the violent animosity that he had aroused throughout a long and active public career. " His present manners and conversation," said Rogers in the declining years of the old radical's life, " remind me of a calm sunset in October." [50] Tooke trusted to the future for the vindication of his principles. " He who sacrifices his good fame to his sense of right," he observed on one occasion, " has still his conviction that some circumstances will hereafter lead to a justification of his conduct, at least with those among whom he would wish to build a memory." [51]

The following characteristic letter addressed to Major Cartwright on December 12, 1800, represents Tooke as a successful gardener, and at the same time reflects his never failing interest in the trend of politics:

My Dear Friend,

I went to town last Friday, on purpose that I might, after so long a delay, deliver the little parcel for you, with my own hands to the Boston coachman. I was half an hour too late; my usual *misfortune*, which truth would call *fault*. However, I left it with a trusty tradesman in Fleet Street, who promised that it should be carefully sent by last Monday's coach. That I might tell you this by last Saturday's post, I got a frank ready: the old misfortune recurred; again too late.

With this frank I will not be too late.

[50] Introduction to the division of Roger's *Recollections* devoted to Tooke.

[51] Rogers: *Recollections*, Boston, 1859, p. 169.

The parcel contains two honeysuckle roots, laid down purposely for you, of the standard evergreen honeysuckle; some white and red strawberries, and many sorts of large gooseberries, which I had from Manchester, where they are curious in that fruit.

I have two sorts of strawberry, which those who gave them to me represent as very extraordinary. If they prove so, you shall next year have some. I am promised by different persons (some of whom, like myself, will probably be always too late) many very curious plants and flowers. When next I see you, you shall tell me whether any of them will suit you.

Whilst we are cultivating our gardens, the *Victualling*-Office, of whose exports the Custom House takes no note, is sending grain and cattle out of the country, much beyond all actual, or probably, possible importation. Thirty thousand oxen in the course of a few weeks past. But Mr. Pitt holds him a jacobin, who ought to be impaled, who suggests that the war may possibly be some cause of the scarcity. I think I may, perhaps, be able to send you some authenticated facts concerning that terrible office, which is starving the miserable inhabitants of this land. You will be better pleased with these roots of bitterness than with the paltry roots I have sent you. I believe the lawyers would say that this letter contains a libel; perhaps they would call it treason, but I should have no objection to be tried and convicted, provided they would permit me, on such trial, to bring to light, by evidence, the operation of this despotic war.

Till the proper time arrives, when truth may be useful, let us go on cultivating our gardens.

J. Horne Tooke.[52]

Tooke, it should be explained, was habitually opposed to the foreign policy of the nation and had much to say in his last years in criticism of the Government's attitude to France. His disapproval of the Administration took a very amusing form shortly after the beginning of the first French war when taxes were levied for its prosecution. The eccentric philosopher of Wimbledon, concluding that a head covering was not essential to his existence, decided to wear

[52] *Life and Correspondence of Major Cartwright*, Vol. I, London, 1826, pp. 261–262.

no hat. Conformity to such a fashion, would, in his opinion, be lending aid to the conduct of an uncalled-for conflict. Since his old hat, however, was not taxed, he inaugurated his rebellion by carrying it under his arm, as if he were going to court. When it was suggested that his individuality in this matter might injure his health, he replied: " No, I am too old for that; for when the hair begins to fall, the skull at the same time begins to thicken; nay, it becomes more thick and more hard by being left without a covering." [53]

The national agitation over Napoleon's possible invasion of Britain was evidently regarded by Tooke as unwarranted. To express his equanimity on the subject he employed a witty comparison. He said that when he was travelling in Italy the post boy cursed all the saints in Paradise and five miles around. " Why five miles around? " the blasphemer was asked. " Because some of them may be at their country houses," was the reply. " When Bonaparte comes to England," said Tooke, " his curse, therefore, will not reach me at Wimbledon." [54] Speaking on another occasion of his retirement from active life, he observed: " When bad times come, I shall take to my garret-window. I shall take no part in them but as a looker on. When the Surgeons are called in, the Physician retires." [55]

The infirmities of old age and physical suffering that was often acute did not, however, cause Tooke to lose his interest in public affairs. The indifference of his countrymen to the sad state of politics was the subject of his conversation and of his correspondence. The following passage from another letter addressed to his colleague, Major Cartwright, reflects his despondency at the national apathy:

[53] Stephens: *Memoirs of John Horne Tooke*, Vol. II, p. 493.
[54] Rogers: *Recollections*, Boston, 1859, p. 168.
[55] *Ibid.*, p. 166.

" The gout, which at this time is furiously upon me, abates
not one jot of my resolution. But the gout affects only my
limbs: I fear you will find it in the heads and hearts of most
of our countrymen." [56]

After his withdrawal from political life, Tooke, who had
already established a reputation for scholarship, added to
his fame by publishing, as we have already noted, a second
volume of his treatise on philology. In his declining years
when ill health confined him to his rooms, he found increasing delight in study and reading. During his convalescence from a severe illness in 1810 he made such
demands upon his daughters as readers that they were
forced to call in outside aid to assist them in satisfying
his literary appetite. According to Samuel Rogers, Tooke
read all books through " and bad books most carefully,
lest he should lose one good thought, being determined never
to look into them again." [57] Despite his decided literary
preferences, he advocated a comprehensive acquaintance
with writers. He was a wide reader. His library, however,
was small, the few volumes which it contained having been
carefully chosen by their owner. The restricted character of
the Wimbledon library led an omnivorous reader like Bentham to observe: " Horne Tooke had a narrow mind. His
library was narrow. A man may be judged by his library." [58]

Among the volumes in Tooke's limited though classic
collection were: a translation of the New Testament " which
was very much though surreptitiously circulated in the reign
of Edward III and afterwards," [59] as Tooke informed Sir

[56] F. D. Cartwright: *Life and Correspondence of Major Cartwright,* Vol. II, p. 137.
[57] *Recollections,* Boston, 1859, p. 156.
[58] *Works,* Vol. X, p. 404.
[59] *Diversions of Purley,* Philadelphia, 1807, Part II, p. 229. (A
Catalogue of Tooke's library was published in 1813.)

Francis Burdett, who had given him the rare manuscript; an old black letter copy of Chaucer's translation of Boethius; a First Folio edition of Shakespeare; and an interleaved Johnson dictionary, made more valuable by manuscript notes. In an entry of his *Diary* for December 22, 1840, Crabb Robinson makes an interesting reference to Tooke's copies of Chaucer's Boethius and the *Trial of Hardy,* which had been bequeathed by their owner to Samuel Rogers: " I went out early, to breakfast with Rogers. A most agreeable chat. He was very cordial, communicative, and lively; and pointed out to us his beautiful works of art, and curious books. I could not help asking, ' What is to become of them? ' — ' The auctioneer,' he said, ' will find out the fittest possessor hereafter. He who gives money for things values them. Put in a museum, nobody sees them.' I allowed this of gold and silver, but not of books; such as his ' Chaucer ' with the notes Tooke wrote on it when in the Tower, with minutes of the occurrences that then took place. So Tooke's copy of the ' Trial of Hardy,' etc., with his notes. ' Such books you should distinguish with a mark, and say in your will, " All my books with the marks set out to so and so." ' I fear he will not pay attention to this." [60]

Knowing Tooke's fondness for unusual texts, Wilkes, who in spite of his many faults was free from rancor, so far forgot his enmity for his former ally as to make him a gift of one of his valuable privately printed works. Tooke's eagerness to peruse rare volumes, it should be said, did not make him a professional hunter of black-letter books, handsome copies, or choice editions, if the prices asked for such treasures were exorbitant. " He detested literary foppery," says Stephens; " his collection was intended for use and reference; not show, curiosity, or splendour. He contemplated large libraries as noble depositories of human knowl-

[60] Crabb Robinson: *Reminiscences,* Vol. II, Boston, 1870, p. 288.

edge, but he often expressed his wonder at the sums lavished on purchases of this kind by men of fashion, who have neither time nor inclination for study: and he has been known to compare a library, founded by one of these, to a seraglio collected for a Tenducci, or a Rausini." [61]

Just a year before his death, when his critical faculties were still keen, Tooke busied himself with making comments on Stewart's recently published *Philosophical Essays*, which contained adverse criticisms of *The Diversions of Purley*. He had " a rod in pickle " [62] for his critic, he informed Stephens. It is probable that Shakespeare, whom Tooke had loved from childhood, was the last author that he read. It is certain, says Stephens, who found him just a short time before his death, correcting his copy of the poet and making notes on the margin, that Shakespeare was the last writer to receive his literary criticism.

The First Folio, it may be noted, was in Tooke's opinion the only edition of Shakespeare worth regarding. Of any corrected text he spoke contemptuously, and he never lost an opportunity to deride " tasteless commentators," [63] who suggested difficulties in the poet's lines where none existed. In his criticisms he distinguished sharply between the work of George Steevens, who had, in his judgment, accomplished much in the field of Shakespearean scholarship, and such editors as Johnson and Malone, who could not be dignified by the name of commentators. The interpretations of " poor Malone " [64] he regarded as " constantly insipid and ridiculous." [65] " It is much to be wished," he said, " that an edi-

---

[61] Stephens: *Memoirs of John Horne Tooke*, Part II, p. 495.
[62] *Ibid.*, p. 419.
[63] *Diversions of Purley*, Philadelphia, 1807, Part II, p. 43.
[64] *Ibid.*, p. 45.
[65] *Ibid.*, p. 194.

tion of Shakespeare were given *literatim*, according to the first folio; which is now become so scarce and dear that few persons can obtain it: for, by the presumptuous license of the dwarfish commentators, who are forever cutting him down to their own size, we risque the loss of Shakespeare's genuine text; which that folio assuredly contains; notwithstanding some few slight errors of the press, which might be noted, without altering." [66]

A comprehensive knowledge of Shakespeare and other dramatists caused Tooke to display much concern, we may add, as to the quality of theatrical productions. For years he was a frequent attendant upon the dramatic performances of his time. He had the privilege of seeing Garrick and other prominent actors, who spoiled his taste, he said, for some of their successors on the stage. The writer and actor, Arthur Murphy, he particularly disliked, because of his interference in the Bigby case, in which, as we have seen, Tooke was interested, and because of his attempt, as Tooke believed, to alienate sympathy from him just prior to his trial for treason.

Even after he had ceased to care for the recreations which they offered, Tooke frequented the playhouses and the coffeehouses. " He would sit an act at the theatre," says Samuel Rogers, " and then adjourn to a coffee-house, and then to the theatre listless and cheerless; and yet a slave to the habit of attending them: and on his return home, when he sat up to read with delight, he would reproach himself for his folly in having thrown away his evening. At last he met with insults in the coffee-houses and relinquished them entirely. He then retired to Wimbledon." [67] Although familiar with criticisms of the most virulent kind, Tooke was not entirely callous to public opinion. His sensitive-

[66] *Ibid.*, p. 42.
[67] *Recollections*, Boston, 1859, p. 154.

ness to personal insult is revealed in the following anecdote also related by Rogers:

> One night after dining with him at Cline's (the surgeon), I ac-
> companied Tooke to Brandenburgh House (the Margravine of
> Anspach's) to see a private play. During the performance, a per-
> son behind me said, "There's that rascal, Horne Tooke." The
> words were uttered quite distinctly; and Tooke was so offended,
> that he immediately withdrew. I went home with him to his
> house on the Common, and slept there, after sitting up very late
> to listen to his delightful talk.[68]

To the end of his existence Tooke found enjoyment in
his books, in his home, and in his friends. Surrounded
during his last prolonged illness, by his family and his
loyal companions, he remained serene and cheerful, though
he knew that his end was approaching. " He advanced
to the close of his life," says Foster, "with a self-com-
placent mixture of pride and gayety. A thoughtful reader
will accompany him with a sentiment of deep melancholy,
to behold so keen, and strong, and perverted a spirit, tri-
umphant in its own delusion, fearlessly passing into the unknown world." [69] That he was entirely without religious
convictions, however, the following assertion attributed to
him would disprove: "I believe in a first cause, because
every other supposition is more absurd." [70]

When he became convinced that his days were numbered, Tooke decided to burn his manuscripts and letters.
The destructive task of consigning to the flames all of the
papers in his possession, except legal documents and expense accounts, occupied him for a month. In this whole-
sale conflagration a manuscript on language, sufficient in
length to furnish forth a third volume on the subject, and

[68] Dyce: *Table Talk of Samuel Rogers*, New York, 1856, p. 127.
[69] *Critical Essays*, London, 1856, Vol. II, p. 192.
[70] Rogers: *Recollections*, Boston, 1859, p. 169.

a treatise on moral philosophy, opposed in principle to that
of Paley, were consumed. In further preparation for his
end, he also supervised the erection on his premises of his
own vault and tomb, for which he wrote the following
epitaph:

John Horne Tooke
Late Proprietor
And now Occupier of This Spot,
was
Born in June, 1736
and
Died
In the   year of his age.
Content and grateful.

Though urged by an acquaintance to add to the inscription
some sentiment expressing his love of freedom, he refused
to alter the wording.

In 1810, when he was at the point of death, he was calm
and uncomplaining though he was perfectly aware of his
dropsical condition and of the ravages already made by
his disorders. To his gardener, who was trying to make
him more comfortable, he remarked: "These gouty legs,
John, in the course of a very short time, will give trouble
to neither you nor me!"[71] To Sir Francis Burdett, who
expressed a hope of his recovery, he replied: "We hope
differently. I am now so far on my journey, that I do not
wish to turn back, in order to proceed again by the same
road, a few months hence."[72]

Urged by his daughters and his friends to exert himself
to live, he finally rallied from this acute attack although
he himself realized fully that the change was but tempo-
rary. No sooner had he begun to improve than he demanded the *Times* and the *Morning Chronicle*, and during

[71] Stephens: *Memoirs of John Horne Tooke*, Vol. II, pp. 388–389.
[72] *Ibid.*, p. 389.

the last two years of his life, in spite of suffering and advancing infirmity, he displayed his accustomed interest in public events. As late as 1811, he made a stand against what he considered an illegal tax of fourpence-halfpenny, imposed on him under the name of "tenantry." He was accustomed to meet all of his obligations punctually, but in this instance his principles forbade acquiescence in the demand of the tax-collector. Others affected by the same illegal procedure followed Tooke's example in rebelling against the unjust tax, and the outcome was a triumph for the Wimbledon landowners.

Tooke occupied himself during the last months of his life with making alterations in his house and grounds. He repaired his stables, paved his yard, papered his house, and refurnished his back parlor, in which he spent a great part of each day. In the midst of additional plans for beautifying his home, he became ill and one of his daughters soon detected the seriousness of his symptoms. His physicians and Sir Francis Burdett were immediately summoned to his bedside. His courage and his calmness never left him, and his interest in public affairs was manifested almost to the latest hour of his life. Notwithstanding his suffering and his critical condition he made earnest inquiries as to the effect on the House of Commons of the motion concerning the punishment of soldiers. Later in the day he became alarmingly worse, but he remained in full possession of his senses to the last. He died on the night of March 18, 1812.

The *Morning Chronicle* of March 21 paid him the following tribute:

Died on Wednesday night about twelve o'clock, John Horne Tooke, at his house at Wimbledon.

This extraordinary man has flourished so long and acted a part in the world so remarkable and diversified, that it is not within our limits to attempt any outline of his life. Neither indeed is it necessary, to those who are at all acquainted with literature or our domestic history for the last forty years, to delineate a man who has been so conspicuous in both.

We consider his literary character to be already immovably fixed, and that there is no man of ingenuity who does not lament to see the close of his philological labours. As a man of wit and general talents, he will be likewise allowed on all hands to stand in the highest rank; as a companion, well bred, affable, cheerful, entertaining, instructive, and in raillery to have been perhaps without an equal.

But when we proceed to his politics, we find ourselves on contentious ground, and feel the embers hot under our feet. Gay and lively in his general habits, here only he was inflexible and severe. Whether it was the love of mankind or impatience of power, let men dispute according to their fancies. It is a sufficient motive for *our* praise that he was constantly on the side of freedom.

We, ourselves, who have always preferred, from love as well as principle, to tread in the footsteps of another leader, may have thought Mr. Tooke culpably fastidious and intractable. But, to say nothing of his just confidence in himself, he must be allowed to have had some ground for caution and distrust in forming connections with public men; for he had supported Wilkes and was betrayed; and had united with Pitt, and was persecuted.

By those who are ready to approve every encroachment of power, his writings may still be termed libels, and his conduct turbulence. Yet the nation has long since come to agree with him respecting the American war, and the " *murders* of Lexington "; and if the judgment of a jury shall be confirmed by posterity, the infamy that was prepared for Tooke may fall on his prosecutors. At any rate, the supporters of future administrations will probably be satisfied with classing him among the Hampdens, the Miltons, and similar disturbers of quiet government and order.

In his public character, he may fairly be allowed the praise of being disinterested, for he exposed himself to sufferings and loss when he failed, without personal advantage from success. Nor let it be thought that his exertions in the cause of liberty were vain, because they were so generally repelled. The abuse of power has no greater restraint than the dread of some stubborn mind, which fines and prisons cannot subdue; and we are persuaded that ministers and even Judges, have sometimes been awed into moderation by a man who not only sacrificed to liberty, but was willing to yield himself up as the offering.

The marked and inveterate hostility which he so long indulged against the purest and most disinterested Patriot of our times, took its rise in the memorable period of 1782, when on the demise of the Marquis of Rockingham, Mr. Fox felt himself compelled to resign in consequence of the appointment of the Earl of Shelburne to be First Lord of the Treasury. Mr. Tooke closely allied himself with and became the active partizan of that ministry; and though in the end he detested the inordinate lust of power, at the shrine of which Mr. Pitt sacrificed every principle of his youth, Mr. Tooke never seemed to forgive the keener penetration of Mr. Fox, in discovering the real character and views of that youthful statesman. Added to which Mr. Tooke had in his nature a jealous and unrelenting enmity to all intellectual endowments superior to his own. He would be master of his circle. He did not envy Mr. Fox his political superiority more than he did Mr. Porson his literary attainments — and this humour was not of a character to be corrected by age. We fear it went with him to his death-bed.

Mr. Tooke was in the 77th year of his age. He had been for several weeks in a declining state, and had lost the use of his lower extremities. A few days ago mortification appeared, and rapidly advanced. Dr. Pearson, Mr. Cline, Mr. Tooke's two daughters, and Sir Francis Burdett, attended on him, and he was informed that his dissolution was approaching. He signified with a placid look, that he was fully prepared, and had reason to be grateful for having passed so long and so happy a life, which he would willingly have had extended if it had been possible. He expressed much satisfaction that he should be surrounded in his last moments by those who were most dear to him. He professed his perfect confidence in the existence of a Superior Being, whose final purpose was the happiness of his creatures. The eccentric facetiousness for which he was so remarkable did not forsake him till he became speechless, and even then his looks wore an aspect of cheerful resignation. A short time before his death when he was supposed to be in a state of entire insensibility, Sir Francis Burdett mixed up a cordial for him, which his medical friends told the Baronet it would be to no purpose to administer, but Sir Francis persevered in offering it, and raised Mr. Tooke with that view. The latter opened his eyes, and seeing who offered the draught, took the glass and drank the contents with eagerness. He had previously observed, that he should not be like the man at Strasburgh, who, when doomed to death, requested time to pray, till the patience of the magistrates was exhausted, and then, as a last expedient, begged to be permitted to close his life with his favorite amusement of *nine pins*, but who kept bowling on, with an evident determination never to finish the game — He desired that no funeral ceremony should be said over his remains, and that six of the poorest men in the parish should have a guinea each for bearing him to the vault which he had prepared in his garden.[73]

Sir Francis Burdett addressed the following note to Samuel Rogers, informing him of the plans for the philologist's funeral:

My dear Mr. Rogers, — Our friend Horne Tooke used to express his desire that his few real friends should accompany him to that " everlasting mansion," which, like Timon, he had prepared for himself. As I know he counted you of that number and as I believe you would like to pay this last tribute to his memory, I take the liberty of acquainting you that his remains will be deposited in his garden at Wimbledon on Tuesday next, the 27th.

Yours very sincerely

F. BURDETT.[74]

As it was found impracticable, however, to inter Tooke in the vault so carefully prepared by himself, he was buried on March 30, 1812, at Ealing, in the tomb of his sister, his body being laid to rest by the side of his mother.[75]

---

[73] Newspaper clipping found with a collection of Tooke pamphlets owned by Holt White — Collection found in the Library of Yale University.

[74] Clayden: *Samuel Rogers and His Contemporaries*, Vol. I, p. 82.

[75] All of Tooke's property was left to his daughter, Mary Harte, who had, no doubt, been instructed by her father to provide for her sister.

BIBLIOGRAPHY

The following list represents the principal sources of the present study. Other authorities have been mentioned in the footnotes.

ALMOND, JOHN: *The Correspondence of the Late John Wilkes with His Friends, Printed from the Original Manuscripts in Which Are Introduced Memoirs of His Life*, London, 1805, Vol. 11.

American Quarterly, Vol. V, 1829.

Annual Review and History of Literature for 1805, Vol. IV, London, 1806.

BARCLAY, JOHN: *A Sequel to the Diversions of Purley; containing An Essay on English Verbs, with Remarks on Mr. Tooke's Work*, etc., London, 1826.

BENTHAM, JEREMY: *Works*, Vol. X.

Blackwood's Magazine, Vols. 33, 34, 47.

BLAKEWAY, J. B.: *An Attempt to Ascertain the Author of the Letters published under the Signature of Junius*, London, 1813.

BLEACKLEY, HORACE: *Life of John Wilkes*, London, 1917.

BOSWELL: *Life of Johnson*, Vol. V, London, 1906 (Birrell Edition).

BROUGHAM, HENRY PETER (Lord): *Statesmen of the Time of George III*, Second Series, Vol. I, Philadelphia, 1839.

CAMPBELL, JOHN (Lord): *Lives of the Lord Chancellors of England*, Vols. VI, VII, VIII, IX, London, 1857.

CARTWRIGHT, F. D.: *Life and Correspondence of Major Cartwright*, London, 1826.

CLAYDEN, W. P.: *Samuel Rogers and His Contemporaries*, Vol. I, London, 1889.

COLERIDGE, S. T.: *Specimens of his Table Talk*, New York, 1856.

CONWAY, M. D.: *Life of Thomas Paine*, Vol. I, New York and London, 1909.

COOPER, CHARLES H.: *Annals of Cambridge*, Vol. IV, Cambridge, 1852.

COURTNEY, W. P.: Article on *Horne Tooke* in *Encyclopedia Britannica*.

DALY, J. BOWLES: *Dawn of Radicalism*, London, 1892.

DYCE, ALEX.: *Table Talk of Samuel Rogers and Porsoniana*, New York, 1856.

FEARN, JOHN: *Anti-Tooke*, Vol. I, London, 1824; Vol. II, London, 1827.

FELLOWS, JOHN: *The Posthumous Works of Junius to which is Prefixed an Inquiry Respecting the Author; Also, A Sketch of the Life of John Horne Tooke*, New York, 1829.

FITZGERALD, PERCY: *The Life of John Wilkes*, London, 1888.

FOSTER, JOHN: *Critical Essays*, Vol. II, London, 1856.

Fraser's Magazine, Vol. I, 1830.

GODWIN, WILLIAM: *Cursory Strictures on the Charge Delivered by Lord Chief Justice Eyre to the Grand Jury*, London, 1794. (First published in the *Morning Chronicle*.)

GRAHAM, JOHN: *Memoirs of John Horne Tooke*, New York, 1828.

GURNEY, JOSEPH: *The Trial of John Horne Tooke for High Treason*, 2 vols., London, 1795.

The Whole Proceedings in the Cause on the Action Brought by the Rt. Hon. Geo. Onslow, Esq. against the Rev. Mr. John Horne, on Friday, April 6, at Kingston, for a Defamatory Libel before the Right Honourable Sir William Blackstone, etc., London, 1770.

HAZLITT, WILLIAM: *Collected Works*, Vols. IV and XI.

Horne Tooke Memorial, published by the New England Society of Brooklyn, New York, June, 1920.

HOWELL, T. B.: *Complete Collection of State Trials*, Vol. 20, London, 1816–1828.

JESSE, JOHN H.: *Celebrated Etonians*, Vol. II, Edition de Luxe.

Journals of the Commons House of the Province of South Carolina, 1769–1771.

JUNIUS: *Letters*, Vol. II, London, 1796.

KNIGHT, WILLIAM: *Letters of the Wordsworth Family from 1787–1855*, Vol. I, Boston and London, 1907.

LECKY, W. E. HARTPOLE: *England in the XVIIIth Century*, Vol. III, New York, 1892.

MACKINTOSH, ROBERT JAMES: *Memoirs of the Life of Sir James Mackintosh*, edited by his son, Vol. II, London, 1835.

MASSEY, WM.: *History of England*, London, 1863, Vol. 4.

MÜLLER, MAX: *Science of Language*, Second Series, New York, 1870.

Notes and Queries, Eighth Series, Vol. XI.

Parliamentary History of England, Vol. XXXV, London, 1819.

PAUL, CHARLES K.: *William Godwin. His Friends and Contemporaries,* London, 1876.

PAULL, JAMES: *A Refutation of the Calumnies of John Horne Tooke including a Complete Exposure of the Recent Occurrences between Sir Francis Burdett and Mr. Paull, In a Letter to the Electors of Westminster,* London, 1807.

Quarterly Review, June, 1812, Vol. 7.

RICHARDSON, CHARLES: *On the Study of Language,* London, 1854.

ROBINSON, HENRY CRABB: *Diary, Reminiscences, and Correspondence,* selected and edited by Thos. Sadler, Boston, 1870.

ROGERS, SAMUEL: *Recollections,* Boston, 1859. Edited by William Sharpe.

Substance of Earl Stanhope's Speech Delivered from the Chair, At a Meeting of Citizens at the Crown and Anchor on the 4th of Feb. 1795, To celebrate the Happy Events of the Late Trials for supposed high Treason: And Published at the Request of the Meeting; Also the Resolutions of the Meeting and the Toasts together with an Appendix By Earl Stanhope Respecting the Trial by Jury, London.

STANTON, HENRY B.: *Reforms and Reformers of Great Britain and Ireland,* Second and Revised Edition, New York, 1850.

STEPHEN, LESLIE: Article on *Tooke* in *Dictionary of National Biography.*

STEPHENS, ALEXANDER: *Memoirs of John Horne Tooke,* 2 vols., London, 1813.

STEWART, DUGALD: *Philosophical Essays,* First American Edition, Philadelphia, 1811.

Tait's Edinburgh Magazine, Vol. 20, September, 1853, " John Horne Tooke and the State Trials of 1794."

TIMBS, JOHN: *English Eccentrics and Eccentricities,* Vol. II, London, 1866, " Oddities of John Horne Tooke."

TOOKE, JOHN HORNE: *An Appeal to the Public Touching the Death of Mr. George Clarke who received a blow at Brentford on Thursday the eighth of December last, of which he languished and Died on Wednesday the Fourteenth of the same month.* By John Foot, Surgeon, London, 1769.

The Controversial Letters of John Wilkes, Esq., The Rev. John Horne, and Their Principal Adherents; with Supplement containing Material Anonymous Pieces, London, 1771.

Epea Ptereonta, Diversions of Purley, Part I. By John Horne

Tooke, A.M.   Late of St. John's College, Cambridge, London.
Printed for J. Johnson, No. 72, St. Paul's Churchyard, 1786.
Epea Ptereonta; or *The Diversions of Purley*, Part I, Second
Edition, London, 1798.
The Diversions of Purley, Part II, London, 1805.
Diversions of Purley, Parts I and II, First American Edition
From the Second London, Philadelphia.   Printed by Wm.
Duane, 1806 and 1807.
Diversions of Purley, with numerous additions from the copy
prepared by the author for publication.   To which is annexed
his Letter to John Dunning, Esq.   Revised and corrected,
with additional notes.   By Richard Taylor, London, 1857.
*Facts Addressed to Landholders, Stockholders, Merchants,
Farmers, Manufacturers, Tradesmen, Proprietors of every
Description, and generally to all the Subjects of Great Britain
and Ireland.*   Third Ed.   London.   Printed for J. Almon in
Piccadilly (1870).
*Genuine Copies of all the Letters which passed between the
Right Honorable, the Lord Chancellor and the Sheriffs of
London and Middlesex and between the Sheriffs and the Sec-
retary of State, relative to the Execution of Doyle and Valine,*
London, 1770.
A Letter to the Editor of the Times, London, 1807.
*A Letter to a Friend on the Reported Marriage of the Prince
of Wales*, London, 1787.   Second Edition.
*A Letter on Parliamentary Reform containing the Sketch of a
Plan.*   Second Edition, London, 1782.
*An Oration Delivered by the Rev. Mr. Horne, at a Numerous
meeting of the Freeholders of Middlesex assembled at Mile-
End Assembly Room,* March 30, 1770, etc. (published anony-
mously).
The Petition of an Englishman, London, 1765.
*Proceedings in an Action for Debt between The Right Honour-
able Charles James Fox, Plaintiff, and John Horne Tooke,
Defendant, Published by the Defendant*, London, 1792.
A Sermon, by the Rev. John Horne, Minister of New Brentford,
London, 1769.
*The Speeches of John Horne Tooke during the Westminster
Election, 1796,* London.
Two Pair of Portraits, Presented to all the Unbiassed Electors

of Great Britain and Especially to the Electors of West-minster, London, 1788.

A Warning to the Electors of Westminster, London, 1807.

TOWNSEND, WILLIAM C.: *Lives of Twelve Eminent Judges,* Vol. II, London, 1846.

TREVELYAN, GEORGE OTTO: *Early History of Charles James Fox,* New York, 1880.

TUCKERMAN, HENRY T.: *Characteristics of Literature,* Second Series, Philadelphia, 1851.

VERITAS: *Horne Tooke Refuted or, the Absurdity of his Calumnious Letter to the Editor of the Times Fully Exposed, In a Letter to John Horne Tooke, Esq., containing also his Letters to Mr. Paull,* London, 1807.

Westminster Review, Vol. 40, Article X, December, 1843.

INDEX

COLUMBIA UNIVERSITY PRESS
COLUMBIA UNIVERSITY
NEW YORK
————
FOREIGN AGENT
HUMPHREY MILFORD
AMEN HOUSE, E.C.
LONDON

COMMENTS

(Please sign your name)